"Christian Warren is a gifted, insightful communicator who has written a critically important book. This book will change the way you lead, your relationships, and in fact your life! As a teacher, coach, and leadership expert with an abundance of inspiration and creativity, Christian is unsurpassed. *Running with the Rhinos* is a must read!"

—Gerry Robert, bestselling author
of *The Millionaire Mindset*

"As a leader, you're always in the spotlight. *Running with the Rhinos* teaches how to be an authentic leader under that bright light. Infused with the mystery of the rhino, this book is a fantastic resource for all people who want to connect more profoundly to those they lead. This book is a thought-provoking and highly practical guide to realizing one's leadership potential that every leader can immediately relate to."

—Bob Proctor, international bestselling
author of *You Were Born Rich*

"Christian Warren, one of today's premier leadership coaches, unlocks the leadership secrets of one of the most powerful animals in the world: the rhino. This is perhaps the most perfect safari guide ever written for leaders. The principles are powerful and have been a key part of my personal journey as a leader for years."

—Lynn Allen-Johnson, author of
Getting Out of Your Own Way

"I believe the difference between average leaders and leaders who change lives lies in the tools they use. In *Running with the Rhinos*, Christian Warren not only provides you with the most effective tools, he also shows you exactly how to use them to build yourself into the kind of leader others want to follow."

—Craig Valentine, MBA, coauthor of *World Class Speaking*
and 1999 World Champion of Public Speaking

"This book could not come at a better time. There is no question in my mind of the importance, inspiration, and practicality of this book. And I cannot think of anyone who could not be positively influenced by reading it. Christian Warren is arguably one of the best leadership coaches working today. In fact, *Running with the Rhinos* may well be one of the most complete books written on the subject of leadership!"

—Jim Sweeny, author of
MLM: A Shortcut to Financial Freedom

"Using his master storytelling skills, Christian Warren shows how to build a strong, high-energy team that can outperform the toughest of market conditions. *Running with the Rhinos* should be required reading for all leaders who are not only looking to raise their ability to influence others but also looking to grow, develop, and inspire their teams!"

—Dr. Tony Smithlin, Founding Director,
Smithlin Chiropractic

RUNNING
WITH THE
RHINOS

RUNNING
WITH THE
RHINOS

Courageous Leadership
for a Complex World

Christian Warren

Cirrus Publishing
Orlando, Florida

Cirrus Publishing
1800 Pembrook Drive, 3rd floor
Orlando, FL 32810-6376
Tel: (800) 324-3228   www.cirruspublishing.com

Ordering Information
Quantity sales. Special discounts are available on quantity purchases by corporations, associations, and others. For details, contact the "Special Sales Department" at the Cirrus Publishing address above.
Individual sales. Cirrus Publishing publications are available through most bookstores. They can also be ordered directly from Cirrus Publishing at the number above or via e-mail at sales@cirruspublishing.com.
Orders by U.S. trade bookstores and wholesalers. Please contact Cardinal Publishers Group: Tel: (800) 296-0481, Fax: (317) 879-0872, www.cardinalpub.com.

Printed in the United States of America

Warren, Christian Daniel, 1964-
  Running with the rhinos : courageous leadership for a complex world / Christian Warren.
      p. cm.
  Includes bibliographical references and index.
  ISBN-13: 978-1-935010-02-9 (hardcover) ISBN-10: 1-935010-02-6 (hardcover)
  1. Leadership. 2. Management. I. Title.
  HD57.7.W374 2008
  658.4'092—dc22   2008027149
  FIRST EDITION
  13 12 11 10 09 08   10 9 8 7 6 5 4 3 2 1

Cover design: e2Impact Design Studio
Interior design and composition: Beverly Butterfield, Girl of the West Productions
Editing: PeopleSpeak

*To my wife, Jami, who unselfishly runs beside me each
and every day. I'm forever grateful for your love,
your support and assistance in putting my voice to print,
and the privilege of being allowed to run like a rhino!
I knew the day I asked you to marry me that my life
would never be the same. Thank you for saying yes.*

*To my four boys, Cameron, Chandler, Connor, and Chase.
You all are my ultimate teachers. Not a single day goes by
that I don't feel gratitude for the amazing relationships
we have with each other. No father could be prouder.*

*To my parents, who taught a little rhino-in-training
to not follow someone else's path but to create
my own and to always follow my dreams.
Thank you for always being there.*

CONTENTS

ACKNOWLEDGMENTS

It has always been in my nature to go for it. To look a rhino right in the eyes and charge! To live by the horn, die by the horn. I've been this way as far back as I can remember, and when I had the opportunity to move forward in the business world, nothing changed. I stayed focused, grew as a leader, and most importantly, had the privilege of developing lifelong relationships.

While writing this book, I had much time to reflect on the individuals who have a lasting impact throughout my life. Even though I cannot acknowledge each one independently, my gratitude extends to all those who taught me how to be a coach, mentor, author, friend, husband, and father. I've received so many wonderful benefits and so much knowledge from each of these teachers. These people have provided opportunities for me to develop, implement, and share the information in this book in a very fresh way.

I understand that a book comes not only from the author's personal life experiences but also from a global network of individuals who contribute directly and indirectly. I especially want to recognize the following individuals for all of their outstanding contributions.

Sharon Goldinger, my chief editor and dear friend, I could not find a better advisor. Your expertise and professionalism gave me the momentum needed to complete this project. Without you, this book would still be sitting on my desk in its original manuscript form. Thank you!

Michael Levin, you are the difference maker. I will be forever grateful to you for taking my original manuscript and shaping it into this book. Your artistry and use of language will help me influence the lives of many and provide them with a foundation to increase their leadership effectiveness. Thank you for lending your talents, time, and incredible energy to this project.

John Trujillo and Bill Apablasa, thank you for your invaluable inspiration, guidance, and helpful words during the initial development of this book. I will always cherish and value our relationship and feel blessed for all that you have graciously given to this exciting project.

Thanks to my entire staff and team at e2Impact, who helped me in so many ways during the entire book development process. Steve Colwell, Don Maxfield, Jason Benson, Jennifer Holmes, Christopher Feagan, Aron Parker, and Rod Wittmier—all my longtime friends, staff, and colleagues—I will never be able to fully express my appreciation to all of you for the impact you have had on this book, though I hope the above words adequately express my gratitude.

And to the single most important person in my life, Jami—my wife, best friend, and partner—I am so grateful that you are always there for me, keeping our little rhinos safe and out of harm's way. In all that we do together, your belief, support, understanding, patience, and love for me is truly remarkable. You have blessed me beyond my wildest imagination.

To my four amazing boys—Cameron, Chandler, Connor, and Chase—oftentimes the lessons I learn from you embody the deepest meaning of the word "leadership." You remind me every day what truly matters most in life.

Finally, to all my readers, success in leadership is not just about ability; it is largely about taking responsibility for the choices you make and for the role you play in the lives of those you lead. Stay true to your personal values, be authentic at all times, and commit yourself each day to raising the level of your leadership effectiveness! Each of you is special and unique and possesses all that is needed to run with the rhinos.

Charge hard.

INTRODUCTION

The Way of the Rhino

A ncient wisdom says that when the student is ready, the master will appear. I never imagined that my master would weigh four thousand pounds and come charging at me with horns on its head!

Truth comes from all directions, in many shapes and guises, and often in surprising ways. This explains how the rhinoceros became my unlikely guru, my guide on my journey toward leadership mastery. And as you read this book, the rhino will become your guide, too.

I saw my first rhino where you probably saw yours—at the zoo. It was an enormous black rhino, and to the pleasure of the small crowd gathered around its enclosure, it was charging intently and fearlessly at another rhino. In truth, I'm not really a zoo person, and for that matter, I'm not all that crazy about wild animals. I went to the zoo for the same reason many people do—because my kids wanted to go. But something about that rhino and the way it charged grabbed my attention immediately. An inner voice said, "Take notice. There's something important to be learned here."

Soon I commenced an in-depth study of the rhino. I checked out books from the library, watched videos, surfed the Web, and made frequent return trips to the zoo. Sometimes I brought a pad of paper and sat for hours outside the rhino exhibit, jotting down notes and sketches of my observations as bewildered families stared in wonder.

The more I learned, the more excited I became as I recognized a host of traits that made the rhino exceptional. Everything I learned about the rhino could be applied to my personal quest to live well and successfully as a leader. Small details of the rhino's attitude, behavior, and appearance, even its third toe and its thick skin, started to carry a deeper meaning for me. The more I discovered, the more I wanted to share these life-altering revelations with others. This book is the culmination of that journey, and it offers you the chance to learn all the leadership lessons that, with the help of the rhino, I've garnered in my own life.

Rhinoceroses may not be the most beautiful of God's creatures (except, perhaps, to other rhinos), but they are powerful and impressive animals. Watch a rhino long enough and you can't help but feel a great deal of respect for its sheer size and strength. Keep watching, however, and you'll find that underneath its imposing exterior is a much more complex animal than initially meets the eye.

If you haven't seen any rhinos lately, keep in mind that they are the second largest land mammal, smaller only than the elephant. Adult rhinos are approximately seventy inches tall measured at the shoulder, weigh one to two tons or more, and have a life span of approximately thirty-five years. They carry their young for about sixteen months, a prospect sure to awe any mother who knows how trying a mere nine months can be. And rhinos mature at a remarkable rate: a baby rhino is capable of eating grass and leaves on its own only a week after birth.

Rhinos have thick skin, three toes on each foot, ears that are almost comically oversized, and smallish eyes. Their massive noses afford them an excellent sense of smell, an important survival mechanism in the harsh world they live in. They use their energy sparingly, rarely engaging in tussles with other species and fighting other rhinos only over territory or female company.

The best-known feature of the rhino is, of course, its horn. In fact, rhino horns are so highly prized in many African, Asian, and Middle Eastern countries that poachers continue to kill these magnificent animals, almost to the point of extinction, despite international laws and treaties forbidding it. In addition, it's becoming harder and harder for a rhino to find a place to call home. In some parts of the world, its natural habitat has been stripped of trees, which are needed for lumber. In India, the land where rhinos live and forage is increasingly being converted to rice paddies to feed an ever-growing population. For all its strength, the rhino, it seems, can't catch a break.

Perhaps what drew me back to the zoo after that first day was the rhino's uncertain plight or the fact that I have always appreciated and identified with the underdog. But as I continued to study rhinos, I learned to admire their every move. I watched them alone and with others—playing, eating, resting, fighting, snorting, charging, shrieking (they have an extensive vocabulary of grunts, snorts, and shrieks), and rolling in the mud. Before long, I began to see rhinos through a different lens than most casual zoo-goers. Yes, rhinos are big and powerful, but they are also soft and diplomatic. They might usually be slow and cautious, but they can be fast and bold when the situation calls for it. They are fierce, strong-willed, and independent but also docile, nurturing, and loyal.

In short, the rhinoceros represents a bundle of contradictions that somehow collectively balance each other and make sense. Before my eyes, the rhino slowly revealed itself to me as a majestic tower of wisdom, the perfect metaphor for what it takes to be a leader in today's complex world. The rhino might not be as large as the elephant, as farsighted as the eagle, as swift as the cheetah, as powerful as the jaguar, or as agile as the mountain lion. And yet the traits it possesses, I realized, are exactly what it takes to succeed as a leader today. The rhinoceros symbolizes the vision, understanding, communication, power, endurance, conviction, support, heart, and, most important, the balance that those desiring to be leaders must integrate into their lives.

We all struggle to find the balance in life that rhinos, no matter how ungainly they appear, achieve effortlessly on their three-toed hooves. We all seek equilibrium between who we are and who we want to become; between our inner world and the chaotic environment we are a part of;, between our work life and our home life; between profit and principle, power and wisdom, strength and compassion, might and heart. Ultimately, how well we achieve this balance determines not only the sense of purpose and joy we will find in life but also the success we will have in leading our organizations, communities, and families toward the future we envision.

The rhino is an endangered species; so is the true leader. Our country, and indeed humanity as a whole, is in a stage of global transformation, and we are at an unmistakable crossroads in history. The choices we make today will dictate not only the quality of life tomorrow for our children and grandchildren but also whether there will even be a tomorrow at all. We often find the world, our nation, our organizations, our communities, and even our families deeply divided about the best road to take, the best decisions, the best approaches. The world's diverse and ever-expanding economy leads many of us to feel a sense of unease and insecurity about the future. This crossroads has become a battleground of conflicting ideas, approaches, and philosophies. All too often, the "right" approach for an organization, institution, or society is sacrificed for whatever is considered the "strongest" approach.

What will bring us back from the brink? The answer is simple: courageous leadership. The root of the word "courage" is *coeur*, French for "heart." Today's most successful leaders, the ones whose visions and programs endure, are not the autocrats and dictators of times past but those who approach leadership as an art form, those able to influence others to buy in to a vision that takes into account not just the ends but the means as well. Almost a century ago, the great author Napoleon Hill wrote in his classic, *Think and Grow Rich*, "No wealth or position or wealth can long endure unless built upon truth and justice."[1] Recent events, such as Enron's collapse amidst a heap of lies and improper accounting methods, have made Hill's words ring truer than ever.

In times past, CEOs ruled with the authoritative flair of the emperors of ancient Rome. No longer. In his book *Revolt in the Boardroom*, *Wall Street Journal* columnist Alan Murray wrote of the post-Enron fall of the imperial CEO. He gave three examples: Carly Fiorina, former head of Hewlett-Packard, who was brought down by her board of directors because she was perceived to be too arrogant, aloof, out of touch, and unwilling to share power and authority; Harry Stonecipher, former CEO of Boeing, who was forced to resign by his board within weeks after the appearance of sexually inappropriate e-mails between the married CEO and a female Boeing employee with whom he was having an affair; and Maurice R. "Hank" Greenberg, who ran AIG, one of America's largest insurance companies, with an iron hand until evidence came to light of financial double-dealing that he had either authorized or tolerated.

If not for the Enron scandal, these CEOs might never have been forced to leave their multimillion-dollar posts and their transgressions might never have come to light. But today, board members of corporations have personal responsibility for any misdeeds by their companies: if the company does something illegal, the fines come out of the board members' pockets. Members of the Enron board had to pay tens of millions of dollars out of their personal financial holdings for their role in failing to investigate more deeply the corporation's financial shenanigans. The subsequent collapse and death of Enron's accounting firm, Arthur Andersen LLP, sent a similar shock wave through the accounting industry. Now accountants are held responsible for all financial statements they sign off on for their clients. In the wake of Enron's demise, formerly untouchable leaders now have to be accountable to all the stakeholders in their world.

What does all this mean to you? As leadership expert John C. Maxwell puts it, leadership is influence. It's simply the ability to influence others to see and do things in a certain way. Today's leader does not have the dubious luxury that top-level businesspeople, politicians, and others in power once possessed: the ability to impose one's will, unquestioned, on others. That mode of leadership is all but extinct. One vivid and potent symbol of its demise was the tearing down of a huge statue of Saddam Hussein in downtown Baghdad in 2003, shortly after the American invasion of Iraq.

The old-style, top-down, no-questions-asked leader is out of date, out of style, out of time. The new leaders recognize that to influence others, they must be able to see the road ahead, create a vision, and find acceptable ways to induce others to share that vision. New-style leaders must be willing to charge ahead when necessary, pull back when appropriate, and "get down there in the mud" with those they lead—just like a rhinoceros.

If a bull or elephant could be viewed as a means of old-style leadership, thrusting ahead relentlessly when provoked, trampling everything underfoot without regard for those who share its turf, the rhino symbolizes the new kind of leader the world needs today: patient, thick-skinned, aware of the presence and needs of others. That's why, to me, the rhino is the perfect metaphor for leadership today. And this is as true for a Fortune 100 organization like Hewlett-Packard, a nation, or a community as it is for a PTA, a high school football team, or a family.

We must all be leaders—we all need to develop and implement visions of the way life *should* be rather than simply follow along with the way life is. The problem is that while the necessary leadership skills are intuitive to the rhino, they must be learned by most of the rest of us. Thus the need for this book. In each chapter you'll find a different aspect of the rhino's nature on display, and you'll see how the lessons this extraordinary animal offers can be put to work in developing your own leadership skills.

"Adaptive Leadership"—a catch phrase in the modern business world—means having a vision, influencing others, and making a difference. The most successful form of Adaptive Leadership practiced now is what many call "servant leadership." Servant leaders recognize that their authority is not a function of how loud they can yell or how frightening they can appear. Instead, today's wise leaders grasp that the essence of leadership is serving others— those on their team, those who work for them, and those in the world around them such as customers, prospects, the community, or the government.

A leader in a family or a community needs the same rhino-inspired skills as an individual who commands a corporation or a nation. In this book, I want to share with you an understanding of servant leadership based on the rhino principles we will discover together. The key word here will be "authenticity." It's hard to get people to act on our vision unless they trust that we are being honest with them—and with ourselves. The Bible, famously quoted by Abraham Lincoln in his "House Divided" speech in 1858, tells us that "a house divided against itself cannot stand." A leader's personality divided into unmatched parts cannot stand. It is impossible to reconcile the appearance of integrity with deep-seated character flaws, or the desire to project an image of honesty with no underlying commitment to the truth.

Society hungers for leaders who can bridge distances between individuals, groups, and conflicting ideas—gaps that often seem insurmountable. This is just as true in the business world as it is in politics, in our communities, and in our homes. Regardless of the scope or size of our spheres of influence, if we wish to be leaders we must reflect and unite all the voices and experiences in our domains, not just the polar extremes. And no matter what political pundits may say, we are not simply red states or blue states, conservatives or liberals, any more than we are just black or white, young or old, educated or illiterate, blue collar or white collar. Rather, we are a people of nuances, subtle differences, and unique characteristics.

We are schoolchildren, baby boomers, Gen Xers, and retired people. We are brown, yellow, beige, amber, and primrose. We are old money, new money, middle class, cash poor, working class, and destitute. We are high school and college educated, self-taught, and PhD's. We are Catholics, Protestants, Jews, Buddhists, Taoists, Muslims, agnostics, and atheists. We are not one thing or the other thing but many shades of the same thing, all doing what we can, in our own ways, to make better lives for our families, our communities, our workplaces, our government, and ourselves.

Wise leaders will see the beauty and strength in these differences, realizing that within this same tapestry of diversity come individuality, perspective, and passion—the unlikely power that will build consensus and drive an organization forward.

It isn't easy being a rhino. Threats from poachers and others who encroach on the rhino's living spaces continue at full force. It's not easy to be a leader today, either. Adaptive leaders must grasp and develop all the skills that the rhino so neatly symbolizes: vision, understanding, communication, power, endurance, conviction, support, and, heart.

Leaders must stake out the high ground above self-interest and personal agenda; they should act upon what they believe and know to be true and right and not just what is popular or easy. To put it another way, leaders must be well-rounded, fully developed, and authentic human beings. That's the new paradigm for leadership throughout the world.

As we explore the mind, body, and heart of the magnificent rhino, I invite you to take a journey toward the realization of your own potential. It's a quest that will inevitably lead you to ask the questions we so often hear about leadership: Are great leaders born or made? Will I uncover something that I already have inside me, or will I be creating something new?

Great leaders are revealed—to others, certainly, but also to themselves. The revelation doesn't happen all at once. Slowly, sometimes without warning and often with just a soft whisper in the ear, a push to reach out, take a step, and make a difference soon becomes a nudge that grows into a call to stand up and make a simple choice: to act or not to act.

That's the moment when leaders must ask themselves a deeper, more profound question: What do I want my life to stand for?

The choice is always ours. We can stay put, or we can run with the rhinos. We can settle for the safety and comfort of the status quo, or we can embrace the challenge to become leaders who will break through the boundaries of mediocrity, going beyond what others are doing and what others expect of themselves, beyond what is ordinary and commonplace, to journey across the bridge from who we are now to what we are capable of becoming.

In this unrealized potential, we will find the power to create, heal, transform, unite, and, above all, lead. We all have the potential to quietly inspire others to follow, not because they have to but because they want to and because they recognize that we offer them a chance to achieve their own goals.

This unrealized potential holds the promise of a richer and more rewarding life—a life of purpose, authenticity, and service. Here we will find the power to make a genuine and lasting difference in the lives of our organization.

How do we get there?

Follow the rhino and let the journey begin.

CHAPTER ONE

The Rhino's Eyes

A Leader's Vision

It's not what you look at that matters.

It's what you see.

Henry David Thoreau

During the climactic finale of *Star Wars: A New Hope*, Luke Skywalker, in his X-wing starfighter, seeks to shoot a photon torpedo into the main power source of the Death Star. Two previous attack runs have just failed, and with Darth Vader closing in, Luke has only moments to hit his target and save the world from the dark side of the Force.

As Luke speeds along the Death Star to take his one shot at success, he hears a voice in his ear. It's Obi-Wan Kenobi, whispering, "Use the Force, Luke. Let go, Luke." At first Luke resists, but soon he gives in and turns off his targeting computer. Using his feelings to "see" the target, he pulls the trigger, firing the torpedo that annihilates the Death Star and saves the Rebel Alliance.

It's a classic movie moment, a triumph of good over evil and light over darkness. But it's more than that. It's also a triumph of knowing over seeing. In this defining moment, Luke no longer needs his eyes for seeing. He enters into the hidden but powerful world of *inner vision*, where trust and knowingness trump fact and reality. Whether you're a Jedi warrior, corporate vice president, U.S. senator, team leader, teacher, coach, mentor, or parent, taking that leap into the world of inner vision is both monumental and terrifying. This is especially so because we are taught throughout our lives to trust only what we can see, feel, and quantify. But, as Marvin Gaye sang in "I Heard It through the Grapevine," we would be much better off trusting only half of what we see and none of what we hear.

In this chapter, we're going to see how the rhino can lead us from the ordinary vision that marks the ordinary human being to the inner vision that is the hallmark of the true leader. This is no small journey; inner vision requires trusting blindly, and most of us simply are not comfortable doing this. Yet with the rhino as our teacher, we will soon see that blind trust is the very power source that all genuine visionaries tap into.

A Chinese proverb teaches that the journey of a thousand miles begins with a single step. For all new leaders, that first step is an inward one, a move to discover our own personal vision—using the mind to know where we're headed and the eyes to see the future to which we aspire.

A map or a compass will show leaders how to get where they need to go, but vision entails knowing where to go in the first place. There is a story of a husband and wife leaving Cape Cod, Massachusetts, at the end of a hot summer weekend. The roads to and from the cape have not kept up with the massive number of people who visit each year, and traffic from the Bourne Bridge up to Boston on a summer Sunday night is snarled, to say the least.

After crossing the bridge, the husband suddenly finds himself driving on a practically open highway at a speed of sixty-five miles per hour. As he glances at all the motionless traffic headed in the other direction, he suddenly develops a sinking feeling.

"We're going in the wrong direction," he tells his wife.

"Yes," she replies, "but look at what great time we're making!"

It doesn't matter how fast you're going if you're going the wrong way. Before leaders can expect anyone to follow them, they must develop that sense of inner vision, that clarity, that blind faith that allowed Luke Skywalker to close his eyes, lock in on the target, and save the Empire.

Ironically, rhinos are not known for having perfect eyesight. Indeed, they can see only approximately fifty feet ahead. Their other senses, most notably their sense of hearing and sense of smell, more than compensate for this deficiency. But are they really deficient when it comes to vision, when it comes to their survival or growth?

Absolutely not. Rhinos' eyes are mounted on the sides of their heads, not next to each other like in human beings and so many other creatures. As a result, rhinos see breadth and depth more easily than do most other animals. In order to see clearly and put together a vision of the terrain, they must constantly turn their heads this way and that. Human beings can become myopic, like racehorses with blinders on, focused only on their speed as they hurtle down what may well be an unsuccessful or unavailing path. Rhino Vision is just the opposite. Rhinos know what they want to do: they want to survive and thrive. In order to do that, they keep a 360-degree watch on everything that's going on around them. Rhinos don't like surprises. So they are always creating, shifting, and refining their vision as the terrain, weather, opponents, and time of day dictate.

For a leader, the shift from seeing what's there to seeing what *could* be there can happen in an instant. In 1992, John Bryant, a highly successful African American banker in Los Angeles, turned on the television to see the neighborhood in which he grew up, South Los Angeles, burning. The not-guilty verdicts of the four policemen in the Rodney King matter had just come down, people were outraged, and the civil unrest that would shake Los Angeles and the nation had begun. If you recall, Rodney King had been the subject of a severe beating by four officers. It was caught on videotape and replayed endlessly on the news. And yet a Los Angeles jury had found the police officers to be acting within the lawful scope of their job and thus not guilty of any crimes against King. The outrage the verdicts sparked, combined with a woefully unprepared Los Angeles Police Department, led to widespread death and destruction throughout the city's poorest neighborhoods, those that could least afford this sort of damage.

Bryant had already made a remarkable journey—from lower-income childhood to television sitcom stardom, appearing on *Diff'rent Strokes* and other shows—and then back down the socio-economic ladder after taking on such a high-and-mighty attitude with the television networks that nobody wanted to hire him again. Once sharing a home in Malibu with the son of comedian Flip Wilson, Bryant found himself living out of his car and working as a waiter in order to make ends meet.

Two businessmen took Bryant under their wing, and although Bryant had no college background, they brought him into the banking business, where he rapidly developed a reputation not only for outstanding work but also for sterling character. Bryant had left the mean streets of South Los Angeles behind him and was now living in luxury on the city's Westside. When he saw the riots and fires destroying so much property in the community of his birth, he was struck with a sudden realization.

The only properties that had been destroyed were businesses. Homes were untouched. The community appeared to be taking out its frustration and anger about the verdicts on the businesses in their midst, which somehow represented the power structure in Los Angeles. Bryant's revelation: people don't burn what they own. He realized that if more people in the inner city had access to home own-ership, they would be able to buy their own homes, care for them better than renters do, and thus increase the quality of life in their neighborhoods.

Bryant achieved that revelation simply by looking within. It led him to charter buses to take Los Angeles bankers to visit the inner city. The bankers, most of whom were white, learned—to their enormous surprise—that most inner-city communities were not gang-ridden drug neighborhoods riddled with bullet holes. Instead, they saw row after row of well-maintained homes and the bombed-out and burned-out businesses. They saw that a huge potential new market for housing loans existed right there in the inner city of Los Angeles. Out of the ashes of the civil unrest, John Bryant's Operation Hope was born.

With the support of the Los Angeles banking community, Operation Hope opened offices in inner-city neighborhoods to work with individuals, couples, and families to help them clean up their financial problems, establish healthy credit records, and make them ready for home ownership. Operation Hope became so suc-cessful in Los Angeles that it soon spread to other cities across the country, and John Bryant, a product of the inner city, found himself honored at a White House ceremony presided over by President George H. W. Bush. Bryant has gone on to become an ambassador to the United Nations and the author of a book about his experi-ences, *Banking on Our Future*. John Bryant did what a rhino does: he moved away from his old way of thinking, looked within, and envisioned what was possible.

Vision provides us with direction, motivation, and a sense of purpose that inspires our journey in the first place. It gets us up in the morning and gives our day meaning. It keeps us motivated, con-nected, and excited. When times are tough, it gives us courage to finish the job we started. Take away this clear understanding of where we are headed and we subject ourselves to the spinning-wheel syndrome of aimless wandering and organizational inertia. Our journey becomes driven by boredom, hesitancy, and worst of all, chance.

Zig Ziglar tells the story of an individual who comes across three workmen digging in the hot sun. He asks the first one what he's doing.

"I'm digging a ditch," he says, wiping the sweat from his brow.

"What are you doing?" he asks the second worker.

"I'm earning twelve bucks an hour," the man replies.

"And what about you?" he asks the third. "What are you doing?"

"I'm building a cathedral," the third worker says clearly.[1]

That's how it is: without a vision, work feels like endless, pointless labor, something we do just for the "almighty dollar." But when we have a vision, even the most menial task takes on new meaning.

Vision is the inward life that shines through a leader, allowing him to influence those within his organization. *Someone* must have inspired that third ditch digger with a vision of how his work would benefit others in the future. Vision is the fuel that drives our actions. It is what turns a simple walk into a trip and a trip into a journey. Take, for example, the tale of eighteenth-century French author Xavier de Maistre, who, after a particularly compelling walk around his room, wrote an entire work entitled *A Journey around My Room*. De Maistre understood the principle of seeing beauty in places where most people don't look; within a few steps he found a whole world of wonderful discoveries. His vision produced a book, a fascinating (and somewhat humorous) work that has been enjoyed by readers for over two centuries. Combine vision with enough passion and heart, and a leader can make a true difference in the world.

A glance at history shows us that all great journeys, big and small, begin in the mind's eye, often with the leader's eyes closed. It goes back to what T. E. Lawrence said: "The dreamers of the day are dangerous men, for they may act their dream with open eyes, to make it possible."[2] Leaders begin with imagination and the ability to see what they want to create before it is created. Putting vision first and action second, leaders gaze across the horizon and imagine the possibilities.

Henry Ford envisioned the assembly line that would revolutionize the nation's workforce and signal the breakthrough of the industrial age, and the Model T became a mass-produced fixture in driveways across America. Before the Golden Arches sprouted up around the world, Ray Kroc envisioned a simple concept: franchising restaurants with a limited menu, fast service, and low prices. Years before women were granted the right to vote, Frances Willard envisioned a political system of equality and suffrage extended to all. Long before millions of Americans marched on Washington, DC, in 1964, Martin Luther King Jr. imagined a world where all men and women would be judged "not by the color of their skin but by the content of their character."[3]

Have there been achievements in which action preceded vision? Certainly. But this "shoot from the hip" style is more the exception than the rule. As leaders, we cannot rely on chance and possibility. Rather, we need to establish consistent and repeatable steps of behavior, beginning with the inward search for what we hope to achieve.

Ready? Then take aim (find your vision) and fire (take action). That's a much more reliable method of moving your team in the direction you want to go. This is conscious leadership, driven by passion and purpose, the twin foundations of any successful accomplishment.

Rhino Anatomy: The Eyes

Everybody thinks that the bat is the most visually challenged animal. But it's not the bat: it's the rhino. The rhino has horrible eyesight. If you want to see the world the way a rhino does, look at an object across the room with your eyes wide open. Now squint until your eyes are almost closed and look at the same object. You now have a fair approximation of a rhino's vision. What can a shortsighted animal teach us about vision and the art of leadership? To answer this question, we must understand how we see in the first place—or, more important, how we *think* we see.

I See What I See

Our eyes are amazing wonders that allow us to appreciate sunsets and gardens, the smiling faces of children, a beautiful painting, a music video, and a million other things. Sight is a gift that gives us pleasure and intimately connects us to the world in which we live. But with our eyesight come the limitations of our physical bodies. One trip to the optometrist and we realize that not all eyes are created equal. Some of us wear glasses. Some of us are nearsighted; some are farsighted. Others have astigmatism or cataracts. Let's take the case of an individual who wears prescription glasses. The moment she takes off her glasses, a seeming distortion of what's real takes place, making it difficult for her to move safely within her environment. The same would be true if she had 20-20 vision and then put on someone else's prescription glasses.

This type of distortion can have a major impact on how we look at our surroundings. As a leader, what you think you see influences your perception of your current situation. If you do not have the ability to assess a situation properly, a false impression may cloud your vision and hinder your ability to choose the appropriate course of action. For example, about ten years ago an earthquake struck northern Italy, an unusual event in that region. In one small town, buildings suffered great damage, but only two deaths occurred—both due to heart attacks. The two individuals who died were so overwhelmed with fear, they must have envisioned that the world wasn't just shaking, it was coming to an end. Sadly, their inaccurate vision of what they were experiencing cost them their lives.

In the same way, a false impression of your current situation can not only be costly but can threaten or destroy your effectiveness, ultimately confusing and sowing doubt among those you lead. Naturally, the reverse is true as well. When leaders are able to perceive reality accurately, they can choose the appropriate course of action, thereby increasing their effectiveness and leverage.

The rhino teaches us that while we must appreciate the enormous gift of our eyesight, we cannot rely on it alone or allow ourselves and our leadership to be limited by it. Like the rhino, we don't always see straight. Unlike the rhino, however, we don't always tilt our heads to change the view and figure out if what we're seeing is true or false.

I Know What I See

Sight comprises observation, perception, and the ability to know. Collectively, these add up to one of the leader's greatest assets: point of view, or the power to see what no one else can see. Like snowflakes, no two points of view are exactly alike. We've all been in situations in which the person we are dealing with is convinced that he is right and we are wrong. He perceives that his point of view is more correct than ours. Sometimes even the simplest disputes of this sort can escalate into highly unpleasant arguments. Most of the time, both people are forgetting the old axiom "There are three sides to every story: your side, my side, and the truth."

It's important for us to remember that behind every viewpoint is an individual with a lifetime of experience. All one's jobs, successes, failures, likes and dislikes, family experiences, friendships, and love relationships affect not only what a person sees but how she interprets what she sees. Ask ten different people to watch a movie, listen to a speech, or read a book, and you will undoubtedly receive ten entirely different perspectives or points of view, each depending on the person's life experiences. Is the stock market headed up or down this year? Is that comedian funny or just offensive? Is that politician a credible individual or a windbag? It all depends on whom you ask and that person's point of view. Point of view is subjective. One person isn't always right or wrong. Because of this reality, Rhino Wisdom teaches us that while we must appreciate our point of view the same way we appreciate our gift of eyesight, we must not rely solely on our unique understanding of a situation or allow ourselves to be limited by it.

The biggest difference between true statesmen and dictators is that statesmen will always seek the opinions of others. They will surround themselves with people who are willing to tell them the truth, not just what they want to hear. By definition, dictators want to be surrounded only by yes-men, and their underlings live in fear that if they disagree or disapprove, their lives will be in jeopardy.

An old expression says, "There's no limit to what you can accomplish if you don't care who gets the credit." If you are willing to listen to the ideas of others, if you are willing to incorporate their thoughts into yours, you will end up with a better product, a better service, a clearer message, a greater opportunity to influence the world.

Leaders must remain in a high state of awareness that their points of view or perceptions are inevitably only partially correct and somewhat skewed based on their own experiences. They must factor that awareness into the decision-making process as they have discussions with others.

I Imagine What I See

Imagination is the most powerful means of sight a leader can achieve. It is the essential bridge to visionary eyesight. Our imagination can take those we lead to worlds they could not envision without us. And while it may initially challenge our comfortable way of thinking, with conscious effort, we can incorporate imagination into our lives. It's said that a genius is someone who shoots at something that no one else can see and hits the target. As leaders, we must realize that if we're going to set our sights on reaching goals we've never seen, then we must aim with eyes we have never used in this manner. A successful author recently revealed that her workspace is composed of just three items: a bare table, her laptop computer, and a white wall behind them both. As she types, she uses that white wall to project mental images of her story as it plays out. It takes a true visionary to turn a blank space into a magnificent tale of human triumph. But that's exactly what a leader does.

The First Principle of Rhino Leadership: Rhino Vision

A leader's goal is not to see but to envision.

Rhino Vision is the art of 20-20 vision. While rhinos may be notorious for their bad eyesight, they have an amazing ability to form a picture of what they think is out there. And that picture can be so crystallized in their minds that they no longer have to see with their eyes to move through their world. Rhinos actually charge with their eyes closed. They rely so heavily on their ability to shape a clear vision, even without the most perfect eyesight, that they can lock on to a target and hit it precisely within inches.

Rhino Wisdom teaches us that we should not depend on traditional sight alone to develop our vision and find our target. Relying solely on our own point of view can create misconceptions. Instead, our ability to cultivate multiple ways of seeing creates an environment in which leaders thrive and charge forward with clarity, speed, and conviction. If we were to express this as an equation, it would look like this:

$$\text{See} + \text{Know} + \text{Imagine} = \text{Vision}$$

Simply put, Rhino Vision is our ability to see, know, and imagine all at once, transforming our straight-ahead perception into a 360-degree state of knowingness, affording us the ability to see in all directions at once. To achieve Rhino Vision, leaders need to utilize the entire spectrum of seeing. This begins with an understanding and mastery of the four elements of Rhino Vision: hindsight, foresight, myopia, and imagination.

Hindsight Vision

The farther back you can look,
the farther forward you are likely to see.
Winston Churchill

Hindsight involves using the past to guide the present and direct the future. Yet when we think of the word "hindsight," we probably think of a Monday-morning quarterback playing the "would have, could have, should have" game. Or we might call to mind a television pundit who, from the safety and comfort of a television studio, criticizes leaders for their missteps. In truth, hindsight is not rehashing or second-guessing but rather achieving a genuine understanding of something after it has happened.

Hindsight is critical to our ability to see the whole picture. It's impossible to have 360-degree vision without seeing behind us as well as in front of us. We must shed light on what works and what doesn't work in our organizations—both our successes and our failures. The key to hindsight is not whether we perceive our successes and failures at all but how we perceive them. That's the difference between leaders who seem to have the Midas touch and those who continually struggle to produce results.

Earl Nightingale, the father of the modern personal motivation movement, tells a story of an alcoholic father with two grown sons.[4]

"I became an alcoholic," one of his sons says. "With a father like that, what choice did I have?"

The other son says, "My father was an alcoholic, so I became sober in a twelve-step program, and today I have a very fine life. With a father like that, what choice did I have?"

In other words, hindsight will not be exactly the same for each of us. Some of us are going to draw more accurate lessons than others. Hindsight says that as leaders we must look beyond our own limitations, shortcomings, and failures. A surefire way to live a status quo life is to avoid and fear failure. Instead, we need to examine our failures and use what we find as fuel to break through our own self-defeating attitudes. Hindsight is not about mastering the world; it's about mastering the "three-pound universe": the brain with which we have been endowed. Hindsight helps train us for the inevitable setbacks that we must experience to help us grow as leaders and reach our maximum potential. After all, the point of success and failure isn't just to make us repeat our successes and avoid our failures. It's to help us become better leaders by giving us a clear understanding of why we succeeded or why we failed.

An Eye on Failure A man succeeds when he realizes that "his failures are the preparations for his victories," Ralph Waldo Emerson wrote.[5] The American attitude toward failure is interesting, to say the least. Do a Google search on "failure in the workplace" and you'll get thousands of hits. Do a similar search on Amazon and you'll find enough books to fill the library of the RMS *Titanic*. Here are some representative titles: *The Road to Success Is Paved with Failure, The Power of Failure, When Smart People Fail, Great Failures of the Extremely Successful*. Failure books are all the rage in business today. Each of them espouses its own theories, and virtually all of them cite similar examples of failures that led to success. The stories are as legendary as they are common: Babe Ruth struck out 1,330 times but hit 714 home runs in the process. Michael Jordan was cut from his high school basketball team before going on to national fame. R. H. Macy failed in retailing seven times before his store in New York became a success. Madeleine L'Engle's book *A Wrinkle in Time* was rejected by twenty-six publishers before going on to win the John Newbery Medal for best children's book. Margaret Mitchell's *Gone with the Wind* received thirty-six rejection letters before becoming a classic. Even Abraham Lincoln was defeated in elections for the legislature, the House of Representatives, the Senate, and the office of vice president before he was finally elected president in 1860.

A less well-known story of failure viewed the right way is that of Theodor Geisel, one of America's best-known advertising cartoonists in the 1920s. He did ads for national brands like Mobil Oil. Yet despite his outstanding success in advertising, Geisel harbored a dream to write books for children. He sat down and wrote a children's book and sent it to more than twenty publishers in New York. Every single publisher who saw the book rejected it.

One day, Geisel was in Manhattan about to head home, having made up his mind to gather all the drawings and the manuscript for his children's book and throw them in the trash. But before he could take that step, he ran into a college classmate. Geisel mentioned that he had written a children's book, but since no publishers had shown any interest in it, he was planning to throw it out. Coincidentally, his classmate had just gotten a job editing children's books at a publishing company, so he invited Geisel to show him his work.

Ted Geisel became known as Dr. Seuss. The book, *And to Think That I Saw It on Mulberry Street*, still entertains and enchants children of all ages. Only one publisher in two dozen said yes, which would give Geisel a batting "average" of approximately .050! But that's no way to judge the career of perhaps the single most beloved children's book writer and illustrator in American history.

Or take the case of Mel Blanc, an unemployed actor who stopped in every week for fifty-one straight weeks at Warner Bros., asking if the studio had voice-over work for him. He was rejected time and again until the fifty-first week, when someone said that the studio had just created a new cartoon and asked Blanc if he thought he could do the voice of a rabbit.

Blanc figured it was worth a try. The rabbit was Bugs Bunny, and the rest is cartoon history.

While these are undoubtedly inspirational lessons of persistence and commitment, hindsight should do more than urge us not to quit. Hindsight should teach us how to *analyze* and *use* our own failures to make us even stronger as individuals.

There is no success in life without failure. True leaders understand this. More important, the success you enjoy as a leader will be in direct proportion to the amount of failure you embrace. An old adage says that if we're not failing, we're not trying. John Wooden, the legendary UCLA basketball coach, quotes the man who coached him during his own college days: "The team that makes the most mistakes usually wins."[6]

If you're not making mistakes, you aren't doing anything! And if you're failing and not learning from your mistakes, you're failing twice. We can't allow ourselves to stagnate in our failures or succumb to paralyzing regret. Katherine Mansfield, a prominent New Zealand author, notes, "Regret is an appalling waste of energy . . . you can't build on it; it's only good for wallowing in."[7] Or as Edwin Louis Cole so aptly put it, "You don't drown by falling in the water. You drown by staying there."[8] It doesn't do us any good to wallow in our failures. As leaders, we must teach our teams not only how to get out of the water but how to use that experience as a valuable steppingstone to the life we imagine.

An Eye on Success   The failure-to-success equation can be written as follows:

Failure + The Right Perception + Perseverance = Success

As Winston Churchill said, "It is no use saying, 'We are doing our best.' You have got to succeed in doing what is necessary."[9]

A door-to-door cosmetics queen with a penchant for pink turns a $5,000 investment into a billion-dollar enterprise. A failed Nevada gold prospector with six employees and two bicycles turns his messenger service into a global empire. A twenty-year-old housewife with no business experience turns a recipe and a dream into a $450 million cultural phenomenon. Whether hearing about Mary Kay Inc., UPS, or Mrs. Fields Cookies, everybody loves a good success story. And in between the glamorous rags-to-riches Fortune 500 stories are thousands of other tales—small, anonymous, unheard stories of men and women who, through their own determination and bravery, found a way to overcome obstacles so that they could have a better life for themselves and their families.

Success stories inspire us and remind us that with hard work, anything is possible. They are educational, providing us with a blueprint for our own dreams. Most important, success stories are contagious: they lead to even more success.

Of course, of all the success stories in the world, none is more important and more powerful than our own. These are the stories we need to tell the most, especially to ourselves. However, even the most successful people often downplay their great accomplishments. This isn't false modesty on their part; it's a sign of their greatness. Successful people don't rest on their laurels. They aren't content to celebrate and relive old victories. Instead, they sweep the trophies into the attic and ask themselves, Where am I going to win today?

But before you allow your own trophy case to gather dust, take a moment to celebrate what you have accomplished because it will remind you that even greater things are in store if you will only keep trying. Sharing your success stories with your team is not only courageous and empowering, but it forces you to stop and observe the how and the why of what you have accomplished, opening doors to even more success than you had before.

How will observing your successes help you become a leader that others will follow?

First, observing successes helps educate the team. By analyzing the individual components of successful strategies, you can discover what specifically is working and what is not. If your team says that it takes X, Y, and Z to be successful but after review you learn that it was only X or some other factor altogether different, then the team's future growth strategy needs to be amended.

Second, observing successes allows you to appreciate them. No team should get so used to success that it becomes complacent and jaded by its own achievements. That's the easiest way for a team to go from "we" to "me." Although you want success to become commonplace, you do not want *the way your team responds to success* to become commonplace. This response leads to arrogance and the misguided belief that because your team has achieved in the past, it will always achieve in the future. Genuine appreciation for your team's achievements creates the necessary passion and enthusiasm while fueling the entire team's commitment to continuing to succeed.

Third, observing your successes allows you to validate the contribution of each individual. Today's most effective leaders realize that an organization is not its bottom-line profits but instead the individuals who make those bottom-line profits happen. This fact needs to be acknowledged and recognized at every opportunity. What kind of recognition, rewards, bonuses, and other "feel good" experiences does your enterprise offer people who succeed? If you are an entrepreneur, providing your team members with a surprise round of golf or a day at a spa pays dividends far in excess of the cost of those tax-deductible items. Such gestures connect us with our workers, humanize our teams, and lead to increased staff retention, higher job performance and satisfaction, and most of all, loyalty, which any good leader will tell you is the ultimate prerequisite for success.

Finally, observing successes gives the team confirmation that it's heading in the right direction. All great journeys should be the manifestation of a concrete mission statement, like President John F. Kennedy's 1961 commitment that we would put a man on the moon by the time the decade was out. And we did! By celebrating your success, you can simultaneously reaffirm your shared mission while communicating your continued optimism for the future and the direction in which you are headed. This not only builds morale but also generates confidence in your ability to take the team where it needs to go in the future.

You don't have to have an elaborate awards banquet to celebrate your successes. Just surprising a team member—preferably in front of her coworkers—with a gift certificate, cash, or some other symbol of appreciation makes a huge difference.

Foresight

Everything changes but change itself.

John F. Kennedy

Foresight, the second element of Rhino Vision, involves anticipating the future. If history teaches us anything, it's that change is inevitable. Successful CEOs sometimes say that leaders have to eat change for breakfast. This is true not just in technology but also in politics, economics, fashion, entertainment, and even morality. The world is changing faster than our imaginations can keep up with.

While change might present incredible opportunities, it's also a scary proposition, especially when you are trying to grow a business and provide for your family. In the blink of an eye, your products and services can turn into something people no longer want or need. In that same blink of an eye, if your business becomes expendable and obsolete, you may be forced to scramble for a new way of life. For example, jobs are being outsourced to India and China at a dramatically increasing rate, which only increases the pressure on workers left behind.

People in today's workforce know that something needs to be done about the rapid pace of change. They're looking to their leaders not to stop change, which is unrealistic, but to keep pace with it. Leaders have two choices: they can adapt to change after it has happened and hope that they're not too late, or they can anticipate change and be ready when it happens. Anticipating change takes skill and courage. More important, it takes foresight.

In 1976, General Motors CEO Elliot M. "Pete" Estes had a plan he called "60-60-60": he wanted General Motors to reach a 60 percent market share for all vehicles sold in the United States and have the company's stock reach $60 per share. And he wanted to accomplish this by his sixtieth birthday. If you had asked Estes back then about Japanese imports, he would have scoffed. "Americans don't want those dinky Japanese econoboxes," he might have told you. "Americans want big cars like the ones we make."

Fast-forward to the present day. You know how the story turns out. Toyota, not GM, is the world's dominant automaker. GM, Ford, and Chrysler combined possess less than a 50 percent market share for cars. This story is an example of a business leader who failed to anticipate change and whose company paid the price.

By contrast, consider the example of General Electric. Under Jack Welch, GE made a critical strategic decision: it would be either first or second in every market it entered, or it would abandon that market altogether. This approach constituted a wrenching change for GE, as many longtime GE divisions and components were let go. But Welch held to his vision, recognizing that in a changing marketplace, being number three or number four would never be profitable. As a result, GE today represents the gold standard for American corporations, and Jack Welch is revered as a business genius.

By definition, foresight is the act of knowing something before it happens. If this sounds like a magic trick, it is! After all, what can be more like pulling a rabbit out of a hat than anticipating the future and seeing what no one else can see? Study the life of any visionary leader and it won't be long before you're asking, How did he (or she) do that? But as Rhino Wisdom will teach us, as is the case with any good magic trick, once you figure out how to see the future, it's easy to do. In truth, there is no magic. Predicting the future is possible for anyone who takes the time and makes the effort to learn how. In fact, incorporating foresight into your leadership practice takes only three simple steps: cultivate, correlate, and anticipate.

Step 1:* Cultivate *the Environment in Which Foresight Can Thrive Foresight is a matter of preparation, training our eyes to see what they need to see so that we can thrive in whatever environment tomorrow may bring. And that takes education and knowledge. As leaders, we must commit ourselves to knowing the information that affects our future. Bill Gates was among the first to recognize that all sorts of products could be created if a computer's operating system and all other software programs are separated from the hardware. Gates saw the future of computing and understood the importance of owning the dominating operating system in that emerging industry. His vision: a computer on every desk. At the time, only the largest corporations owned their own mainframes, which took up entire rooms.

Gates not only saw the future, he acted upon it. And while it might be easy to think that Gates's gaze into the future was purely a matter of timing, none of his innovations would have happened had he not been so immersed in the computer industry in the first place. This is an important lesson for all of us. We can't look into our future with only half the answers, any more than we can complete a puzzle with only half the pieces. A solid understanding of the future requires facts, figures, and analysis. It demands that we become experts in our chosen fields. If we're not actively learning everything there is to know about our businesses, our foresight will be limited at best.

We must commit to staying current in our fields of expertise by reading the latest books, current biographies, and historical perspectives. We need to attend trade shows and seminars and join professional organizations. We need to do whatever it takes to stay on the cutting edge of our businesses. If we don't do it, who will? Our competition, that's who.

Step 2: Correlate *Events of the Past with Those of the Present* The next step in our pursuit of foresight is to understand how events of the past created the environment of our present and how the events of the present will create the environment of tomorrow. This is correlating, or finding cause and effect. As Isaac Newton put it in his third law of motion, "For every action, there is an equal and opposite reaction."

Mark Twain once said that a cat who sits on a hot stove-lid "will never sit down on another hot stove-lid again—and that is well; but also she will never sit down on a cold one anymore."[10] Often, we mix up the law of cause and effect just as much as that cat does. If we get "burned," we never want to try anything new again. But that's exactly the wrong lesson to learn. Just watch a baby try to take his first steps. He'll fall and fall again and sometimes get hurt in the process. But he'll keep trying until he's mastered the art of walking. As adults, we've got considerably more advantages than a toddler: we have the ability to study the past and discern its true meaning. All we need to do is avoid hot stoves in the future and we can cook up anything we want. Understanding how the causes of the past align with the effects of the future allows us to methodically grasp what will happen, even before it happens. To cultivate this powerful tool for your leadership practice, study every aspect of the current activity in your organization (events, attitudes, behaviors, successes, failures). Then work backward to find the specific root cause for each of them. Make a list and be as specific as possible.

Now study the same current activity and, working forward, draw specific conclusions as to how you believe these actions will be manifested in the future. For example, look at your sales pipeline, not just the bottom line of how many sales your team is closing and how much those sales are worth. Instead, take a look at the other end of the funnel. What kind of prospects is your team contacting? Are they really the right people for your business? Should you be going after a more lucrative market? It's tough to improve results at the narrow end of the funnel until you've examined what's going into the broad end. The key isn't necessarily to fix or change anything but purely to understand how one action causes another.

Finally, study the law of cause and effect in your day-to-day activities. Every meeting, telephone call, e-mail, argument, and smile is an action that leads to another action. If you train yourself to see these cause-and-effect principles in your daily routine, you will be better able to see them in larger events as well.

Correlating is an incredibly empowering tool that helps you understand the seeds of your individual successes and failures. The sooner you realize how your actions and reactions connect back to your life and shape your future, the sooner you will begin to see the emerging patterns that allow you to anticipate future events.

Step 3:* Anticipate *the Future Foresight must be proactive. It requires conscious effort to anticipate and direct what the future will look like. Organizations, teams, small groups, and individuals need to engage in forward thinking in order to anticipate problems and capitalize on opportunities. Doing this requires strategic planning and forecasting capabilities, which can develop only if forward thinking is an integral part of the organization.

As a leader, take the opportunity to start your own forward-thinking R&D (research and development) department. For technology, communications, and pharmaceutical companies, R&D is part of their lifeblood because if they can't offer the latest, fastest, and shiniest new products on the block, their customers may go elsewhere to find them. To keep up and stay relevant, these companies are forced into bold and innovative thinking.

For example, pharmaceutical companies are always engaged in a race against time: eventually their lucrative new drugs will lose their patent protection, and their profit margins will disappear as generic versions compete in the marketplace. This sense of urgency should apply to every organization no matter what business you're in, no matter what products or services you offer.

If you had a sudden realization that your organization was going to be entirely obsolete in a year's time, you'd start developing contingencies immediately, wouldn't you? Think about how differently business is conducted today compared with just one, five, or ten years ago. Today's leader needs to create a "necessity mind-set" without any prompting from the marketplace. This is not to suggest that you should conduct your business fearfully, always thinking you are just one lost client away from shutting your doors. But as the Boy Scouts remind us, you need to be prepared for what lies ahead. Adopting an R&D mentality helps you prepare for the future and demands that you take critical time to experiment, challenge existing beliefs, and play "what if." This forward-thinking approach will allow you to stay ahead of the curve, helping you not only to anticipate future challenges but to create the appropriate strategies for dealing with them.

Myopia

All thought is a feat of association; having what's in front
of you bring up something in your mind that
you almost didn't know you knew.
Robert Frost

Many scientists believe that rhinos have poor eyesight because their ancestors lived in dense forests. The thick cover of plants prevented the animals from seeing very far in any direction, making good eyesight unnecessary. For today's leader, too, a little shortsightedness is a good thing. "Myopia" may mean shortsighted and narrow-minded, but for truly visionary leaders it also implies an intense focus on the essential elements that are right in front of them. That focus is myopia, the third element of Rhino Vision.

Our lives are stuffed with so much to do and see, past and present, far and near, that we have lost our ability to just stay in the moment and concentrate on what needs to be done to move our organization forward. Myopia asks that we take our cue from the rhino, putting up trees around us so that we will pay attention to what is right before our eyes. Like the glasses that are sitting on your head while you're looking for them or the lost keys that were in your pocket the whole time, most of life's ideas and solutions are as close as your fingertips. You just need "rhino eyes" to see them.

Myopia asks each leader to *stay in the moment*. Forget about the past. Ignore the future. Focus only on now. Of course, this doesn't mean you cannot use the past and the future to help you grow, as you do with foresight and hindsight. It only means that you can't allow yourself to get permanently stuck.

We all know people who are stuck in the past, athletes or businesspeople living off former past glories and accomplishments or people crippled by failure and regret. We probably know just as many people stuck in the future, living off the promises of what might be (the right job, a perfect relationship, a promotion, or retirement) or crippled by fear of what might happen (unemployment, divorce, disease, or death). You might think of a businesswoman who is so focused on work that she misses valuable time with her children or of a recluse who won't venture to the corner store for fear of being struck by a car. The past and future contain realities we must contend with, but we cannot permit our minds to stay there too long. If we do, not only do we deplete our energies, but we deny ourselves present-moment awareness and with it, the power to focus on the gems that are right in front of our eyes.

Here's a practical suggestion: Take an informal survey of your own thoughts. See how much time in any given day you spend regretting the past (or fantasizing about past glories) or wandering off into the future, worrying about problems that are most likely never going to happen. If you can increase the time you spend thinking about the present a little bit every day, you're doing a huge favor for not only your team or organization but also yourself.

Spend time on what matters. A little-known disease is spreading among organizations today. It's wasted effort—also known as inefficiency—and it's characterized by a poor use of time and a lack of focus. As leaders, we need to be conscious of how we spend our time and when our attention seems to drift. We need to actively focus our resources and energies on what really matters, on the items that drive the business and allow us to reach our goals. In his book *The 4-Hour Workweek*, Timothy Ferriss reminds readers of a century-old rule first proposed by an Italian philosopher named Vilfredo Pareto. In 1906, Pareto began the research that led to the realization that *80 percent of our results come from only 20 percent of our efforts.*

In other words, when we come to work, we spend so much time sharpening pencils, categorizing e-mails, shuffling sales leads, or simply spilling coffee on our pants that we end up being productive only a small portion of the day. What if we were able to achieve a much higher degree of efficiency? What if we were able to expand that 20 percent figure to 30, 40, 50, or more? Wouldn't that be exciting?

Focus on one task at a time. Two objects can't occupy the same space at the same time. We have all tried to master the art of multitasking. Yet multitasking is nothing more than constantly switching gears, going from one focus to another focus. Switch gears long enough and often enough and you'll eventually burn out the clutch and leave the car sputtering on the side of the road. Yes, multitasking has its place. For busy leaders, there is no way around it, but for visionary thinking and leadership, your view needs to be uncluttered as much of the time as possible.

Your ability to think forward depends on your patience to focus on just one task at a time. It takes discipline. The next time you're on the phone, don't open your e-mails and start replying while you're only half listening to the conversation. Many people consider it a badge of honor that they can do two, three, or more activities at the same time; mothers are the quintessential example of skilled multitaskers. But the human mind wasn't built for such activities. It's just not worth the effort. And in the business realm, while you're doing six things at once, your competitor is doing just one: focusing on beating you.

Imagination

> Imagination is more important than knowledge.
> It is the preview of life's coming attractions.
> *Albert Einstein*

With hindsight, foresight, and a generous dose of myopia, a leader's vision becomes sharp and formidable. But to realize the true power and potential of Rhino Vision, a leader needs imagination. While foresight deals with assumptions as they relate to data, human behavior, and trends, imagination shows us what is possible regardless of what everyone else believes is either improbable or even impossible. In the words of Walt Disney, "If you can dream it, you can do it."[11] And as Nike says, "Just do it."

Imagination is the ability to see what isn't there, to form images and ideas in your mind, which, when combined with a clearly defined plan and hard work, gives you the power to bring life to your dreams. Imagination is what created the Sistine Chapel, cured polio, and put a man on the moon. It's what put a Starbucks in every shopping center and a computer on every desk. It has given us every major advancement and accomplishment since the beginning of time. And yet many believe that imagination is the province only of genius and visionaries. In reality, it's accessible to anyone and everyone who chooses to use it and incorporate it into their leadership practice. All it takes is following a few simple guidelines.

Listen to Your Heart The idea of listening to your heart might seem nebulous and new age, but the heart is the only place to begin a journey that aims to make a genuine difference. With your heart comes your passion, gut, intuition, and instinct—the part of you that knows the path you should be taking. The heart is the source of your power. If you aren't operating from this place of strength, then you are a leader without vision. And a leader without vision is just a manager, implementing someone else's will. As a true leader, you need to trust and listen to your most valuable asset: yourself. Only then can you allow your heart to lead you where you need to go.

Ever wonder why compact disks have a maximum run time of approximately eighty minutes? It's because the most popular piece of classical music in Japan is Beethoven's Ninth Symphony. If you're in Japan on New Year's Eve, you can find orchestras playing its finale, "Ode to Joy," in practically every corner of the country. The president of Sony Corporation, Akio Morita, was annoyed that every time he wanted to listen to Beethoven's Ninth on his record player, he would have to interrupt his enjoyment of the piece and turn the record over halfway through. So he tasked his engineers with devising a memory-retention device that would hold a piece of music as long as Beethoven's Ninth, or approximately eighty minutes. And thus the compact disk was born.

The creation of the compact disk, and the Sony Discman and the myriad of CD players that followed, was not initially a *business* decision. It was a decision that came from the heart of a music lover who happened to be running one of the world's largest technology companies.

Color Outside the Lines Admittedly, coloring outside the lines is a cliché that ranks right up there with thinking outside the box. But it's a powerful and liberating instrument, bringing profound truth and important lessons to every leader. Coloring outside the lines means that no rules, no limitations, and no right or wrong way to do something exist. It also means challenging old rules, old realities, and old ways of thinking. Too often, organizations won't allow new ideas to bloom because they have a policy or procedure already in place, whether it's working or not. Multiply that same logic among our families, churches, schools, and government, and the result is a pandemic of everyone thinking the same way.

As a leader, you need to challenge the rules, practices, traditions, and paradigms of your organization. You don't necessarily need to defy them, but you do need to challenge them. You need to ask where the beliefs about your organization came from. Why do we operate the way we do? Where do all the programs, concepts, and projects originate? And do the reasons still exist for them to be there? This challenge to existing truths and realities will free your mind for innovation and change.

Throughout history, most great innovations shattered some preconceived thought or broke some established rule. Christopher Columbus broke the rule that said the world was flat. Albert Einstein broke the rule of Newtonian physics. Henry Ford broke the rules on how society manufactures its products. Apple Computer broke the rules about how a computer is supposed to look. Charles Schwab broke the rules about how we buy and sell stocks on Main

Street. And Kathrine Switzer broke the rule that only men could run in the Boston Marathon, persevering even when officials attempted to physically pull her from the race. History is rich with rule breakers, so take a risk and break some rules of your own.

Adopt an Imaginative State of Mind   Rhino Wisdom teaches us that there is more to vision than what is right in front of our nose. The most profound state of seeing is the imaginative state. Unfortunately, we are a culture that creates and rewards realists. We value what we can hold in our hands, what we can see, hear, and touch, none of which helps us adopt an imaginative state of mind.

To enter this state of awareness, you need to change the way you look at the world around you. You must leave your MBA at the door, along with all your titles, the initials after your name, your sense of self-importance, and all preconceived ideas. You need to stop taking the world so seriously.

In the words of the Persian poet Rumi, "Sell your cleverness and buy bewilderment."[12] With bewilderment comes wonder and the empowering sense that you live in a world where your dreams can come true. If you don't believe that, if you cringe at the sentimentality, then how will you create a vision you can expect others to follow? You won't. Rather, you must strive to become a leader who wholeheartedly believes that what seems improbable to most is inevitable. Do that and the world will follow you anywhere.

After Steve Jobs dropped out of college, he audited a few courses, including one on calligraphy. As a result, he learned the history of fonts, which at the time was an arcane topic of interest only to those in the publishing industry. When Jobs later designed Apple's personal computers, he included a range of fonts based on his experiences in his class. He had a vision of computers that created not just documents but *beautiful* documents. As a result, archcompetitor Microsoft had to build fonts into its operating systems. And today, whenever computer users sit down at a computer, whether it's a PC or a Mac, a range of fonts awaits them. What could be more improbable than the expectation that what comes out of a computer could be beautiful? But that was Jobs's vision, and it worked out—most likely far beyond even his expectations.

Ask, What If? In order to use our imagination, we need to ask, What if? "What if what?" you might ask. It doesn't matter. It's a fill-in-the-blank question that comes out of your own personal and organizational needs. What if you zigged instead of zagged, turned left instead of right, reversed directions, changed procedures, did it this way instead of that way? What if you rewrote your mission statement, changed your organization's name, moved the business to Hawaii, and gave away free lunches on Thursdays? The specifics aren't important. What matters is the process. There are no right or wrong what-if questions and no rules other than this: engage in asking what-if questions as often as you possibly can. Aim to make your question as far reaching and illogical as possible. What-if questions should ask us to suspend assumptions and allow us to enter into an altered state of seeing.

And while you're at it, make your answers just as far reaching and illogical. Don't stop with just one answer or two, but try for five, ten, or twenty answers. Push yourself to keep going. It's like drilling a well: you'll never know what you'll hit—when that idea light bulb will go on—unless you dig a little deeper. What-if thinking is your reminder that you don't always solve a problem by seeing it in a normal way. Rather, you often solve problems through play and experimentation. When Hofstra University on Long Island was being built, the concrete paths between the buildings were added last. The school's designers wanted to see where people walked; once they knew, that's where they laid down pavement. See where people take you, and then see where you can take them.

Schedule Time to Imagine

You aren't what you eat. You are what you put in your Palm Pilot or iPhone. We schedule our days with what's "important": meetings, phone calls, travel, exercise, social events. But how much time do we spend stretching our imaginations, pushing ourselves to see things from different perspectives? It's not enough to say that we need to use our imaginations. We need to create the time to use our imaginations. Imagination is a muscle, and like all muscles, it's either "use it or lose it." Make a firm commitment to set aside time every day to ask what-if questions and to daydream, imagine, and visualize the future you want to create.

The Wisdom of Rhino Vision

Rhino Vision teaches you not to be limited by your outer vision or by what others believe you can or cannot see. As a leader, you must learn to see not only with your eyes but with the inner knowingness of your heart and mind. Today's leaders have no choice but to close their eyes, play "what if," and dream big. What if you could create the company you wanted, the world you wanted, the you you wanted? What would that look like? How would it feel? Put these thoughts in your head and play them over and over until they're so clear you can touch them. These wild and bold imaginings will become the vision that begins your journey of a thousand miles, from where you are now to the enlightened leadership it is your responsibility to create.

A FINAL RHINO THOUGHT

The imagination has no limitations,
so be optimistic. Be courageous.
Be bold. Be yourself.
Follow your heart.
And know that your vision can
change the world.

CHAPTER TWO

The Rhino's Ears

A Leader's Ability to Listen

Listening is a magnetic and strange thing, a creative
force . . . When we are listened to, it creates us, makes
us unfold and expand. Ideas actually begin
to grow within us and come to life.

Barbara Ueland

alt Disney envisioned a magical amusement park emerging from the orange groves of then-sleepy Anaheim,
California. The park would enable visitors to experience
the small-town America we were leaving behind; the exciting technological advances of the future, which were rapidly approaching
back in the 1950s; and the greatest amusement park rides on earth.
His park would stir the imagination and excitement of people of all
ages. But his legacy wouldn't have been possible had he been unable
to persuade bankers and industry experts, all of whom initially pre-
dicted disaster, to invest in his dream. After all, who would actually
pile their children into the car and drive all the way to *Anaheim*? Just
about everybody in the world, as it turned out.

Martin Luther King Jr. envisioned a world of equality, one in
which men and women of all backgrounds could sit together at the
table of brotherhood. But his legacy would not have been the same
had he lacked the extraordinary ability to communicate a vision of

nonviolent resistance. Not only did he have a dream, he had a message.

Steve Jobs envisioned a sleek, more user-friendly computer, one that would transform information processing. But the Apple revolution wouldn't have happened without Jobs's ability to convince artists, designers, publishers, and students that his was the personal computer "for the rest of us."

These individuals were great leaders not only because they held a crystal-clear vision of where they were going but also because they understood that their success depended on selling that vision. They understood that you can't be a leader if you don't have any followers. And without dedicated team members, eager investors, and loyal customers, there can be no CEOs. In short, leaders must learn how to *sell their vision*, which is the next step in the leader's journey.

How well you sell your vision becomes the single most critical factor in determining whether you realize your organization's goals. As a leader, you must remember that you need people who believe in your vision and are willing to back that belief with a sacrifice of their time, talent, and energy. Team members want more than paychecks. They want to feel important. They want their work to be valued and their ideas to be respected. They want to be heard. They want to be recognized. Your job as a leader is to synergistically provide an atmosphere in which your team or organization can thrive.

Consider the story of some prisoners of war who were forced to move a huge mound of dirt from one side of the prison yard to another. Although the task took a long time, they were able to complete it with no problem and without any loss of health or vitality. But then the order came to move the dirt back to where it used to be. At that point, the prisoners realized that their strenuous efforts were for no particular purpose. This is when their health began to break down, when despair set in, and when death followed.

This is an extreme example but a telling one. People need to feel that their efforts matter—that they aren't just digging a ditch but building a cathedral, to come back to the story mentioned earlier in this book. And it's up to leaders to convince their team members that they have a vision worth following.

First, leaders have to realize that selling a vision isn't just a matter of *telling* it to their people but instead *connecting* it to the organization they lead. This connection is the key to communication, a process that involves speaking and listening, giving and taking. Meaningful communication is a two-way street. Ideas and feedback need to flow between the leader and the team so that the vision becomes not "mine" or "yours" but "ours." This creates ownership, buy-in, enthusiasm, passion, and persistence—the essential ingredients for long-term success. Contrary to popular belief, communication doesn't begin with speaking. It begins with listening. Listening is always the first step in effective communication. In fact, without listening, communication cannot exist at all.

Listen to Your Team Members

If there is any one secret of success, it lies in the ability
to get the other person's point of view and see things
from that person's angle as well as from your own.
Henry Ford

It's one of the oldest and wisest axioms in business: listen to the individuals in your organization who are making things happen. Find out what they want and then deliver it. That's how you create loyalty and grow a business. We need to listen to every single man and woman on our team. We need to find out what drives them to get up in the morning. What can we do to help them succeed within the organization and provide for their families? How do they feel about their coworkers and leadership team? What about the organization as a whole and the role they play in it? Do they feel empowered? inspired? bored? fed up? Do they feel they can make a difference in their organization's future? The answers to these questions are the keys to unleashing a team's potential.

Employees are naturally more receptive to leaders who listen. When people feel that their leadership team truly cares about them and their opinions, they're happy to work harder for the benefit of the organization. Take the leadership example set recently by the executive vice president of a technology company. Company employees were eager to heap accolades on their leader, noting that she had an amazing ability to motivate her team and was always available to lend her professional expertise. She was responsive to workers' comments and concerns, always working with them to improve the office environment. But what truly endeared the executive to her employees was the fact that she supported them in their lives *beyond* the office.

After learning that one of her staff was to participate in his first triathlon, she came to the race to support him. A few days afterward she presented him with a framed picture and a gift card to an athletic store. He was touched at this show of affirmation and support. Here was a leader who knew how to listen to her team members by showing that she appreciated what was important in their lives.

The degree to which you listen to your employees and understand their needs and motivations is the degree to which you can help them succeed. And as is the reciprocal nature of life, the more you help them, the more you will help yourself and your business. It's not just good business practice; it's good people practice. The most enduring, memorable, and successful leaders have always been men and women of principle who value the people who work for them.

Nancy Lieberman is considered by many to be the greatest female basketball player in American history. After being part of a silver-medal-winning team at the Olympics and after an outstanding career in the fledgling WNBA, Lieberman went on to coach the Detroit Shock. She says that on whatever level she played, she would always take her teammates to lunch. As the point guard, it was her job to distribute the ball to the shooters, so she would ask her shooters, "How do you like getting the ball? Do you like it up high or down low? Do you like getting a bounce pass, or do you like getting it in the air?"

These seem like such obvious questions to ask, but how often in professional basketball, or in basketball at any level, do you think questions like these are asked? Probably not very often. Because Lieberman was taking the time to find out how her teammates felt most comfortable, she was setting them up to succeed. She wasn't telling them, "It's my team and this is how it's going to be: you're going to get the ball the way I want to give it to you." That's not communication. Instead, she opened a dialogue with them by asking what it would take to make *them* comfortable. That's true leadership.

Herb Kelleher founded Southwest Airlines with the vision of giving people who couldn't afford to fly the ability to do so. But Kelleher's dream came true not only because of the attractive ticket prices he offered but because of the loyalty he earned from the people who worked with him. From the beginning, Kelleher's business strategy revolved around the simple idea that he would give his staff the same respect and care that he expected them to give their customers. Kelleher understood what all visionaries know: the road to realizing your vision begins with a workforce that feels valued and understood. The only proven way to take your team on a journey is to create a desire for them to want to go along.

Begin your journey with the undeniable premise that the best way to lead others is with your ears. Listening—and the understanding it brings—will make a profound difference not just in your team's life but in your own as well. Listening is the power behind your vision.

Rhino Anatomy: The Ears

As we discussed in the previous chapter, just because rhinos don't have 20-20 vision doesn't mean they don't know what's going on. They learn in other ways. While rhinos' eyesight may be less than perfect by human standards, their hearing is exceptional. In fact, the rhino's ears are a biological wonder, seemingly designed for optimal listening. Rhinos have round, cupped ears with long tubes pointing toward what they're listening to—just like funnels for sound. What's more, they can swivel their ears around, rotating them to pick up sound from any direction. Their ability to hear so well is a matter of consciously shifting their attention to what they should be hearing, coupled with their ability to master the delicate balance between active and passive listening. Rhinos have much to teach us about the art of listening, but first we need to understand how we hear in the first place—or at least, how we think we hear.

I Hear What I Want to Hear

Hearing, simply put, is the ability to perceive sound. Someone speaks or music plays, and it registers in the brain. While this definition is accurate enough, I suspect the folks who wrote the dictionary never played the childhood game of "telephone." A child whispers something to the next child, who whispers it to someone else, and around the circle it goes until the message reaches the last person, who usually ends up with a message that's entirely different from the one that began the process. Somewhere along the line, the message always manages to become watered down or distorted. While you could chalk it up to garbled speech, bad memory, or an assortment of outside distractions, another possible culprit cannot be ignored: *we hear want we want to hear.*

A salesperson spends twenty-five minutes with a prospect in an electronics store, explaining all the features of six different wide-screen televisions. At the end of the demonstration, the salesperson asks, "Which one do you like best?"

The prospect vaguely nods toward one of the televisions.

"Does that mean you want to take it?" the eager salesperson asks breathlessly.

"Well," the prospect says, sounding uncertain, "I like that one, and I'll call you tomorrow if it turns out that my wife says she likes it, too, and if it goes with the drapes, and if we can afford the payments on our credit card, and if it isn't raining so that it doesn't get wet when it's being delivered, assuming my kids don't need an extra year of college . . ." and so on and so forth.

But the salesperson didn't hear anything after the words "I'll call you tomorrow." He heard what he wanted to hear—that he made the sale. He ignored all the obfuscations and conditions that the prospect placed on the "sale." A more experienced salesperson would have understood exactly what was going on: the prospect was saying, "No, I'm not ready to buy at this time." But the salesperson in this example immediately jumped in front of his laptop and booked tickets to Hawaii because he was convinced that with this "sale" he had just won the prize for top salesperson of the month.

Similarly, an eager young attorney could learn a lot by listening to a senior partner's advice, but she might miss the constructive criticism if she lets her ego, fed by years of academic success, get in the way. A team leader so driven to meeting his sales goals might miss out on crucial feedback from his team members. An executive who invites only her friends onto her board or advisory council most likely won't hear the diverse points of view that other members of her organization have to offer.

While we may hear the good, easy-to-digest, and congratulatory messages that satisfy our own self-interests, we often ignore the "uncomfortable stuff" we most need to hear. If we're not careful, we can become victims of selective hearing and lose out on the wisdom and experience others have to offer and are actively trying to share.

In M. Night Shyamalan's brilliant psychological thriller *The Sixth Sense*, the main character (played by Bruce Willis) is fundamentally affected by the fact that he hears only what he wants to hear. All the relationships in his life—his slowly decaying marriage, his business contacts, and his friendship with Haley Joel Osment's character—are deeply influenced by his inability to see and listen to anything beyond the world he wants to see and hear.

Rhino Wisdom teaches us that we must be open to hearing everything and not allow our own preconceptions, prejudices, or preferences to hinder our ability to be good listeners.

I Hear What Others Want Me to Hear

Over two thousand years ago, Buddha said, "At the bottom of things, most people want to be understood and appreciated."[1] These words are as true today as ever. We all want to be listened to and genuinely heard. We all want to know that somebody cares about what we have to say. Unfortunately, many of us think we're too busy to stop and really listen to what someone else is trying to say. We interrupt, finish their sentences for them, think about something entirely different, or just walk away. And if we don't walk away, it's probably because we're so busy thinking about what we're going to say next that we aren't paying attention in the first place.

Have you ever been part of a lunch group and noticed that one person talks more than everybody else combined? Someone might start talking about her recent vacation in Italy and how great it was. While good listeners will give her a chance to share her experiences, conversation hogs will quickly turn the dialogue back to themselves, stealing her thunder. "Oh, I've been to Italy twice!" the word hog will blurt out. "I visited Milan, Florence, and Rome, and I've had lunch with the pope—twice!"

Of course, not only does that empty the lunch table, but it leaves the original speaker feeling drained and less willing to speak up the next time around.

Rhino Wisdom teaches us that we need to lose that selfishness and impatience. We must stop hearing through our own experiences and start hearing through the speaker's experiences. We need to stop hearing what we want to hear and start hearing what others want us to hear. Listening is not about what's in it for us but what we can do to help others be understood. It's said that the hand that is most open to give is most open to receive. Likewise, the ear that is most open to listen is also most open to receive knowledge and learning. This higher level of purposeful hearing is what begins to connect the listener to the speaker, and it is the first step on the road to creating meaningful communication with those in our organization.

I Hear What I Need to Hear

Good leaders work hard to obtain the information they need to keep a finger on the pulse of their organizations. But as leaders, we must recognize that we hear a lot of things that don't matter to us or don't do anything to help our organizations move forward. While the rhino teaches us that we should listen with open ears, we also need the wisdom to know what information to accept and what to

reject. Our job is to become discriminating listeners, able to separate the noise from what truly matters in our lives.

For animals in the jungle or on the savanna, the ability to discriminate between wind blowing through leaves and the crackling
of twigs indicating the impending arrival of a predator is the difference between life and death. Like the rhino, we must think on our
feet and quickly process what we hear. This is the wisdom of the
rhino: training ourselves to hear only what matters.

"In one ear and out the other" is an old expression often applied to lazy husbands and irresponsible teenagers, but actually it
is an important and valuable tool for listening. Rhino Wisdom
teaches us that we must take in only what is essential, disregard-
ing the rest, so that what remains is the information that will lead
us closer to the truth.

One of the most important political events of the twentieth
century was the discovery of the Watergate break-in in 1972. Back
then, President Richard Nixon was running for reelection. A group
of operatives working for the Committee to Reelect the President
had broken into the Democrats' political headquarters in the
Watergate Hotel office and apartment complex in Washington, DC.
But the crime might never have been noticed were it not for an
astute security guard named Frank Wills. Wills had already made
his rounds through the Watergate once when, passing the door to
the Democratic Party campaign office, he noticed that a small
piece of tape had been placed over the lock. A security guard in a
complex as big as the Watergate has a thousand things to notice.
But out of all the bits of information available to Wills, he focused
on this one piece of evidence. That small piece of tape told him
that something was amiss.

Wills's ability to discern the wheat from the chaff, to tell meaningful information from meaningless information, led to the arrest

of the perpetrators and an investigation that ultimately brought down the Nixon White House.

The Second Principle of Rhino Leadership: Rhino Hearing

A leader's goal is not to hear but to understand.

Rhino Hearing is understanding what we hear. Nobody cares if you can hear a pin drop across the room or a hummingbird flying miles away. When it comes to hearing, what matters is how well you hear what is being said. For the enlightened leader, hearing is about understanding what your team is telling you and then figuring out how to take that information to drive your vision forward. These skills take practice. Unfortunately, they have never been a prerequisite for earning an MBA, and too often they are the last skills a leader will consciously work to improve. When was the last time a leader you know enrolled in the latest listening workshop?

Yet whether we admit it or not, listening is critically important to our communication strategies. Therefore, it's something we can't take for granted, nor can we assume that it will always be there. Listening is a muscle that needs to be used and stretched or it will deteriorate and wither away, and with it, the foundation on which we build our organizations. As leaders, we must commit to turning listening into an art form, cultivating our power to hear what we need to hear.

Back in the 1980s, when answering machines could record conversations on tape, a University of California researcher invited his students to bring in the minicassettes from their devices. The researcher, Gerald Goodman, then listened to the cassettes to hear conversations recorded after someone who had been screening calls picked up the phone. He discovered that there was often just a minuscule amount of time between the moment when one person stopped talking and the next person started. How much active listening could people really be doing if they only needed a microsecond in order to make their next point?

Funnel Listening

The greatest compliment that was ever paid to me was when one asked me what I thought, and attended my answer.

Henry David Thoreau

When it comes to listening, only one rule is absolute: don't sit back and wait for others to talk. Listening is a proactive process that requires the leader to both *engage* and *direct* the voices in the organization. The rhino's funnel-shaped ears show us how the process works. Typically, a funnel is a cone-shaped instrument with a large opening at the top and a small tube at the bottom used to guide substances into containers. But for the rhino—and the leader—the word "funnel" becomes a verb meaning to actively move or direct something into and through a narrow space.

Rhino Wisdom teaches us that the key to communication is to proactively seek out and encourage the voices in your organization. Your front-line personnel must feel as if they literally "have the ear" of their team leader, that you are receptive to their ideas and concerns. Funnel listening gives you the tools to address these concerns, a platform that allows individuals to open up and share the insight, experience, and wisdom they have to offer. Becoming a listener is built on the premise that every person with whom you talk is not only unique and valuable but has the potential to transform your organization into something magnificent. If you treated all people as if they were potential diamonds in your organization, every conversation would immediately take on a new significance.

We can learn a lot from the story of how Finbarr O'Neill brought leadership back to Hyundai. It was 1998 and the company was selling fewer than a hundred thousand cars a year in the United States. Worse still, the organization didn't have a CEO for months as the parent company searched without success for someone to bring Hyundai back to life. O'Neill had been general counsel since the company's founding in 1985 and was appointed interim president. At the first meeting with his dealers, he found himself in a hotel conference room facing a group of angry people. What vision did he lay out for them? None.

He didn't tell the dealers what they were doing wrong. He didn't even tell them what he planned to do in order to turn sales around. Instead, he stood up and asked one simple question: In what direction did they think the company should be headed? After a moment of silence, the room erupted in shouting and finger-pointing.

As the dealers started launching their complaints, O'Neill took out an easel and a pen and began writing down what he heard. By the end of the meeting, he had recorded over one hundred different suggestions. He smiled at the group, picked the top ten suggestions, and then promised that he would deliver on those ten action items. Only after O'Neill had listened to what the men and women in the group had to say did he speak and act. In return, the dealers responded with respect and support for their new leader. Not long afterward, a reinvigorated Hyundai began its march back toward profitability and excellence.

It doesn't matter if you're the CEO of a major company or if you run a small team. The principle remains the same. You need to show your people that you are willing not only to hear them but to *listen* to what they are saying. Acting on what they say sends a message that you hear more than the sounds coming out of their mouths; you hear the truth behind their words.

In the same way that the rhino teaches us to see without our eyes, we must learn to hear without our ears. To become master listeners, we must embrace funnel listening, hearing not with our ears but with our mind, eyes, heart, and mouth.

Listen with Your Mind The fastest way to stop the flow of a conversation is to enter it with a closed mind. In other words, you already have all the answers, the best ideas, and all the information you need to know. Your opinion is already formed and locked in concrete. Your mind is rigid and clogged, guaranteeing that nothing will move through it. On the other hand, if your mind is open, flexible, and accommodating, anything can move through it, including the free exchange of ideas.

As leaders, we must firmly resist the temptation to allow past experiences to affect what we hear. This means banishing the editor, silencing the judge, and putting aside the opinions and preconceived ideas that live in our heads. An open mind is like a raging river that knows where it's going but welcomes and encourages other rivers to join it so that it can become more powerful than it already is. As a practical suggestion, when entering a conversation where you think you already know the answers, tell yourself this: "I now intend to set aside everything I think I know about this topic in order to learn something new."

Listen with Your Eyes Poets say that the eyes are the windows to our souls. And if you think about it, you might agree. After all, one look at someone's eyes and you pretty much know what they're thinking. People can't hide how happy, surprised, or interested they are any more than they can hide how impatient, condescending, or bored they may feel. With your eyes you may check your watch or the clock on the wall or look around the room, out the window, and off into space. You may roll, squint, and rub your eyes when you're bored or uninterested. If you're really bold you might even shut your eyes to tune out the speaker.

Through the eyes, you will find the quickest way to break off or improve the flow of communication within your organization. Speakers are often advised to make eye contact, but this advice is equally important for listeners. Eye contact is the bridge to your audience. Use it genuinely and you've taken one giant step toward making a true connection.

A case in point is the senior minister who picked up the new junior minister at her home the Sunday morning she was to deliver her first sermon. As they were driving to church, the senior minister asked his younger colleague, "Do you have the notes for your sermon?"

"Right here." The junior minister took her notes out of her planner.

"Hand them to me," said the senior minister.

The junior minister did so, and the senior minister took them and threw them out the window of the car.

"Why did you do that?"

"Now you won't have any excuses for not making eye contact with the congregation," he said.

As a result, the junior minister gave a sermon that was far better than the one in her notes. That's because without notes to keep her from making eye contact with her audience, she was able to follow carefully their mood, register their reaction to what she was saying, and tailor her talk to meet not just her needs as a speaker but their needs as a congregation.

Listen with Your Heart Treating all people equally is especially important when it comes to listening. The way we listen to a washroom attendant should be no different from the way we listen to the

CEO of a Fortune 500 company. The moment we think there is a difference, we create a value system that says some people aren't worth listening to. In so doing, we immediately create a giant gulf between speaker and listener.

We need to take ourselves off whatever pedestal we've put ourselves on, and we need to remind ourselves that it takes a lot of courage for people to open up and share their ideas. The least we can do is receive what they say with gratitude and respect, whether the speaker is an executive or the individual who cleans his office late at night. Good leaders aren't condescending or impatient. Rather, they focus on making the speaker feel important and valued. Because of this, they have free access to the hearts and minds of all the people in their organizations.

Listen with Your Mouth An old saying is that we're given two ears and one mouth because we should listen twice as much as we talk. While this may be a cliché, it's also good advice to live by. Talking too much or too quickly can be a major roadblock when you're trying to encourage others to open up to you. It's impossible to have two-way communication when one person does all the talking.

Leaders must resist the urge to dominate a conversation. Whether this manifests itself as an impatient desire to finish other people's sentences or an automatic impulse to turn the focus of the conversation back to yourself, it is both unnecessary and counterproductive. Interrupting others happens only when we possess a false sense of importance. And although some people believe that the one who responds fastest is the smartest and wittiest, it is certainly not the secret of success for most achievement-oriented leaders. The most effective way to listen with your mouth is to keep your mouth shut.

On the other hand, sometimes you need to speak up. You often can help a conversation partner with a few affirming words. You can always seek to gather more facts and details or encourage elaboration with questions like, What happened next? and How does that make you feel? And it never hurts to clarify and validate the speaker's meaning with a simple "So what I hear you saying is . . ." That said, you should never take over the conversation and make it about you. Good listeners know when it's appropriate to use a few words to put people at ease and when it's best to use silence to open the channel for better communication. Any good therapist knows that sometimes patients just want to be listened to, while at other times they need professional feedback. Either way, the affirmation that comes when one human being truly listens to another has the power to change corporations, organizations, and personal relationships. Sometimes a simple "I'm sorry" or "I understand how you must be feeling" can change the entire course of a relationship.

Rhino Filter: Behind the Noise Is Wisdom

The key to knowing how to listen well is knowing what to listen for. Once your team feels as if they have your ear, you need to know what to do with the information they give you. To be perfectly honest, you won't need everything they'll give you. The world is indeed filled with a lot of superfluous noise, and you must figure out which parts of it you need to have. You do this using a Rhino Filter.

As we've discussed, rhinos have the innate ability to take in the sounds they need to help them survive. In our leadership practice, the Rhino Filter helps us sort the good from the bad, determining what we should let go "in one ear and out the other," and what we need to hold onto as truth.

Imagine if all your thoughts, fears, emotions, and prejudices were left unchecked and allowed to flow out of your mouth. You'd become a boring windbag with no one listening to you or caring about what you had to say. And it wouldn't even matter if behind all the noise were a few nuggets of truth.

Unfortunately, some individuals don't know how to turn off the flows, keeping their mouths moving when they shouldn't. And while it would be easy to just turn away and ignore them, as a leader, you can't be so dismissive. You need all your people, even the ones with "leaky faucets." Fortunately, with a little work, you can learn to filter out what you need to know from what you don't.

What You Don't Need to Listen To

Your Rhino Filter can help you sift out negativity, backbiting, and gossip—three kinds of conversation you definitely don't need to listen to.

Negativity   No matter how important or noble your vision may seem to you, you're bound to meet people who think otherwise, who say what you're doing is impractical, misguided, or foolish and, of course, that it can't be done. While these folks may genuinely disagree with the direction in which you are taking the organization, more often than not they're just too comfortable with the status quo to want anything to change. Now, you can't expect to prevent fear, complacency, or any other negative feeling from rearing its ugly head, any more than you can expect everyone to walk around with rose-colored glasses on all the time. Still, you must be vigilant in your attempt to keep negativity and doubt from seeping into the consciousness of your organization.

Negativity is a contagious virus that spreads from one mouth to the next, disempowering everyone and everything in its wake. Your job is to stop it. You can begin by realizing that the best way to prevent a virus from spreading is not to let it enter the body in the first place. You must stay proactive, keeping your organization healthy and vital by focusing your energy on nurturing a positive, can-do attitude. And this means that all the "can't-do" comments—and the whole string of excuses that usually come along with them—should go in one ear and right out the other.

Along the same lines, you have to be vigilant about whom you are keeping in your organization. It doesn't matter how good a person's work product is if that person is infecting the general atmosphere with an endless stream of negative comments. People think they're being funny when they're being sarcastic, but the Greek root of the word "sarcasm" is *sarkazein*, meaning "to tear flesh." There's nothing funny about that!

Backbiting Most of us spend more time at work than we do at home. By extension, our work colleagues become like a second family to us. While this is generally a good situation, it can also be challenging, leading to the same petty squabbles and occasional fighting that happens at home. You might say it's not in your job description to interfere in your team's interactions. But the time will come when you find yourself playing the role of parent to your team, deciding whether to step in and stop the fighting or let them deal with matters on their own. And as any good parent will tell you, the technique is simple and straightforward: don't believe everything you hear, don't take sides, and unless someone is going to get hurt, let the parties settle their differences on their own.

Many squabbles will undoubtedly reflect the competitive work environment. We live in a cutthroat world where the difference between getting ahead and finding ourselves left behind is often a matter of inches. Today's competitors seek every advantage possible, and some people think that gives them permission to step all over the next person. This is where pettiness can move to a new level. Consciously or not, your team members may feel that they need to compete for your attention, even to the point of sabotaging one another to steal the spotlight. Are you allowing them all the opportunities they need to be heard without competing for your time?

Backbiting, along with faultfinding and finger-pointing, are unsubtle ways for your team members to remove the competition and get ahead. And while it's natural to be competitive, you can't allow this sort of destructive competition to take root in your enterprise. It's demoralizing and counterproductive, especially for those team members who won't take part in it. And once it's allowed to gather steam, it takes on a life of its own. Instead of allowing this sort of behavior to become a part of your organization's culture, you must send a loud and clear message that backbiting will not be tolerated. There is no better way to do this than through your refusal to listen to it in the first place.

As a seasoned listener, you must discuss the hidden agendas that underlie so many conversations, as well as the negative attacks that go along with those agendas. If you lend an ear to everyone in your organization, you can help overcome the challenges of petty and even vicious office politics and foster team spirit.

Gossip   During a recent stand-up comedy show, a female comic talked about how she'd recently quit smoking. "Do you know why I miss smoking?" she asked the audience. "It's not the cigarettes. It's because now I don't know anything that's going on at work. If you ever want to know the gossip at the office, check with the smokers—they know *everything*. Without my old smoke breaks, I haven't the faintest clue who's dating who and what people are saying!"[2]

Whether you're inhaling secondhand smoke with your gossip or taking it plain, gossip can be toxic stuff. And it's easy to "bite" when people throw you a line about someone else's personal life or something they heard at the water cooler. But as a leader, you have to let the gossip go and rise above it.

In truth, gossip is even more insidious than backbiting. Why? Because we have talked ourselves into believing that gossip is fun, harmless, and universal. We all do it. And yet we all know better. Not only does gossip divert people from work and decrease productivity, but it is often malicious, causing resentment and pain for the targets. Ultimately, gossip demoralizes an organization and puts a stranglehold on the leader's vision.

As an artful listener, you must resist the temptation to take part in gossip. Remember that just because you don't gossip yourself doesn't mean you're not a part of it. If you listen long enough to the empty chatter of others, you are by tacit agreement just as much a part of it as if you were doing the gossiping yourself. The Bible reminds us not to be a "talebearer among your people."[3] Nor should we be one who listens to those tales!

Perhaps the most damaging effect of gossip on a leader is this: if you engage in enough gossip, you can almost certainly guarantee that you will eventually lose the trust of those around you. Others may laugh and feel a momentary bond with you, but down deep, they know what we all know: whoever gossips to you will eventually start gossiping about you.

What You Need to Listen To

A good filter is not just about keeping out "conversational impurities." It's also about letting in the good dialogue that will drive your organization toward its vision. This process begins by understanding what you need to hear. And it begins not with the question, What's in it for me? but with the better question, What's in it for them? How does your vision benefit your team members?

THE WHAT'S-IN-ITS

Being an influential leader begins with listening, which is all about letting others influence you. Good leaders know that the power of influence begins with their followers. Your team members have to believe in you and trust you, and you can make that happen by giving them a voice. You can give them a voice by applying these "What's-in-its."

What's in It for Me?

It's easy to deride the camel as a "horse designed by committee," but how many truly great inventions or discoveries occurred thanks to one individual working alone? Columbus sailed to America, but he had the crews of three ships alongside him. Steve Jobs came up with the idea for the iPod, but he had numerous people to design the case, implement and license the technology, work with the music companies, and so on. Even the most solitary geniuses can't afford to go it alone.

Every U.S. president has had his cabinet—leaders he has chosen to give him guidance and advice. Whether you're running the country or a small team, you need to listen to different and opposing points of view. Leaders gain legitimacy by listening to their followers and allowing those followers to help them lead. Take advice from your followers. See where they are right. Helping your team not only lets you get ahead but empowers your team members to find their own voices, expressing their opinions, observations, and concerns.

What's in It for Us?

Ultimately, you and everyone on your team want your organization to succeed. So look for great ideas, whatever their source. It's not always the people at the top or the Ivy League graduate who has the best information. A resourceful secretary, not an MIT-trained engineer, invented Liquid Paper. So don't forget to listen to the receptionist who's been taking customer-complaint calls for the last twenty years. And don't ignore the forty-year veteran whose retirement everyone eagerly awaits. These people may have much more to offer than you realize.

What's in It for No One?

Although you want to tune out the noise of negativity, backbiting, and gossip, good leaders also need to remain on the lookout for the sources of disunity in the ranks of their organizations. Be aware so that you can recognize these situations and put a stop to them.

People who work for you and with you have families, careers, and ambitions. They want a better life, just as you do. The entrepreneur or leader takes more risks and thus reaps more rewards, but everyone has the same goals: financial security, happiness, meaningful work and a meaningful life, and peace of mind. It's natural for those around you to wonder whether your vision will lead them not just to your goals but to theirs. Instead of questioning their motives, it's better to understand their motives and work to satisfy them. Keep your ears open and listen for the answers, reminding yourself that the quickest way to get people to help you with your own goals is to help them reach theirs.

The Law of Rotating Ears

Courage is what it takes to stand up and speak;
courage is also what it takes to sit down and listen.
Winston Churchill

Funnel listening means putting your ear to the ground and seeking out every voice in your organization. But there's more to becoming a good listener than simply engaging people and getting them to speak up. Take listening to the next level by moving toward the sound. You'll hear in different ways, and ultimately you'll be able to slow down and hear yourself.

One of the best ways to lead others is by listening to them, but you can't just sit around and wait for people to knock on your door. People are often intimidated by those in leadership positions. Perhaps they don't want to be perceived by their fellow team members as being bootlickers or worse. If you're going to enjoy two-way communication with your team, it's up to you to initiate it. Having "rotating ears" means that you have to go out and meet people where they are. Good leaders create opportunities for people in their organizations to be heard, and they know how to draw people out.

Create Opportunities

Listening is a proactive process, so get out of the boardroom and into the break room. Open your door and invite people in. Maybe even make them a cup of coffee. Don't expect or assume that your team will come to you. Go to them. Make it easy for them to open up, demonstrating that you are actively searching out what others have to say. Like the rhino, rotate your ears and move toward the sound.

Ask Questions

Just because someone isn't saying much doesn't mean he doesn't have anything to say. Good listeners know when it's appropriate to step in and ask the right questions to put people at ease or focus a conversation. For example, you might be talking with a shy individual who's having trouble opening up when you notice a child's photograph on her key chain. Ask if she has kids, and she'll start talking about her three daughters. Before you know it, she'll feel comfortable enough to share an idea for improving customer relations that you might never have thought about on your own. Like the rhino, you need to rotate your ears and find out what your people have to say. And if they're not comfortable initiating the conversation, you can give them a gentle nudge with your rhino horn!

Hear with New Ears

Don't underestimate the importance of unspoken words. They can be even more valuable than what's coming out of the mouths of your team members. In fact, a lot of the real dialogue going on in an organization takes place silently. As rhinos shift their heads to hear, you, too, must shift your ears from side to side to better hear what is being said—and what is not being said. You need to become adept at other types of listening:

- *Listen between the lines.* Some individuals within an organization may be afraid to say what they really think. They might be afraid of being fired or demoted or singled out. Others aren't sure about what they are saying. In either case, you need to listen between the lines and hear what people aren't saying. It's the subtext that matters most.

- *Listen to body language.* You already know that there is more to what people say than what comes out of their mouths. You may tell me that my presentation was good, but I'm not really going to believe you if you were rolling your eyes when I gave it. As the expression goes, "What you do speaks so loudly that I can hardly hear a word you're saying."

- *Listen for morale.* Do people come to work early and volunteer to stay late? Or do they drag themselves to the office in the morning and leave a cloud of dust behind them at 5:00 p.m.? You can learn a lot about your organization by listening for the level of morale around the office. Are individuals enthusiastic or grumpy? Are they looking for more projects or feeling over-worked? If you're a leader, how can you not know this?

- *Listen for attitude.* Do coworkers get along, or are they competitive and catty? Do people go out after work together, or are relationships strictly business? When people work and play together as a team, you'll be able to make your vision for the organization come true. A law firm in Boston held a softball game for its new hires and their assistants to create more of a "family feeling." However, even while the game was being played, the rigid caste system of most law firms was never far from anyone's mind. Associates deferred to partners, new hires deferred to associates, and assistants deferred to just about everybody. When a sudden thundershower drenched all the players, the attorneys and assistants repaired to the nearest pizza place to get out of the rain and grab a bite to eat. With their baseball attire and hair soaking wet, suddenly the walls came down, and they acted like a group of people out having an adventure instead of a law firm observing rigid demarcations between salary levels and job titles. If you want your team to work like a team, let them go out and play like one!

- *Listen for feelings.* Some leaders assume that the workplace is no place for feelings. But the reality is that we are all human, and life happens. Let's look at the example of a team member who had earned a reputation for being a team player with stellar ideas, a lot of creativity, and a great work ethic. He started arriving late to work, a team member complained about a change in his attitude, and he submitted a sloppy draft that barely met an important deadline. This type of behavior went on for a few months as his higher-ups sat in their offices trying to figure out what to do. Then one day, the individual in question walked into his boss's office and apologized for his behavior. He explained that his father had passed away and he had really struggled with the loss. Still, he felt ashamed at how he had let his personal life affect his work product. Although the man could have been more forthright with his managers earlier on, the organization's leaders could have taken a more proactive, responsible role. After "listening" to the uncharacteristic behavior, the man's supervisor should have taken the initiative and asked him what was wrong. With good people, there is almost always a good explanation for a change in work habits.

Hearing Yourself

Good leaders work at becoming good listeners, and good listening takes place every day. If you're listening right, you'll be taking in a lot of information, feedback, opinions, and suggestions. And you'll evaluate every bit of information through the Rhino Filter as you figure out what to make of it. But after all your workers have gone home and you've turned out the lights to leave your office, you'll have a chance to do one more type of listening. That's when it's time to rotate your ears inward and listen to yourself.

Take some time every day to reevaluate your vision and figure out how what you've learned from your team fits into the long-term picture for your organization. Usually, you won't find yourself wanting to make drastic changes to your strategic plans. But occasionally, something you heard or learned will make you think a little and perhaps retool your vision a bit. It's important to develop the habit of actively listening to yourself at the end of the day. As you let others share in your vision by sharing their voices with you, you will become more intuitive. It's important to tune in to yourself and give your own voice a chance to speak up.

The law of rotating ears helps you to take listening to the next level. It teaches you that you need to create opportunities for listening and become a more active listener. It also helps you hear past the spoken words to understand the truth hiding in the shadows and to take time to look inside yourself for that still, small voice you always need to listen to—your own.

The Wisdom of Rhino Hearing

Effective leadership calls on you to take listening to a new level by listening "outside the box." You must hear with new ears that better connect you to the people who work for you: the men and women who not only will follow you today but will help you build your vision for tomorrow. They have so much to offer you, and you have a lot to listen to. Listening is the first step in communicating your vision. In today's world, it's all but a lost art, and those who wish to be true leaders must work hard to master it.

A FINAL RHINO THOUGHT

*No one has all the answers, and you cannot
achieve your vision alone. Even great leaders
need other people to follow them. Leaders
also need other people to help them lead. See
the wisdom and talents of everyone around you.
Surrender your ego. Remember that listening
brings knowledge. Listening brings understanding.
Listening brings loyalty. Listening is the
power behind your vision.*

CHAPTER THREE

The Rhino's Mouth

A Leader's Message

Words are just words. Without heart
they have no meaning.

Chinese proverb

A s we discussed in the last chapter, communication is a two-way street. For you as a leader, it needs to begin with listening to the inner voice that creates your vision and to the outer voices that will help bring that vision to life. Now it's time to put an audible voice to the vision. It's time to direct your people down the road you want them to take. Your voice is more than your words; it's the map that tells everyone in the organization exactly where you're headed. And like any good map, it must be clear and accurate. You can't give people poor directions without expecting them to become lost in the underbrush. And while your voice needs to be strong and unambiguous, it also needs to be lively and exciting.

As William Shakespeare said, "Strong reasons make strong action."[1] For our purposes, strong reasons combined with passion make for even stronger action. In other words, leaders need to inspire. Ever since we were children, we've been warned not to be fooled by the trappings of image: pretty clothes, a quick smile, smooth words, a handsome face. We've been told countless times not to judge a book by its cover; to always listen to the message, not the messenger; and to pay attention to substance, not style. At best, these adages represent half-truths. And herein lies a contradiction of leadership. Yes, we need to offer substance in the form of a genuine vision that others can follow. But if we're going to truly influence those around us, we also need to sell that vision. And selling a vision is often a matter of perception.

It's what those around us believe.

So while the inside of the book matters, so does the outside. How we say something is as important as what we say. Whether Mel Gibson as William Wallace is inspiring his army to fight in *Braveheart* or John Belushi as Bluto Blutarsky is urging his fraternity brothers to take on the Omegas in *Animal House*, without the speaker, the message wouldn't be the same. We are all unique, not just in what we have to say but in how we say it.

This isn't advocating Hollywood slickness or disingenuous polish. A leader needs to speak the truth; that's not negotiable. If she doesn't, all the makeup in the world won't do any good. Sooner or later, everyone will find out. On the other hand, once the message is in place, the leader's task becomes a matter of communicating the message.

A beautiful story illustrates the importance of truth in communication, especially as it pertains to leaders who seek to deliver a powerful message to their workers about doing what is right. As the story goes, a successful CEO was growing old and knew it was time to choose a successor to take over his business. Instead of choosing one of his directors or his children, he decided to adopt a different approach.

He called together all the young executives in his organization for a meeting. "The time has come for me to step down and choose the next CEO of this company," he said. "And I have decided to choose one of you."

The young executives were shocked, but the CEO continued. "Today I'll be doing something a little untraditional. I am going to give each one of you a seed—a very special seed. I want you to plant the seed, water it, and come back here six months from today with what you have grown from the seed I have given you. I'll judge you based on the plants that you bring, and the one I choose will be the next CEO."

One of the junior executives was named Jim. Jim took his seed home and excitedly told his wife about the opportunity. She helped him get a pot, soil, and compost, and he planted the seed. He carefully watered the seed every day and checked whether it had sprouted. After about two weeks, some of the other executives began to talk about their seeds and the plants that were beginning to grow. Each day Jim dutifully checked his seed, but nothing was growing.

Three, four, and five weeks went by, and still nothing had grown in Jim's pot. By now, others were talking about their plants with great pride and gusto. But Jim still had nothing to show for his efforts. He felt like a complete failure. The months passed, and Jim slowly realized that he must have somehow killed his seed. Everyone else bragged about his or her small tree or tall plant, but Jim had nothing. He didn't say anything to his colleagues. He was embarrassed, so instead of mentioning it to anyone, he just continued to water and fertilize the soil. Deep in his heart, he desperately hoped that the seed might still grow.

After six months, the day came for all the executives to bring their plants to the CEO for inspection. Jim told his wife that he wasn't going to take in an empty pot, but she asked him to be honest about what had happened. Jim felt sick to his stomach at the thought of the humiliation he would surely face, but he knew his wife was right. So with slouched shoulders and a pained expression on his face, he took his empty pot to the boardroom.

When he arrived, he was amazed at the variety of plants grown by the other executives. He saw beautiful and exotic plants and flowers of all shapes and sizes. Jim hugged his empty pot to his chest as his colleagues tried to suppress their laughter.

When the CEO arrived, he surveyed the room and greeted his young executives. Jim tried to hide in the back. "My, what great plants, trees, and flowers you have grown!" exclaimed the CEO. "And today, one of you will be appointed as the next CEO."

All of a sudden, the CEO spotted Jim at the back of the room with his empty pot. He ordered him to come to the front.

Jim was terrified. He thought, "The CEO knows I'm a failure! Maybe he'll fire me!" But he stepped to the front of the room and bravely faced his boss. The CEO then asked him what had happened to his seed, and Jim told him the entire story, not holding anything back.

The CEO asked everyone to sit down except for Jim. He looked at Jim for a long time before finally announcing to the room, "Behold your next chief executive! His name is Jim."

Jim couldn't believe it. He couldn't even grow his seed. How could he be the new CEO?

His boss provided the solution to the puzzle: "Six months ago, I gave everyone in this room a seed. I told you to take the seed, plant it, water it, and bring it back to me today. But here's the catch: I gave you all boiled seeds. They were dead—it was impossible for them to grow. And yet all of you, except for Jim, have brought me trees and plants and flowers.

"When you saw that the seed wouldn't grow, you substituted another seed for the one I gave you. You were afraid of failure, afraid of disappointing me, and unwilling to admit that you might have done something wrong. Jim was the only one with the courage and honesty to bring me just a pot of dirt with my seed in it. I have dedicated my whole life to this business, promoting an ethic of honesty, integrity, courage, and forthrightness. Today, Jim has proven to me that he is the only one who also embodies these characteristics. Therefore, Jim will be the new CEO."

The CEO's choice reflected his commitment to his message. Of course in this case, the CEO must not have done a very good job communicating this message to his junior staff if only one of his young executives was honest enough to bring in a barren pot. Ideally, a leader should be able to sell his vision to all his followers. The sharing of this vision leads to great accomplishments.

Communication Matters

If communication with others didn't matter, we'd never have meetings or face-to-face interactions. We would just e-mail the blueprint of our vision to everyone in the organization, along with clear instructions. But where would that leave us? What if Martin Luther King Jr. had skipped the march on Washington and instead sent an instant message?

> IM to all Americans from MLK re: = ity for all.
> Had a dream. All rise up. Free at last (3x).

It doesn't have quite the same effect as his famous speech, does it? And although Dr. King's actual words are still poetic and powerful when we see them on paper, his spoken words were even more stirring. When people speak, we get a glimpse into their hearts and the causes they believe in. Intention, passion, and commitment—these are what give communication power and open the gateway to influencing those around us.

Of course, you don't need to be a famous speaker to communicate your message. The rhino can teach leaders many ways to inspire others. You don't have to have the eloquence of Dr. King or the good looks of Mel Gibson or the swagger of John Belushi. You can be yourself: shy, quiet, loud, boisterous, simple, pompous. It doesn't matter. What matters is that your message gets across the most powerful way possible, preserving the integrity of who you are as an individual.

We began the process of communication with the art of listening. Now it's time to start talking. It's time to speak up and inspire those around us to follow.

Rhino Anatomy: The Mouth

We should all have rhinos in our gardens. Like a John Deere lawn mower, the mouth of the white rhino is a wide, square-lipped instrument, ideally suited for eating grass. Indeed, the white rhino isn't even white: the word "white" in its name is actually a corruption of the Dutch word for "wide." Besides eating, rhinos use their mouths for communicating. Using an elaborate combination of grunts, growls, pants, squeals, whines, puffs, snorts, snarls, and gasps, rhinos are the master communicators of the animal kingdom. If rhinos are mad, you'll know it. If they're happy, you'll know it. If one is in the mood for romance, well, another rhino will get the idea. Rhinos speak their minds—but only when they have something to say. We can learn from their reserve as well as their speaking abilities. But first we must understand how we talk—or, more important, how we *think* we talk.

I Say What I Think I Mean

Whether making an off-the-cuff remark in an elevator or an impromptu speech at a team meeting, leaders talk all day long. And with every word we speak comes the potential to build up or detract from both our vision and our sphere of influence. And while we may think that we always say what we mean, many times we don't. When we're busy, distracted, or rushed, sometimes we don't think before we talk. Other times, we become so emotional that we don't realize that we're speaking not from the truth but from anger, fear, humiliation, or countless other word-distorting feelings.

As Ann Landers advises, "The trouble with talking too fast is you may say something you haven't thought of yet."[2] And the trouble with talking from emotion is that your words become not what you mean but how you feel and because of that, they can lose their power. While it's perfectly acceptable to share your feelings, you should consciously choose when to do so. There should be no accidents. This not only keeps your emotions in check but also gives your emotions and feelings purpose and conviction.

I Say What I Mean

There's more to talking than words: there is meaning, the message a leader wants to deliver clearly. This message must be well thought out, an example of deliberate communication that leaves as little room for misunderstanding as possible. Think back to the 1992 presidential campaign, which President Bill Clinton won. One sign in Clinton's campaign office said, "It's the economy, stupid." This statement was a little harsh, but it was a very clear reminder that the way to win the election was to stay focused on the most important message.

The good news is that great communication is often brief. Think about the Gettysburg Address delivered by President Abraham Lincoln in 1863. Less than three hundred words, it moved a nation and still retains enormous power almost a century and a half later. The bad news is that succinct communication isn't always very exciting. Not every leader is an Abraham Lincoln! A brief statement may clarify and educate but often at the expense of empowerment and inspiration. A leader's words therefore must be more than utilitarian. They must serve a greater cause, emotionally connecting the listener to the leader's vision.

I Mean What I Say

There is more to communicating than meaning: there is connecting. You can create the most well-written and powerful speech in the world, but unless the audience believes in the man or woman behind the words, the message will fall flat and take the audience on a journey to nowhere. Your team will follow you only to the degree that they believe in you, not just your words.

When rhinos howl to tell other creatures to get out of the way, we know from both the sound and the intensity that they mean business. Likewise, your message must be empowered by both the meaning and the conviction that stand behind it. The intent behind your words is what the listener hears. "I mean what I say" is more than a simple declaration of conviction: it is what happens when well-thought-out words are combined with passion and heart.

Leaders seek this higher, nobler kind of communication. Think about the most successful corporate pitchmen in the last several decades: Dave Thomas, the founder of Wendy's; Frank Perdue of Perdue Farms; and Lee Iacocca of Chrysler. When each of these individuals came on television to advertise his product, we believed him—and we believed *in him*. These men came across as sincere, hardworking, and trustworthy. Even if you hit the mute button and just watched them instead of listening to their words, you probably would have come away impressed. And you might have bought a new Chrysler automobile, some Perdue chicken, or a Wendy's burger!

As with any good habit, this kind of communication takes practice and conscious effort. More than that, it takes honesty and leaders' willingness to put their passion on display to the organizations they serve. In other words, we all need to find our own unique voice. The rhino will show us how.

The Third Principle of Rhino Leadership: Rhino Talk

A leader's goal is not to speak but to inspire.

Rhino Talk is the art of using your voice. Communication starts with being yourself, which sounds simple, doesn't it? Unfortunately, if you attempt to accommodate all those around you, trying to be all things to all people, your words become watered down and you lose your voice in the process. In this case, your job is not so much to find your voice as to reclaim it.

When rhinos talk, the animal kingdom listens, and not just because rhinos weigh one to two tons and have deadly horns. The other animals listen because rhinos' every grunt, growl, and squeak serves a purpose. This teaches leaders to speak deliberately and to consciously deliver the message that needs to be heard. This efficient, streamlined manner of communication is Rhino Talk, a guideline for interacting and communicating within your organization. Follow it, and others will follow you.

Rhino Talk actually starts with the kind of listening and understanding described in the previous chapter. But now, as you begin to share your voice, you need to finish the connection, reflecting back the needs and concerns of the people in your organization while simultaneously sharing your vision. Reflecting back doesn't mean saying what others want to hear but instead showing them that they have been heard and understood. Your ability to communicate this understanding and empathy may not alleviate everyone's concerns, but it will go a long way toward letting people know that they are not alone, that someone has their best interests at heart.

At the end of the classic boxing movie *Somebody Up There Likes Me*, Paul Newman, playing the role of Rocky Graziano, says the title words. The setting is the ticker-tape parade that New York is giving him in honor of his winning the heavyweight boxing championship. When he points skyward and says, "Somebody up there likes me," his wife replies, "Someone down here, too."

Our team members need to know that somebody up there—their leader—likes them, cares about them, and has their best interests at heart. But the leader must also be the person "down here, too," the supportive and nurturing presence they need on a daily basis. People want to believe that they are more than pawns being pushed around a chessboard, that their individuality and their unique contributions matter. When they do believe, spreading your vision becomes a lot easier, whether you're speaking one-on-one, to a small group, or to a whole roomful of people.

Rhino One-on-One Communication

The essential principle of all communication is simply this: *everyone matters*. In fact, your communications with your entire organization will be only as successful as your ability to communicate with each individual in the organization. The art of one-on-one communication can be synthesized into one clear objective: honor and value the individual within the organization. Dick Cavett, one of the leading television hosts in the 1960s and 1970s, used to make the comment that when he was broadcasting, he wasn't talking to all the people out in "television land." Instead, he knew that he was having an intimate, one-on-one conversation with each viewer— a conversation multiplied millions of times over because of his popularity.

Remember that even when you are speaking to a large group, you are in fact having multiple simultaneous one-on-one conversations with the people in that group.

The sounds rhinos make to other rhinos are entirely different from the sounds they would make to a human or another animal. Rhinos choose their modes of expression based on the animal they are speaking to. In the same way, you wouldn't speak the same way to a kindergartner as you would to a Harvard graduate. Nor would you speak the same way to a dockworker as you would to a nuclear scientist. It's not that one person's better than another. But people's life experiences make them different, and they listen, learn, and experience truth in different ways.

A first-year team member in your organization will not listen or respond in the same manner as someone who has spent his or her entire forty-year career there. A part-time worker listens differently from a full-time worker, and someone who just got demoted certainly listens differently from someone who just got promoted. People who love their jobs listen differently from those who hate their jobs. Leaders need to hinge their communication strategies on the realization that all of their listeners are different and are listening with different ears. Then, taking their cue from the rhino, leaders need to adapt their communication style to meet people's different needs.

By recognizing the uniqueness of each listener, a leader can avoid the two most common traps of personal communication: treating everyone exactly the same and communicating in the same old way.

"You're All the Same to Me" You know the symptoms: suddenly you can't differentiate between the person on the phone right now and the caller you spoke with a few minutes ago. It's as if everyone in your organization has blended into one nameless face because you're too busy and too distracted to notice the individuality of different people.

By the very nature of their position, leaders are stretched in all different directions, forced to deal with day-to-day minutiae and big-picture vision issues. And because of this constant tug of war, leaders have a natural tendency to think of people in terms of teams, divisions, units, and groups. In their struggle to get the job done, they all too often reduce individuals to data in an Excel spreadsheet, lumping them into the same box.

The result is inescapable: the more you treat individuals the same, the more your communication reflects that sameness. You begin to talk from a global level, not a personal one. You see demographics, not personalities; similarities, not differences. Eye contact becomes minimal because everyone looks the same. Your ears become shut because you've heard it all before. Smiles become insincere and laughter sounds forced, all because you believe nothing new or interesting is being said. Your world becomes impersonal, methodical, and automatic, and those around you see you as cold, aloof, and arrogant—certainly not the most efficient way to communicate!

What's the remedy? The first step is to admit that this can happen to even the best of us. We can be so blinded by our big-picture responsibilities that we forget the power of the individual.

While a certain amount of insulation comes with the job and is almost inevitable, you cannot have any meaningful communication if you do not see value in your conversation partners—on a global and an individual level. You therefore must stand vigilant against your own aloofness and arrogance, whether real or perceived. The best way to do this is to become proactive in your efforts to engage your team members on an individual level. Take time to know people's names. Find out their interests, strengths, hobbies, and family backgrounds. Harvey Mackay, author of *Swim with the Sharks without Being Eaten Alive,* recommends creating a dossier on a file card with each worker's personal information: spouse's or partner's name, children's names and birthdays, outside interests, and so on. As the expression goes, people don't care about what you know until they know you care.

It's hard to verbally acknowledge the individual uniqueness of every single person in your organization, especially if your organization is large or covers a wide geographic area. But you can always do more. And the more you do, the stronger your connection will be to the entire organization.

"It Worked Before" Some leaders tend to repeatedly fall back on the same automatic language, habits, and thought processes they've used successfully in the past. Here you'll find the language of "always," "every time," "without exception," and "because." It is a stagnant environment of business and business communication as usual, where we say and think the way we do for the simple reason that we've "always done it that way."

What's the remedy? *Think before you speak.* Always ask if there is a better, more efficient, livelier, or fresher way to say something than you're used to. You may be surprised just how familiar your team members are with your verbal tics! They probably know them better than you do. Change your language and figures of speech:

use analogy, storytelling, and metaphor to get your points across. As the captain of the starship *Enterprise* said, "Boldly go where no man has gone before." Spice up a speech with poetry, dazzle your audience with alliteration, and pack your words with a punch. Actively seek out alternative ways of conveying ideas and messages to your team members and colleagues. You can't have out-of-the-box thinking if you're always speaking from within the same box.

Ultimately, leadership is about getting the most from your organization using the talents and gifts of your people. But this can't happen unless you recognize and speak to the uniqueness of each individual.

Rhino Small-Group Communication

The same truths that apply to an audience of one also apply to a small group: with one additional note. We need to consider two audiences: the individuals making up the group and the group as a whole. And there is always a group entity, a living, breathing organism that changes every time one person enters the room and another person leaves. To maximize small-group communication, leaders need to be aware of both the individuals and the group. It's a balancing act that can best be achieved with the following suggestions.

Manage the Bad Cells If a group is indeed a living, breathing organism, then like any organism it is going to have good cells (individuals) that enrich and nourish and bad cells that destroy and diminish. These "cancerous" bad cells can infect a group and wreak havoc the same way good cells can perform miracles. While the simple solution is to remove the bad cells, any human resources department will tell you that that's not always easy or possible.

Instead, you need to manage and minimize the counterproductive cells. Biologists teach us that bad cells can be split up or infused with good cells in order to transform them. When and how to do this will be as varied as your individual situation. The key is not to let a bad cell destroy your team. Experiment. Try different strategies. And don't give up until your entire team is healthy again. Understanding group dynamics is an art that not only makes communication easier for the leader but also improves the power and effectiveness of the group.

Don't Speak to the Lowest Common Denominator Almost any teacher with a disruptive or negative student in class will tell you how much better and more productive the class is when that student is gone. She'll also say that she spends more time on that one student than on practically all the others combined.

While you should not write off any team member, you should also not direct a majority of your attention toward one person or negative force. You could spend a lot of time trying to convince, cajole, placate, or subdue that individual, but if you did so, you would be ignoring the positive influences of the group. Here's a rhino word of advice: *feed the good cells, not the bad cells.* Not only does this approach allow more efficient communication, but it is the best way to get the bad cells to become good cells.

Don't Speak to the Loudest in the Group It doesn't matter what size or type of group you're leading. You can always be certain that there will be all kinds of individuals in your group—every type of personality, will, and talent that you can imagine. You must make an effort to recognize all the individuals in the group, not just the loudest or most opinionated, the most eloquent or dominating. This includes the soft-spoken, the timid, and even the downright inarticulate, with a special emphasis on including people who don't agree with the rest of the group.

Use Other People's Time Wisely If you want people to value what you have to say, *value their time.* We tend to speak longer in a group setting than we do in one-on-one situations. It's easier to ignore the bored and vapid looks among a group than a similar expression on one person's face. Don't take twenty minutes to say something that you could say in five. Leadership naturally encourages strong egos, and with strong egos comes the inevitable risk of falling into the "I love to hear myself talk" trap of communication.

Don't be like the comedian who walks into the kitchen for a midnight snack: he opens the refrigerator door, the light goes on, and he does a twenty-minute set. That kind of communication is wasted on butter, milk, eggs, and fruit. It doesn't go over any better at the office. Say what you need to say, and then move on. People will respect you more. And with that respect will come a willingness to listen and follow.

One of the great sports announcers in recent history is Pat Summerall, who was teamed with John Madden for many years on National Football League football and Super Bowl broadcasts. Although Madden is beloved for his effusive conversational style, Summerall commands the respect of football fans everywhere for his utter economy of words. While another announcer might use dozens of words to express the idea that a running back has caught a pass, is in the clear, is at the forty-yard line, the thirty-five, the thirty, and so on, Summerall would use just three words: "And he's gone." Pat Summerall is a master of Rhino Talk.

Rhino Large-Group Communication

Not everybody's going to love you. Lots of people go to the zoo to see the giant pandas, the spider monkeys, the lions, the penguins, the polar bears, but how many people head to the zoo because they're excited to see the rhinos? Rhinos are typically the animals you see on your way to seeing something else that you'd rather see more. Even if you're a rhino, not everybody's going to love you.

When speaking to large groups, you can't take every individual in the room aside and have a one-on-one conversation over a cup of coffee. Instead, you need to speak to the collective will of all the individuals in the room. This is the one time when it's okay to make generalizations and address the group consciousness.

Before leaders speak, they assess. What does the group want? What does the group need? Wise leaders know the answers and address them. In so doing, they are more often than not addressing the individuals in the group as well.

It's also important to know the collective sensibilities of the group. This will help you determine the appropriate tone, language, and style for your speech. Is it appropriate to tell jokes and stories to your group? Or does the group need just the cold, hard facts? Is the group informed, educated, interested, tired, bored, fed up, hung over? The more you know, the more you can address and meet the entire group's needs.

Ron Kenney is one of the most successful comedians in show business, even though you may never have heard of him. He works regularly in Las Vegas, at top resorts in Hawaii, and at the best comedy clubs around the country. He gets a disproportionate share of corporate bookings as well. Why does Kenney appear so often? Because he can be counted on to work within the limits of the group. Certain kinds of humor that would play well in a club would be a disaster in a corporate setting or even in front of certain resort audiences. Ron Kenney is a successful communicator—and a deeply admired comedian—because he always knows his audience, and knowing your audience is the first of the rhino's five commandments of communicating.

The First Commandment: Know Thy Audience Whether it's one person, twenty people, or a thousand people, your audience is anyone who comes to hear what you have to say (whether by choice or otherwise). How successfully you communicate with these individuals depends on many factors, the foremost of which is your ability to know the nature of your audience.

The Second Commandment: Know Thy Message Whether the message is a vision of "where we're headed" or the specifics of how to implement a new program, most leaders know what they want to say and what they believe their organizations need to hear. But your role as a leader doesn't end there. You need to make your message as clear and obvious as you can. Are the front-line personnel hearing exactly what you want them to hear? To make sure your message has no ambiguity, commit to taking the following steps when you communicate:

- *Rewrite the message.* Any good writer will tell you that the real secret of writing is rewriting. Blaise Pascal once apologized to a friend for his verbosity, saying, "I have only made this [letter] longer because I have not had the time to make it shorter."[3] As Pascal knew, brevity is often more powerful than loquacity, and being concise requires a little extra work and revision. Leaders need to not only write and rewrite but also rethink and redo their message until it's exactly what they need to say. This is a trial-and-error process that depends on the results you get from the next step.
- *Test the message.* Is what you think you're saying what others are hearing? Are you connecting? And if not, why not? Which part isn't getting through? Be open to feedback, which is critical in streamlining your communication and determining your overall success. If the members of your organization can commit to eval-

uating performance, numbers, and goals, they should certainly be able to evaluate communication as well, starting with yours.

- *Eliminate ambiguity.* The speaker's platform is no place for mixed signals, uncertainty, or vagueness in communication. Include clear expectations in all your messages, along with the advantages and benefits you offer. All communication is selling, so you must be continually aware of your listeners' need to know what's in it for them. Finally, never forget that communication is a map of where you want your organization to go. So make it a good map, with road signs, markers, and, of course, rest stops!

- *Incorporate the four most important words.* When said and meant from the heart, "we" is the most empowering word in the English language, holding within it the ability to break down barriers and connect your audience to your vision. "We" says that you can't do it alone: you need others and you value the contributions of everyone in your organization. Use the word as often and as honestly as you can, and watch how your audience responds with renewed ownership, passion, and commitment.

  "Please" and "thank you" are the next most important words. Their use is not an empty display of etiquette and kindness. Instead, saying thank you and please shows respect to the men and women to whom you're talking. You could argue that such words are unnecessary: after all, your audience consists of paid professionals who are expected to do their jobs. But communication involves perception, and the image you present to those around you will determine how successful your communication is. If you seek lasting and meaningful communication, you must speak out of respect and appreciation for those around you. And you must let others know and feel that respect. As Gladys Bronwyn Stern said, "Silent gratitude isn't much use to anyone."[4]

The Third Commandment: Know Thy Purpose While the idea of knowing your purpose may harken back to high school speech class, it's as pertinent today as it was then. Communication is always taking place, whether you're doing it consciously or otherwise, whether you have purpose or not. Be fully aware of why you are opening your mouth to speak. The rhino squeaks to be noticed and squawks to keep someone away. There is no wasted sound or lost effort in a rhino's communication.

We need to emulate the rhino and stop wasting our time on useless chatter, gossip, backbiting, negativity, and other communication that doesn't move us forward. We need to know why we are communicating in the first place, which is generally for one of four purposes: to entertain, to inform, to bond, or to persuade and inspire. And the more we fulfill all four purposes, the more successful our communication will be.

Entertain a Little It's never wise for someone who isn't good at telling jokes to start a speech with a rehearsed joke simply because it's expected. Instead, the best humor flows naturally from the situation at hand. For example, if everybody in the room has been grousing about the fact that the air conditioning isn't working, say, "When our organization says it sweats the details, we really mean it!" and then loosen your collar to visually emphasize your point. This puts people at ease; shows that you "feel their pain," in Bill Clinton's terms; and, most important, shows that you care.

Leaders aren't hired to be stand-up comedians or lounge singers, and team members aren't being paid to be entertained. Yet the more interesting we make our communication, the more receptive others will be to it. For most of us, being entertaining is simply a matter of being prepared, spending time practicing what we're going to say and how we're going to say it. It's astonishing how many people speak with little or no rehearsal, expecting others to listen for no other reason than the fact that they're sitting there and have no choice.

Of course they have a choice! They can let their minds drift off, or in today's technological era, they can whip out a BlackBerry or iPhone, tune you out completely, and have conversations with people in the room or anywhere else on the planet. Never forget how easy it is for audience members to pretend that they are listening. Adding a little polish and pizzazz to what you say not only shows respect for your audience but also begins to bridge the gap between the audience and yourself.

Inform a Little Getting your message across as clearly as possible is your number one priority. So, get rid of anything that doesn't serve or enhance that message; for example, throw away your long bullet-point agenda or, worse, your script. When you're boring, you water down your objectives. Instead, focus on the vital elements of your message, remembering these three axioms of sharing information:

- *Less is, indeed, more.* It's true—we don't need the kitchen sink. Details, specifics, and minutiae might be fine for strategic planning and board meetings, but these are often unnecessary and even counterproductive in larger settings.
- *When possible, communicate information in stages.* The more complex your message, the easier it will be for your audience to digest it in smaller doses. Don't believe that just because you understand something well, your team will, too.
- *Teach, don't preach.* If you want genuine buy-in and learning to happen, stay off the soapbox. Nobody wants to be looked down upon. The fastest way to make people tune out is to tell them how to act, think, and feel. Communication is an eye-to-eye, mutual sharing of ideas. Giving major pronouncements from a

podium doesn't produce a message that lasts. Instead, empower your listeners to draw their own conclusions from the stories you tell.

Bond a Little "Communication" comes from the word "commune," which means something held in common. Your obligation as a leader is to find out what you have in common with those in your organization. Common ground not only unites different points of view but makes progress possible. Of course, common ground doesn't develop by accident or by itself.

As is true for all communication, common ground must be facilitated or created, and this requires that you make the first move. Mixing and mingling within your organization won't kill you, although it may feel awkward at first. The story goes that when Richard Nixon was president, a motorcycle rider in his motorcade went down and was injured. The motorcade came to a halt, and one of Nixon's advisors told him to say something encouraging to the motorcycle rider, who, after all, was only there to protect the president. "Go out there and express some gratitude," the advisor said.

"So, uh, how do you like your job?" the hapless president asked.

Genuine mixing and mingling with your team is always a good idea. No one is suggesting road trips to Mexico or Jell-O shots after work. Rather, you merely need to use those moments that life presents us as opportunities to connect. They could include a conversation on the elevator, a few words while waiting for a cab, or a question about a photo on someone's desk. Always display an interest in what your people say and do. Caring creates goodwill, which inevitably leads to good business. People listen to those they like and to those they think genuinely care about then.

Engage, Persuade, and Inspire a Lot Leaders should seek to have a dialogue, not a monologue. This means give and take. When you speak, you should elicit a response. Somebody needs to stand up, move, act, walk away, become angry, laugh, or respond in some other manner. Something needs to happen. It's action you're after, and that happens only if you're able to engage, persuade, and inspire others:

- If you aim to engage others, you need to openly invite those around you to share their opinions and feelings. This requires that you ask open-ended questions, always searching for and listening to answers.
- If you aim to persuade others, you need to provide clear and compelling arguments for following your direction, once again focusing on what's in it for them and how your proposed course of action will benefit their lives.
- If you aim to inspire others, you need to find your true voice, recognizing that you can inspire others only by first inspiring yourself.

Erin Gruwell's work shows that when we can truly engage and inspire others, great things will happen. In 1994, this recent college graduate began student teaching at Woodrow Wilson High School in Long Beach, California. She was assigned the "problem kids," mostly minority students who were expected to flunk out long before graduation. Her class challenged her from day one. But as she got to know her students, she discovered the kinds of things they faced on a daily basis. Domestic abuse, gang violence, and constant prejudice from authorities made up a fundamental part of their existence. All had lost at least one friend or family member to gang violence; many had lost three or four people. Intrigued by their stories, she embarked on a new project: she asked the students to start keeping journals of their lives.

The students' attitude about coming to school and participating in class changed drastically. This project signaled a major turnaround as the students eagerly began expressing their tales of sorrow, drama, and triumph. Gruwell had succeeded in engaging her students in their education by making it applicable to them. She persuaded them to write their own histories, and then she heard and validated their voices, acknowledging that each individual had a story that deserved to be heard. Her success story later inspired the 2007 movie *Freedom Writers*, starring Hilary Swank.

The Fourth Commandment: Know Thy Instrument A thousand books on the subject of public speaking all contain pretty much the same information. Public speaking is the number one fear in our nation, and we've been told over and over again to just picture the audience in their underwear and we'll be all right. Anyone who has been involved in leadership for very long is also likely aware of the five basic suggestions made by those books on public speaking: eye contact, strong projection, good posture, proper body language, and confidence. In other words, we know what needs to be done. We just need to go out and do it.

In truth, even with this knowledge, most of us don't make time to improve ourselves as speakers or don't think the matter's important enough. Leaders need to realize that how we communicate our message is a critical element of our success. We need to be good at it. It's not a luxury or a choice but an absolute necessity.

If you knew there was one tool that could help you motivate your organization, create loyalty and buy-in, and improve staff retention, morale, and productivity, wouldn't you want that tool? Well, you already have it! It's called your voice, and it's your ticket to corporate productivity and success. Okay, it may not be the entire ticket, but it's a big piece of it.

This chapter isn't meant to offer step-by-step instructions on how to speak. Instead, it is a loud and forceful call to action: put your attention on improving your speaking skills today. It doesn't take much effort to do this. Follow these three simple steps and you'll be well on your way:

1. *Find as many different speaking opportunities as you can.* These could include local chambers of commerce, Optimist clubs, or community colleges. Open your eyes and you'll find speaking opportunities everywhere. Choose something you're good at—whether it's golf, team building, or needlepoint—and offer a free topical seminar at a local library. Are you a member of a key club or Rotary Club? Put together a twenty-minute lecture and present your idea to the board. Teach a cooking class at a community center, or give a presentation at your son's or daughter's school. You can find countless ways to garner public-speaking experience while giving back to the community at the same time.

2. *Continuously seek feedback and suggestions on how to improve.* Professional musicians would never play without asking others—typically other musicians on their skill level or higher—how they sound. And yet few leaders ever think to ask those around them how they sound. Let go of your ego and ask people how you're doing. Make sure you ask those who will tell the truth instead of telling you what you want to hear.

3. *Get help.* Join Toastmasters, buy a video, hire a private coach, read books: do whatever you need to do. Learn what it takes to be a good speaker, and then consciously apply what you learn. Practice inspiring your own image in the mirror and give empowering pep talks to your showerhead. Leadership demands that we seek improvement, and here's your opportunity.

Greek history offers the example of Demosthenes, who was such a poor public speaker that he hit upon the idea of putting pebbles in his mouth and trying to speak through them. He became one of the greatest public speakers of ancient Greece. Another great communicator from whom we can learn an important lesson was Frank Sinatra. Sinatra admired the sonorous sounds of trumpeter Harry James, an early band leader. Sinatra wanted to improve his own breath control, so he taught himself to swim entire laps in the pool underwater, thus forcing himself to be able to hold—and expend—more breath. As a result, Sinatra was able to sing longer phrases and to hold notes longer than any other singer of his era (and perhaps of any era). What do you need to do to improve your speaking skills?

Mastering your voice is one of the most important skills you can learn as a leader. Being a good public speaker translates into being energetic, passionate, and involved. Failing to be a good public speaker translates into being timid, uncertain, diffident, and ultimately, unemployed.

As a further suggestion, watch for newspaper and radio advertisements about daylong seminars on success or peak performance that offer a multitude of high-level speakers. Typically, you can buy a ticket to one of these events for $20 to $25, and you can hear a roster of world-class business leaders, politicians, sports-figures-turned-motivational-speakers, and others. Peter and Tamara Lowe started the Get Motivated seminars more than twenty-five years ago with this precise goal in mind.

When you attend such an event, don't just listen for the message; notice the speaking style of each speaker. How does the speaker approach the platform? How does she create and maintain rapport with the audience? Does she rely on jokes, or is she more serious? What's the balance between warmup material to make the audience feel comfortable and the actual time that the speaker devotes to the message? Become a connoisseur of great public speaking. It's a skill that will serve you well for the rest of your career.

One kind word can warm three months.

Japanese proverb

The Fifth Commandment: Take the Rhino Pledges While the first four commandments will take you far in communicating your vision, they mean nothing if you don't follow the fifth and final commandment of communication, which is the key to Rhino Talk: take the rhino pledges.

Finding your voice is the leader's path to inspiration. Inspiration is not something you can magically turn on and off, casually deciding to incorporate it into your leadership practice. For the most part, either you have it or you don't. More than anything else, inspiration depends on where your voice is coming from. Does it resonate with the truth that comes from authenticity, integrity, and boldness? Or are you reading a speech that was written by some faceless individual in your department of corporate communications?

Today's new leaders need to find their inspiration in the only place they can: within themselves. Inspiration, like character, is not made. It's revealed when you make the choice to speak from your highest self. Finding inspiration begins with three pledges you must make to yourself:

- *Pledge authenticity.* Robert Louis Stevenson said, "To be who we are, and to become what we're capable of being, is the only end in life."[5] Shakespeare said, "To thine own self be true."[6] Authenticity is the path to being your true self. It means not letting the job, the title, the money, the power, the difficulties and challenges, or any other outside influences turn you into something you're not. Authenticity is the inner harmony that becomes your power when what you say, think, and do coincides with what you believe. *Pledge authenticity and you will inspire those around you with honesty, warmth, humor, and sincerity.*

- *Pledge integrity.* Integrity is the simple act of doing what's right when no one else is watching. It's having a code of ethics that asks you not just to say the right words but to live by them—to say what you mean and mean what you say. Sophocles said that he would rather "fail with honor than succeed by fraud."[7] *Pledge integrity and you will inspire those around you with the power to speak the truth; then stand behind your words.*
- *Pledge boldness.* While leaders have sacred responsibilities to the people and the lifeblood of their organizations, they can't play it safe—not with their words and not with their vision. They can't tiptoe into the water. This means that they can't hide behind double-talk and mixed messages. Leaders must be bold, unafraid to challenge those who need to be challenged, to say what needs to be said, to ask more of themselves and those around them than they ever thought they could. *Pledge boldness and you will inspire those around you to step out of their comfort zone and do what needs to be done.*

The Wisdom of Rhino Talk

From a children's fight on a playground to a global war and just about everything in between, the problems in our world often stem from a failure to communicate clearly and powerfully, without egos or hidden agendas. As leaders, so much is out of our hands and out of our control that we must take every opportunity to seize and master whatever we can control. This begins with our voice—what we say, how we say it, and how our message affects those around us.

Rhino Talk teaches us the power of communicating with 100 percent "in-the-moment" awareness, choosing the right message for the right individual, and then infusing that message with passion and honesty. Commit to that power and you can turn your every word into a work of art. And in the process, you can transform the lives of the people you lead and the organizations under your care.

A FINAL RHINO THOUGHT

*On average, we speak five thousand words a day.
And behind every word is power: the power
to divide, wound, separate, and attack or the
power to unite, encourage, motivate, appreciate,
and inspire. Choose your words wisely, and
believe them, stand by them, become them.*

CHAPTER FOUR

The Rhino's Horns

A Leader's Power

There are leaders the people fear, there are leaders
the people hate, and there are leaders the people
love, but when the best leaders of all have finished
their work, the people say, "we did it ourselves."

Lao Tzu

T he leader talks; the people must listen. The leader orders; the people must obey. The leader tells a joke; the people must laugh. Such are the spoils—and the dangers—of power. As Abraham Lincoln said, "Nearly all men can stand adversity, but if you want to test a man's character, give him power."[1] More than money, power corrupts, destroys, and blinds. On the flip side, power is also the engine that drives our vision and allows us to realize our dreams. With power comes force, strength, energy, authority, influence, and, most important, action. For all its infectious trappings, power enables, power builds, and power gets the job done. Without it, we could back out of the driveway in a car loaded with willing passengers, but with no gas in the tank we would sputter and go nowhere.

Power is indeed a mighty sword. And leaders need to wield it with care and responsibility. Leaders need to be bold and strong yet cautious and sensitive, mindful that true power is more than the use of force. It's the catalyst that in its most noble form will influence others to do something for the good of the entire organization.

King of the Castle

Ah, to be the king of the castle. To live your life at the front of the line. To make the most money and have the nicest office, the nicest car, the nicest home. You're seated first, listened to and admired, emulated, beseeched, coddled, and fawned over. And the best parking spot is always yours. Yes, it's good to be the king.

There are indeed perks to being the top dog—or the "top rhino." The only problem is that most of those perks are tied to the job and not the person. The power that leadership brings comes and goes, lasting only as long as the board of directors will put up with you, the stockholders find value in you, or the people will vote for you. Power based on what others give will always be as ephemeral and short lasting as fame. A famous poem by Percy Bysshe Shelley speaks of the once-great leader Ozymandias, whose power and reputation were gone, leaving behind only a broken statue in the desert sand.

While power certainly gets the job done, it may well mean nothing outside the organization you operate in. If that pops your balloon, it's only because your power was a balloon in the first place. And a balloon always deflates quicker than it inflates.

In contrast to Ozymandias is Leonardo DiCaprio's character in the movie *Titanic*. In one scene, DiCaprio and Kate Winslet are leaning over the bow of the doomed ocean liner. DiCaprio throws his arms out wide, letting the ocean wind hit him in the face. He shouts, "I'm the king of the world!"—a bold statement for a man who has no money, status, or fame (and is about to be swallowed up by the icy waters of the North Atlantic). And yet with the woman he loves at his side, he declares himself the planet's ultimate ruler. Expecting nothing, needing nothing, and wanting nothing, his character embodies Rhino Power.

Rhino Power is the energy that comes from within, the power that no one but yourself can give you. It is the power to be content and satisfied, the power to be who you are.

As esoteric as that may sound, leaders would be wise to realize that this is the only power that matters. All other forms of power are only illusions. A strong engine doesn't make a car agile. The driver does. Heavy metal door panels don't make a car safe. Again, the driver does. A steering system doesn't take the car to its destination. It's the driver still. Likewise, a title or position doesn't make you strong. You make yourself strong through the intelligent use of power. Power's only a tool, and how you use it or misuse it will dictate the success of your organization's mission.

Rhino Anatomy: The Horns

The word "rhinoceros" is derived from two ancient Greek words that mean "nose" (*rhino*) and "horned" (*keros*). This is only fitting, since the rhino is the only animal on earth with horns on its nose. Rhino horns, made up of thousands of tiny strands of keratin, are hard all the way through. But interestingly, as strong as they are, the horns are attached rather loosely to the rhino's head. As a result, if a horn hits something hard, it may be knocked off. If this happens, the rhino can grow another horn, which, as we shall see, is an important lesson regarding what constitutes power in the first place.

Unfortunately, the extraordinary horns that make rhinos unique are also dangerous for them. Rhinos have faced extinction because poachers crave their valuable "golden" horns, said to have legendary aphrodisiac qualities. Power is no different; it can be as seductive as it is intoxicating, creating leaders who knowingly or unwittingly do anything to get it and keep it. Successful leaders must be cautious and able to understand their own power and its capabilities to build or destroy.

The rhino can show us the way, but first we must understand how we use power to lead—or, perhaps more important, how we think we use power to lead.

I Lead with the Power of a String

Whether we like to admit it or not, most leaders have invisible strings that they hang over the heads of the individuals in their organizations. Dangling from each string is a carrot, which in most cases comes down to either a person's need for security or desire for a perk or incentive. The carrot is not just a paycheck; it's a promotion to the corner office. It's not just a raise, but a plum assignment and a trip to the Bahamas. Sometimes it's just the authority to sit at the right hand of the throne, to have the ear of the top dog. Whether it's spoken or unspoken, implied or explicit, with a wink and a smile or a slammed fist on the desk, this is leadership by fear, coercion, and even blackmail. However, it's like pouring bad gas into a car: it'll keep you going for a while, but eventually it's going to destroy the engine and ruin the vehicle.

Of course, the people in your organization should have tangible things to work for. No matter the job, the position, or the company, there has to be something in it for everyone. People should respond to motivation and incentive. Money does talk. That corner office speaks to the soul of the workaday executive. The right use of incentives is not only valuable, but it's essential for every leader. In fact, it is the cornerstone of capitalism. The abuse of incentives—relying on them to make people listen and follow you in the first place—is corrupting. As soon as you need to dangle a carrot to get others to act, your power is diminished because it is based on something outside yourself.

I Lead with the Power of the Mind

Who is the most valuable, sought-after individual in the organization? The one with all the answers, of course. The person who knows something that can make the lives of those around him easier. Maybe it's the organization leader, or perhaps it's the leader's longtime assistant, who knows all the policies and procedures—and how to get around them. Information is power. So is knowing how to get things done, find solutions, and provide insight. It doesn't matter what field you're in—homemaking, teaching, selling, or running a nuclear submarine—life is about finding answers, and anyone who puts them on a platter for you with a nice little bow around them is somebody you want to be around.

Of course, more important than just having the right information is empowering your organization with that information. Do you give people just what they need to know, or do you show them how to use it? And even more important, do you show them how to find the information they need for themselves?

I Lead with the Power of Me

As long as there are problems, crises, and broken parts, there will always be a need for the leader's expertise and know-how. But when the problems are solved and the parts are fixed, do you run the risk of not being needed as much? Do you become expendable? Does your stock diminish? Of course not—at least not entirely. But the exaggeration drives home a critically important point. Your role as a leader is to be more than the organization's know-it-all and fix-it person. You need to set the tone, policies, and vision. And this calls for a different, more nuanced type of power: the power that comes not from what you know but from who you are. This kind of power comes when people identify with you and admire what you stand for. It comes when people trust you and feel good about being around you, wanting to roll up their sleeves and work beside you. Use the power that comes when people want to follow you. It's not power through extortion, domination, manipulation, retribution, or even education. It's power through inspiration, and with it comes the energy to move mountains.

In our complex world, leaders would be wise to empower the people in their organizations in as many ways as possible. And while that may mean using money, position, and even fear once in a while, their ultimate aim should always be to use power consciously, certain of their motives and confident in their outcome. Leaders must learn to contain and direct their power so that its influence will affect the greater good of the organization. They must learn that true Rhino Power comes from the mastery of the horns.

The Fourth Principle of Rhino Leadership: Rhino Power and the Mastery of the Horns

A leader's goal is not to *be* the power
but to *direct* the power.

Rhino Power is the energy that comes from within. The fact that the rhino can lose its horns and then easily grow them right back is an important lesson for us all. Power is not the horns. The horns are just a symbol of power. Power resides in the leader. The horns are like the title that comes and goes as easily as someone enters and leaves an organization.

Contrary to popular opinion, sports culture, or even world politics, power is not achieved by being tall, strong, fast, popular, or rich. The headlines may tell another story, but don't believe it. You know that the better team wins the Super Bowl, most wars are won by the stronger country, and the wealthiest producers win Academy Awards. But that type of power is temporary. It lasts only as long as the quarterback is strong, the country keeps it resources, or the producer makes money for the studio. As soon as those attributes disappear, the power vanishes as well. History teaches us that fortunes change and the tide turns, and with these changes, power grows or diminishes.

Lasting power is gained by understanding a simple premise: power is not something that others can take from you or give to you. It is only what you give yourself. You can begin with the mastery of the horns: seven commonsense, readily available principles. The only question you must ask is, Will I choose to accept these principles or not? Will I live them or not? The choice is yours.

The choice you make here will determine the leader you will become.

The Emperor Has No Clothes and the Michael Jordan Effect: Ability Is Power

The creation of a thousand forests is in one acorn.

Ralph Waldo Emerson

Casey Stengel, the great baseball manager, once said, "Ability is the art of getting credit for all the home runs somebody else hits."[2] Such is the temptation that comes from believing your power originates from what others do. While you should take pride in knowing that your efforts help others become more efficient, remember that the power that drives you ought never begin with what someone else brings to the table. Instead the question is, What do you bring?

A parent, coach, teacher, conductor, or leader may set the stage and foundation for greatness to arise. But the child, player, student, musician, or team member makes it happen. You may be great in your own right but only in your right, not through the achievements of others. The power of ability begins and ends with your own competencies, your own ability to have the answers, solutions, and information that will drive your organization to grow and prosper.

If you're feeling inadequate, like the emperor with no clothes, then it's time to jump out from behind your desk, find out what skills you are lacking, and go get them. It's a simple equation: the more expertise you bring to the table, the more competent you become. This chain reaction leads to more trust and respect from your organization.

Consider the example of Rick Ankiel, a young pitching phenomenon with the St. Louis Cardinals. He was young, he was gifted, and he was wild. He had all the physical tools that an individual needed to become a highly successful major-league pitcher, but something in his mental framework kept him from achieving greatness. Neither he nor the coaching staff of the Cardinals understood it. Before long, Ankiel went from being a flamethrower to a flame-out, another prospect whose career had turned into a trivia question. Yet Ankiel never gave up. He desperately wanted to return to the major leagues, and at age twenty-eight, Ankiel began a comeback with the Cardinals—as an outfielder. He learned all the skills he needed to succeed as an outfielder and hitter, skills that he might have possessed, though perhaps not at the major-league level, when he initially came up as a starting pitcher. Today, Rick Ankiel is a success story, a starting outfielder, and a tribute to the fact that he recognized his own shortcomings, did something about them, and never gave up on himself.

The true power behind ability has nothing to do with competency. It's not about the skills and talents you have but about how you use those skills and talents. You could take all the valedictory speeches ever written and reduce them to one simple message: strive to realize your potential and achieve what you're capable of achieving. If you could infuse one message into your organization, it should be this one: we all have gifts. How many of us take the time to unwrap those gifts and see what's inside the package? How many of us live up to our true potential?

Outside of commitment and loyalty, what you want most from the people in your organization is for them to become the people you know they can be. The quickest way to get the most out of your team is not by intimidating them with a whip and a gun but by setting the standard. As Mahatma Gandhi said, "You must be the change you hope to see in the world."[3] If you want those around you to get the most out of themselves, you must do it for yourself first. Your failure to do so will lead to organization-wide mediocrity. Nothing shuts off the power faster than doing just enough to get by. People notice, and in time they will do the inevitable, lowering themselves to the example you have set. You can coast only one way: downhill.

Great leaders excel at their own game, live up to their own potential, and, in the process, inspire all team members to live up to their potential as well. Almost every player who ever shared the court with Michael Jordan has said the same thing: he made them play better. This is what top-down management is all about. Your ability not only powers the engine to get things done quickly and efficiently but also inspires and instills confidence in those around you. Like a ripple in a pond, that can-do feeling spreads throughout the entire organization. It's the most powerful type of leadership there is—leadership by example.

Skip the Lights and the Camera: Action Is Power

As the expression goes, there is always room at the top. This statement is unequivocally true. It doesn't matter how crowded, competitive, and cutthroat your chosen field may be. The road to success is not as crowded as you think, and for very good reason. Most individuals, while they love the promise of gold at the end of the rainbow, want nothing to do with the hard work it takes to stay on that road. In short, they don't act.

Earl Nightingale tells the story of a woman who approached an opera singer after a recital.

"I'd give anything to sing like you," she gushed.

The singer eyed the spectator and said, "I gave up my adolescence and teenage years to sing and study music ten hours a day in a conservatory. While all my friends were going to college, I was attending another conservatory, where I devoted ten hours a day, six days a week, to my art. I've honed my talent my entire career so that I could put on the performance I gave today. I gave everything I had to sing the way I do. I'm not sure that you could say the same."[4]

The singer's remarks are a little harsh, but the point is clear: as leaders, we must always take the first step, to lead by example. JoAnn Falletta began studying music at age seven and went to a conservatory when she was eighteen. She studied hard and practiced constantly. Falletta was extremely gifted and capable, but her lifelong dream of being a conductor met opposition on all sides. Her teachers at the conservatory discouraged her from being a conductor, telling her that no woman had ever succeeded in the field. But Falletta stayed committed and paid her dues, continuing to do well in her courses and taking any opportunity to remind her superiors of her goal. Her diligence and ability paid off: today she is director and conductor for both the Virginia Symphony Orchestra and the

Buffalo Philharmonic. She has paved the way for other female symphony conductors to follow. Falletta had to start at the bottom and deal with a lot of small-minded people, but she kept plugging away until she achieved her dream.

Forget fame and fortune; pick up a broom and start sweeping. Nothing drives your organization's engine like action, doing what needs to be done. Today, people think of Colin Powell as one of our most decorated military and most honored political leaders. Few people know that one of his very first jobs as a teenager was sweeping up at the Coca-Cola bottling plant near his home in the Bronx, New York. Powell devoted himself to sweeping so thoroughly that when he went back for the same job the next year, his boss remembered him and singled him out for advancement. If you want to sweep up the glory, the best way to start is by sweeping up the floor. You're demonstrating to those around you, above you, and below you the level of your commitment. Like ability, the power to act creates a ripple effect in your organization. It not only takes care of the job that needs to be done but inspires others to get in the game as well. More important, action almost single-handedly defeats that great cancer of all companies and organizations: inertia.

You remember the law of inertia from high school physics class: a body in motion stays in motion, but a body at rest—and here's the key part—*stays at rest*. How often have we seen organizations stalled in their tracks, paralyzed by the four sedatives of corporate lethargy: overthinking, second-guessing, group thinking, and status quo? In their jointly authored book, *Why We Want You to Be Rich*, Donald Trump and Robert Kiyosaki write that the American middle class is on the verge of being squeezed out of existence, and that our nation is slowly dividing into rich and poor. Why is this happening? Because the problems that we face—high foreign debt, the healthcare crisis, and other issues—have been around for decades but are only getting worse because the government lacks the courage to take action to solve them. By standing still, we solve nothing, and by failing to solve problems, we only make them worse.

Similarly, the demands of Wall Street force corporate executives to "manage for the quarter," to do whatever they can to maintain or inflate their stock prices without regard for the long-term well-being of the companies. By contrast, Japanese companies are managed not with a ninety-day focus but with a hundred-year plan. Now that's foresight!

We've all been victims of one or more of the four elements of corporate lethargy. Like a deer in headlights, we are frozen in place until our competitors have passed us by and it's too late to recover.

Napoleon Bonaparte said, "Over-preparation is the foe of inspiration."[5] After conquering half the world, the man knew something about getting things done. Leaders certainly need to be cautious and practical, but they can't overprepare, overthink, overguess, overanalyze, and overrely on the status quo. Sometimes leaders need to just get in the game and "start doing." As the Chinese proverb says, "Be not afraid of growing slowly. Be afraid only of standing still."[6]

Earlier, I mentioned *Star Wars: A New Hope*. In the sequel, *The Empire Strikes Back*, Yoda, the Jedi master, tries to instill in Luke Skywalker the means of engaging the Force, the greatest power in the universe. He says to his young student, "Try not. Do or do not. There is no try." The point remains timely and important: be a leader of action, not words. Don't be afraid to jump in and make mistakes.

The doubt, uncertainty, and fear within an organization can be erased with one decisive action from its leader. Today, Rockefeller Center is one of the great business addresses in the world. But few people realize that it was built at the height of the Great Depression, at a time when there was serious doubt as to whether the capitalist

HOW FAILURE EMPOWERS LEADERS

Failure can be one of the most empowering lessons. Why? Because we can learn by observing our mistakes.

We Can Recognize the Ruts, Habits, and Even Traditions Holding Us Back

Leaders need to look closely at their organizations' practices and see which ones are fostering growth and which ones are just getting in the way. As Albert Einstein is said to have observed, "Insanity consists of doing the same thing over and over and hoping for a different result."[7]

For example, in 1988 at the Democratic National Convention, the governor of a small state had the unusual opportunity to make a speech in prime time. He blew it. He talked way too long and committed the cardinal sin of speakers: he was boring. Did he quit politics as a result? No. Instead, he learned a lot about how to make a speech the right way. Perhaps you've heard his name: it's William Jefferson Clinton.

The past can be a comfortable and safe place to hide. It can also be a roadblock to innovation and growth. A leader understands that on the path to success, failure is unavoidable. Every one of us at some point has made a mistake and then second-guessed himself or herself, saying, "I absolutely blew it." The greatest part of being human is that we will make mistakes. To err is human, right? Leaders will closely observe their mistakes and learn the lessons that create positive changes, so that the next challenges presented will result in different outcomes.

We Have an Opportunity to Reframe the Concept of Failure

We don't always need to look at failure as being an unsuccessful attempt. How about looking at failure as a yet-unattained goal or as one more step toward eventual success? Unfortunately, most people don't live up to their full potential because of their constant fear of failing. Bill Russell, whom many consider the greatest center ever in the National Basketball Association, used to throw up before every game he played for the Boston Celtics. Did he have a fear of failing? Evidently. Did he let it get in the way of one of the greatest careers in basketball history? Absolutely not.

One of the most famous moments in the NBA came in the 1965 division finals. John Havlicek reached in and deflected an inbound pass to seal the Celtics' victory over the Philadelphia 76ers. This moment was memorialized by announcer Johnny Most, who screamed, "Havlicek stole the ball! It's all over. Johnny Havlicek stole the ball!" Havlicek tells the story that prior to his steal, Bill Russell, normally the surest of ball handlers, had taken the ball out of bounds after a Wilt Chamberlain stuff. Russell threw the ball inbounds and hit a guy wire that held the basket in place. The ball went back to the 76ers, who trailed by one point. During the ensuing time out, the Celtics huddle could have been one of fear and despair. After all, the 76ers would get the ball at half court and had enough time left to score two points, which would win them the division championship. Instead, Havlicek recounts, he looked Russell in the eye as if to say, "Don't worry about it. I'll pick you up. I'll do something." And that's when Havlicek went out and stole the ball. The rest is history.

In the same way, reframing allows people in an organization to reenergize their efforts, turning their attention from short-term pain to long-term success. It also encourages individuals to take risks they might otherwise have avoided. Success, prosperity, and growth in our lives find their genesis in our failures and in the mistakes we make.

Leaders neither shut the door on their failures nor obsess over them endlessly. Instead, they observe their failures and analyze them, understanding that they are not defined by the mistakes. Leaders understand that failure is subjective and that a leader can always turn a failure into an opportunity to create a more purposeful and meaningful life.

We Can Learn from Our Failures

One of the most important lessons that we can learn from failure is that it is a temporary event. How much attention we pay to failure determines the length of time that we will still be dealing with it. Leaders have the ability to isolate failure and not to take it personally. This is a common ability among top athletes: pitchers who give up a grand slam, basketball players who get "posterized" (when they fail to defend against a slam dunker), or quarterbacks who give up a big interception. The most outstanding athletes, professional and amateur, have the ability to shrug off a bad play and move on.

Perfectionists have a mind-set that does not allow for self-forgiveness. Successful athletes—and successful people in every realm—realize that any failure is just a passing event, not a life-defining incident. True leaders also understand that the greater the obstacles to overcome, the greater the personal satisfaction and reward that awaits. Of course, dealing with any adversity in our lives takes time, effort, and the ability to overcome setbacks.

The best approach is to have reasonable expectations so that we don't have our feelings hurt when everything doesn't turn out exactly as we planned. When we have this mind-set, failure presents a golden opportunity for continued learning and growth, without which personal change and evolution would not be possible.

We Gain Perspective and Strength

Having a proper perspective toward failure is essential, especially if we find ourselves defining who we are in accordance with the failures we experience. "Stinking thinking" is a phrase associated with feelings of failure and negativity. Leaders need to break through negative thoughts and beliefs and create a new pattern of thinking. The great movie director Frank Capra reportedly said that he had a very difficult time directing his first picture because everyone from the cinematographer to the gaffer and the best boy kept coming to him and asking for guidance about where to set the camera, how to do the lighting, and other matters. Capra quickly realized two things: first, no one went away angry if he made some sort of decision at all, even if he had no idea what he was talking about, and second, his "batting average" would be at least .500. Capra's ability to make educated guesses and turn them into quick decisions led to the creation of many of the most beloved movies in American history, including *It's a Wonderful Life*, *Harvey*, and *Lost Horizon*. Stinking thinking would have told Capra, "You don't know the answers to their questions, and you never will. Give it up." But instead, Capra hung on and made decisions, and the results speak for themselves.

How do you overcome the kind of obsession with failure we're talking about? First, take yourself out of the failure picture. Let's be honest: it hurts to fail. It can hurt both emotionally and physically. The secret to charging through failure, rhino-style, is in deciding to change your association to it. Once you understand that failing at something does not mean for a second that you are a failure, you establish a position of strength.

For many, fear stops all forward progress. It creates paralysis or prolonged procrastination. Breaking the cycle of failure assures us that while we cannot avoid fear, we certainly can learn from it. We can reverse the damage that it does to our lives, and we can create an environment that allows us to move forward in a more positive and predictable way. Reflecting on our experience from a new vantage point allows us to break down failure into specific elements, which can then be dissected and analyzed, helping us to determine the specific root cause for the failure.

What does a coach do after a tough loss? He watches the film of the game. And then he watches it again and again and again. It's not just an exercise in masochism or futility. A good coach knows that if he keeps studying the film, he'll see where the breakdown arises, and then he'll be able to address his team and offer them a way out. We don't have to run toward failure, but we don't have to run away from it, either.

Put it all together and we begin to see a fundamental shift in how we might view peak performance in a leader's life. It has been proven time and again that the difference between success and failure is minimal. In baseball, the difference between a baseball player who earns $300,000 a year and one who earns

$3 million a year is only one extra hit out of ten. That's it. You can take this analogy and apply it to any situation in life.

Success is not reserved for special people, nor is failure, by the way. The only definitive difference between achievers and those who struggle is how they approach, handle, and perceive their failures. That's the secret. As Michael Jordan said, "I've missed more than nine thousand shots in my career. I've lost almost three hundred games. Twenty-six times I've been trusted to take the game-winning shot and missed. I've failed over and over and over again in my life, and that is why I succeed."[8] Or as Wayne Gretzky said, "You miss a hundred percent of the shots you never take."[9] For today's leader, failure must become a part of success.

system would even survive. It took enormous courage and foresight to spend the money to build the many office towers of Rockefeller Center, and John D. Rockefeller Jr. spared no expense: he used the finest materials; brought in the finest artists to create spectacular murals; and otherwise made the buildings as splendid, modern, and attractive as could be. As the song goes, "They all laughed at Rockefeller Center." Not anymore.

If I Only Had the Nerve: Courage Is Power

As leaders, we may have the ability, intellect, and wisdom to know what needs to be done to drive our organization forward. But it's only with courage that we are able to act. Who are the most admired people? Generally, they are those who stand for something when it is not easy or popular, who will do what nobody else wants to do, who will speak their minds when no one else will, who will act from a sense of purpose when others are acting strictly out of self-interest. We admire those who derive motivation from the simple premise that we should say and do only what is right and true. In an ideal world, those people are our leaders. Those people are you.

Rosa Parks showed us what courage is all about when she refused to give up her bus seat to a white person in Montgomery, Alabama. The year was 1955, and she knew she was not just defying convention but risking personal harm. She knew her life wouldn't be easier because of her choice, but she made it anyway. "I did not get on the bus to get arrested," she said. "I got on the bus to go home . . . My feet weren't tired. I was tired—tired of unfair treatment."[10] Hers was a simple, honest act of doing what she knew was both right and true. In that courageous act of protest, Parks galvanized the civil rights movement. Such is the power of courage. As Helen Keller once said, "One can never consent to creep when one feels an impulse to soar."[11]

The Courage to Do What We Don't Want to Do We all have an Achilles heel, an area in our lives where we feel lacking and vulnerable. We may deny it or go to great lengths to hide it, but we can't escape it. What we fear has a way of catching up to us. Our choice is simple: we can avoid our fears or deal with them head-on. As Mark Twain said, "Courage is resistance to fear, mastery of—not absence of fear."[12] Whether you're afraid of speaking in public, having to fire someone, espousing an alternative viewpoint, or telling people that they're not doing a good job, you must do what is right for the organization, even when it's hard—and even more so when it's unpopular.

President Gerald Ford made an unpopular decision when he pardoned his predecessor, Richard Nixon, of all crimes. The move was intensely unpopular with much of the nation. Many people believed that Ford had secretly promised Nixon a pardon in exchange for Nixon's nominating him for vice president when Spiro Agnew resigned in 1973. Others believed that Nixon had committed terrible crimes and that letting him off the hook was setting a terrible example for all law-abiding citizens. Ford said that he never looked back on his decision and always knew it was the right one. His motivation was to spare the nation the spectacle of a former president sitting in the defendant's chair in a courthouse. As he put it, "Our long national nightmare is over."[13] Before long, many Americans came to see the simple wisdom of his choice. The nation was indeed spared the spectacle of a former president on trial, and America was able to go about its business, putting the bitter, partisan memory of the Watergate debacle behind it.

While moments of courage like this may be our most trying times, they will also be our most telling. They will do more than solve our immediate problems. They will define our legacy, as the pardon did for Gerald Ford. More than that, these experiences will make us stronger, creating a source of power inside us that is unconquerable.

The Courage to Do What Others Don't Want Us to Do From grade school to the Fortune 500, peer pressure hits us where it hurts—in the ego. Whatever age we are or whatever position we may hold, no one wants to be derided, scorned, or ostracized. No one wants to be disliked and on the outside looking in. Unfortunately, that sometimes comes with the leader's job. Our role is not always to be loved but to be respected. And ultimately, we must make our decisions based on what is best for the organization as a whole. Occasionally, a leader realizes that if the organization is to survive, then a large number of people must be let go, regardless of their years of service or their loyalty to the organization. This is the difficult, often-thankless task that leaders must face.

We leaders will make unpopular decisions. In a world where nothing is black and white, we will often make mistakes. We're human and we're not always going to get it right. Yet the world is more tolerant of a leader who makes a mistake than a leader who does nothing at all and allows problems to pile up unsolved. When we do stumble or falter, we will require even more courage to continue to make the tough decisions. But continue we must.

A leader's real power does not come with grand and monumental acts but with the small acts of courage of everyday life. This is the courage that comes with every choice we make to treat people fairly when no one is watching, to keep trying when we don't immediately succeed, to go the extra mile when no one asks us to, to take risks and make sacrifices. Most people don't see this type of courage because it happens far away from the glory and glamour of the red carpet, the corporate jet, or the rally with thousands of pumped-up team members. Yet we cannot expect to be courageous when everything is on the line unless we cultivate the spirit of courage in everyday life.

It Is Better to Give Than to Receive: Empowering Is Power

> A great manager . . . makes you get more
> out of yourself. And once you learn how good
> you really are, you never settle for anything less
> than the very best.
>
> *Reggie Jackson*

On the album *Abbey Road*, the Beatles sing, "The love you take is equal to the love you make." This sixties wisdom perfectly captures the reciprocal nature of love and is equally applicable to power. We might update the lyric to read, "The power you take is equal to the power you give."

It's not as catchy but just as true. Our power does indeed grow stronger the more we give it away and share it with those around us. It doesn't matter how strong or powerful we are. There is a limit to what a leader can accomplish. There is only so much time and energy to do what needs to be done. If we wish to extend our power, we need to extend our power base and leverage our abilities through the talents and energy of others. We do this through the act of empowering.

To empower means to give people a sense of confidence in their ability to make decisions. Empowering others allows them to develop their own strengths and capabilities, and it fosters an atmosphere in which they can improve their self-esteem. No matter what your own definition of empowerment may be, empowering begins with encouragement. Encouragement is more than a pat on the back. It's making those in your organization feel important and valued. You can never really know the impact that a few kind and sincere words of encouragement have on someone. As Emerson said, "Our chief want in life is somebody who shall make us do what we can."[14] This is why parents, teachers, coaches, and leaders have become our most valuable resources, society's most powerful enablers. Of course, encouraging words do more than boost morale; they give confidence. And with confidence comes the power to achieve greatness.

Every time you offer encouragement to your team, you're also sending them a message that you are watching—not only when they're late or underperforming but when they do something good. This simple form of acknowledgment carries the potential to make the individuals on your team want to do a better job. Oprah Winfrey once noted that you know you're on the road to success if you would do your job even if you weren't paid. If your team members love what they do, you're doing something right as a leader, and you have the potential to extend your own power.

Once you have fostered an atmosphere of value and contribution, you must move to the next level, which is creating a culture of power sharing. Paradoxically, to truly empower, leaders must relinquish control of their own power. As much as it may go against the grain of who you are, what you might have learned in business school, or what you see of Donald Trump or other symbols of power in the media, if you are to increase the scope of your power, you must learn to give responsibility and influence away. You can begin with both collaboration and delegation. Lip service collaboration is not the answer. Instead, you need a meaningful meeting of the minds—not a delegation of tasks but a delegation of genuine responsibility. And you know exactly what the difference is.

Leaders are obligated to foster a climate of shared responsibility for their organizations' missions. In other words, you need to send a clear and simple message that you can't do it alone, that you need others. And while you're sending that message, you'll also send one more: if responsibility is shared, so is the credit and the rewards for success. When you give people their due, you empower them all over again. At the end of the day, you certainly need to hold people accountable. You need to guide them, show them the way, and be there to support them. Of course, at the same time, you need to let them go, allowing them to experience and feel their own power, to know what it means to rise to the occasion. Each time they do, their power, your power, and your organization's power become deeper, stronger, and more effective.

The Square Root of Pi Is Apple:
Play and Creativity Are Power

Albert Einstein said, "Imagination is more important than knowledge."[15] And where imagination goes, play and creativity must follow. Unfortunately, play has never been a valued quality in leadership circles. Golf notwithstanding, most people in the business world make a sharp delineation between work time and playtime. And they have all too little playtime! The business world also fails to properly value daydreaming, doodling, playing make-believe, or coloring outside the lines. Yet creativity in all its oddly absurd manifestations is essential for leaders who hope to harness their true power.

Take a look at Superman: faster than a speeding bullet, more powerful than a locomotive, able to leap tall buildings in a single bound—all powerful abilities. And yet Superman's real power lies in his x-ray vision—the ability to see what no one else can see. We discussed vision as a source of power in chapters 1 and 2. This same power comes with creativity. This is the power that turns a leader into a visionary and offers the ultimate competitive edge.

When we think of business leaders, it is hard to imagine anyone having a better time than Richard Branson. The founder of Virgin Records, Virgin Atlantic, and other extraordinarily successful business ventures, Branson has taken a hot-air balloon around the world, envisioned a new airline that takes passengers into space in order to cut transoceanic travel time from hours to minutes, and exercised a strong sense of creativity and play. Branson is famous for his collection of notebooks: he jots down every intriguing idea that comes to mind, and more often than not, he finds a way to turn these ideas into successful and exciting businesses or equally successful and exciting fun activities. American business leaders would be wise to emulate the spirit of Richard Branson when trying to loosen the reins and create new visions for their businesses.

You can certainly get through a brick wall with will power, determination, and hard work, but this approach takes a lot of energy and isn't foolproof. As President Ronald Reagan once said, "It's true hard work never killed anybody. But I figure, why take the chance?"[16] Navigating a wall can often take other skills, such as finesse, outside-the-box thinking, and the creative ability to put a square peg in a round hole.

Remember that you don't have to crash through a brick wall to get to the other side. There just might be a door! If not, perhaps there's a window you can crawl through. Or maybe you can just go around the wall. You need to see the wall and its surroundings in new ways, to see new possibilities and solutions, and you need to suspend all beliefs. You need to rearrange mentally what's in front of you, to challenge existing principles, ideas, rules, and strategies in order to see the truth, beauty, and uniqueness missed by others. Countless children are pigeonholed as dyslexic and are viewed as having a learning disability. Neurosurgeons point out, however, that dyslexia is not a learning disability: it is a different way of learning. Many of America's most creative and successful business leaders are highly dyslexic. Isn't it possible that the automatic rearranging of letters, numbers, and words that they see gives them a vision of the world far different from anything that "normal" learners experience?

As a leader, you need to create the time and space to look at your organization from as many different angles as possible. You need to surround yourself with creative people not so you can abdicate responsibility but so you can augment and inspire your own creativity. If all you have around you are people who always think in the same way, you're bound to continually get the same-thinking results. Remember that the hallmark of all creative thinking is to *keep digging*. When looking for solutions to problems or new ways of doing something, you can't always settle for the first answer. The real magic often comes from the second, third, or fourth idea. Of course, after digging, you might go back to your first idea, but you will do it consciously, recognizing the merit of the original idea even more.

All organizations strive to be unique. Creativity is the path to that uniqueness. It makes you powerful and lets you see what others can't see.

Leave Your Power Behind: No Power Is Power

> I hope our wisdom will grow with our power,
> and teach us that the less we use our power,
> the greater it will be.
> *Thomas Jefferson*

The enemy of power is burnout or exhaustion, which will inevitably lead to performance malfunction, usually characterized by bouts of boredom, predictability, ineffectiveness, inertia, and downright crabbiness. Fortunately, there is a remedy: *leave your power behind*.

Of all the horn-mastery principles, this is the simplest, and yet it's the hardest to adopt. It all comes down to embracing one life-altering sentence made up of eight simple words: There is more to life than your career.

If you eat, breathe, and sleep work, then your entire identity, including your power, is wrapped up in your career and title. As a leader, you need to leave your work and power at the office. Insist on having a life outside of work: time with family and friends, exercise, hobbies, interest in the world beyond your workplace. This separation from your power gives you emotional balance, a respite from the all-or-nothing business climate in which you are absorbed every day.

Take the example of U.S. senator and presidential candidate Barack Obama, who called his wife to tell her that he'd achieved a great success on the Senate floor. His wife's response?

"We have ants."

"Ants?"

"Yes, we have ants . . . in the bathroom and the kitchen. So on your way home, can you pick up some ant traps?"[17]

Obama says he just laughed and realized that he may be one of the most successful political leaders in America, but as far as the ant was concerned, he was just another guy with a kitchen full of food.

Focusing on aspects of life other than work invigorates you and keeps you fresh and excited. If you are fresh and excited outside of work, it only makes sense that you would carry that attitude into work, helping you to avoid the pitfall of burnout. This separation of power also gives you your "legs": it helps you to stand up and be strong without the power of a title. Think of a millionaire rock star with his entourage of back-scratching flatterers. He has no need to call on his inner strength because he's given whatever he wants, thanks to his celebrity. But take away the success and he finds that his power and strength must now come from who he is and not what he does. If you're not used to it, it's not easy to make that transition. It takes practice to be your true self.

As a leader, you will never be able to cultivate real Rhino Power unless you leave behind your job—and, more important, the power that is attached to it. *It's a simple principle with big results. Try it. It's empowering.*

Stand for Something: Purpose Is Power

What pushes you to get out of bed in the morning and face another day? Is it ambition, the need for recognition, fame, and money? Or is a sense of purpose, duty, or a higher calling?

The answer you give will fundamentally determine the amount of power you will possess in order to realize the mission of your organization. Martin Luther once said that even if he knew the world would end tomorrow, "I would plant a tree today."[18] Such is the power of purpose, to do what needs to be done, to do what your heart tells you must be done, to live your day with the conviction that what you do matters. As William James wrote, "The great use of life is to spend it for something that outlasts it."[19]

Leaders who find a higher purpose in their missions will have power beyond their wildest imaginations. It's impossible to truly believe in something and not find the power to make that dream come true. According to Margaret Mead, "If we are to achieve a richer culture, rich in contrasting values, we must recognize the whole gamut of human potentialities, and so weave a less arbitrary social fabric, one in which each diverse human gift will find a fitting place."[20]

The Wisdom of Rhino Power

Al Capone said, "You can get much farther with a kind word and a gun than you can with a kind word alone."[21] Capone probably never understood the emotional fragility of the human psyche, or perhaps his mother never told him he could catch more flies with honey than with vinegar. In either case, the world has changed. The symbol of power is no longer the sword, nor is it the gangster with a Tommy gun. The symbols of power are now the individuals themselves.

Leaders have more responsibility than ever before, and with that responsibility comes the opportunity to shape and influence their organizations and the lives of the people in their care.

This takes more than power. It takes Rhino Power.

A FINAL RHINO THOUGHT

Only the strength, confidence, creativity, and power we give ourselves really matter. Our inner power sets us apart, fuels our mission, and allows us to accomplish what we never dreamed of.

CHAPTER FIVE

The Rhino's Feet

A Leader's Endurance

Those who endure, conquer.
Anonymous

I f history has proven anything, it's that within every man and woman lies the power to endure, to keep going when all seems hopeless and lost. Humanity has collectively endured every imaginable obstacle: famine, earthquake, tsunami, war, terrorism, starvation, poverty, disease, desperation, loneliness, and heartache. We have endured with uncompromising tenacity and perseverance, living up to the challenge of Winston Churchill, who urged his generation to "never give in—*never, never, never, never.*"[1] We Americans have created a society that has shown how much we can endure, and in so doing, we have clearly illustrated what we were capable of achieving.

Of course, we are also the same people who can't live without our cell phones, laptops, or PDAs. We're the first to hit the snooze button in the morning, quit a diet at the first sight of fudge, and call in sick with a bad case of the sniffles. We are a paradox, both tough and pampered, resilient and fragile.

135

The explanation is most likely a matter of what's on the line—the difference between what has to be done and what we can get away with doing. In crisis after crisis, we have proven just how deep we can dig and how much we can accomplish. When the crisis passes, so too vanishes our power to endure and, with it, the miracles we can achieve.

We're Not All Marathon Runners

To lead is like being a runner. Anyone can put on athletic shoes and start running. The world has a place for joggers, but we also need long-distance runners, those with the vision to gaze far down the road and the endurance not to quit until they arrive at the finish line. Of course, that's easier said than done. The task can seem overwhelming and even impossible, an achievement meant only for the chosen few.

That statement has a kernel of truth: leadership isn't for everyone. It takes a select breed, individuals who are willing to step up and do what needs to be done to prepare themselves for a long-haul journey. Having a vision, a plan, and the best intentions isn't enough if a leader can't sustain the energy to finish the race. In our results-driven culture, we either make it happen or we don't; we either go partway or all the way. This, of course, puts an enormous amount of pressure and weight on today's leader.

In years gone by, college football coaches were idolized and forgiven the occasional losing season. Today, the shelf life of a football coach at a major university program is no more than a couple of years. The message from the administration, the alumni, and the fans is "Produce or be gone." The same is true for the CEO of a major business enterprise and for practically any one of us in a leadership position. We have less and less time to prove ourselves to more and more constituencies, who are often in conflict with one another.

The rhino teaches us that to carry this weight, the heavy burden of a long journey, we must have the strong foundation to support it. If the journey of a thousand miles starts with a single step, then the key to endurance is our feet.

Rhino Anatomy: The Feet

How does a six-foot-tall, four-thousand-pound rhino run at speeds of up to thirty-five miles an hour? The answer can be found in the rhino's perfectly constructed feet, the ideal foundation not just for running but also for endurance. Rhinoceroses, like horses, belong to the scientific order Perissodactyla, a name that comes from the Greek words meaning "odd toed." In plain English, rhinos have three toes on each foot. The middle toes support the rhinos' enormous weight.

Through the lesson of Rhino Endurance, we will learn to support the heavy weight of our own responsibilities and, in the process, discover what real endurance is all about. But first we must understand how we endure in the first place—or how we think we endure.

We Endure for the Sake of Self-Preservation

Nothing else is like rising to the challenge that comes when we have no choice. Fail to endure and you don't eat. Fail to endure and you lose your job. Fail to endure and someone else will take over your business.

An example of this kind of fear-based endurance comes from former New York mayor Rudy Giuliani, who admitted that when

9/11 occurred, New York did not have a plan for what to do if planes slammed into the World Trade Center. A situation like this, although it had been on Osama Bin Laden's planning board for months, if not years, had never crossed the minds of anyone in New York. Yet the city had been the scene of numerous terrorist attacks in the past, including the 1993 bomb attack at the World Trade Center itself.

Giuliani says that the city could have wallowed in fear, but instead it turned fear into the most productive action possible: planning. Although it had no specific plan for what took place on the morning of September 11, 2001, New York indeed had plans for what should happen if the subways shut down, the hospitals were overwhelmed, the United Nations was attacked, and so on.

As a result, Giuliani and his team were able to combine these various plans into a new, cohesive approach to deal with the reality of the terrorist attacks. The process of getting the city back on its feet in the minutes, hours, days, weeks, and months after the tragedy might not have been smooth, but at least it was well-orchestrated.

When our backs are against the wall, we get done what we need to get done. This is even more true when our family's safety or our livelihood is on the line.

We Endure for the Sake of Self-Respect

Type A leaders don't need to step to the front of the line because they're already there. These competition-driven individuals persist because refusing to give up or take no for an answer is in their very nature. They're persistent, tenacious, strong-willed, and downright stubborn. These qualities collectively become "I'll prove I'm the fittest" ego-based endurance. Lance Armstrong, the seven-time winner of the Tour de France, endured and continues to endure abuse, whispers of drug allegations, and outright pure hatred from many in the French media. This is because he, a foreigner, came to France and for seven straight years took its crown jewel to its more prestigious rival, the United States. "Everyone wants to know what I'm on," Armstrong said of the drug allegations. "I'm on my bike . . . six hours a day."[2]

Who wouldn't give anything to have an army of Lance Armstrongs join their organization?

We Endure for the Sake of Self-Realization

As Friedrich Nietzsche said, "He who has a why to live for can bear almost any how."[3] What keeps great leaders going is not fear or ego but personal growth and a meaningful mission that they believe in. For them, endurance becomes a matter of both a purposeful goal and their personal ambition to realize their potential. It's "I'll achieve what I can" principle-driven endurance, and not only does it work, but within the realm of this mind-set, unimaginable achievement takes place.

Reinhold Messner is one of the greatest and most fearless mountain climbers to ever live. He's not only climbed Mount Everest, but he has done it alone, once without oxygen. He has endured temperatures of forty degrees below zero and winds over one hundred miles per hour, all while scaling some of the highest and most dangerous peaks in the world. In one day, he endures more than many of us will endure in a lifetime. While he undoubtedly endures for the sake of survival and, no doubt, because of a healthy ego, he endures mainly because it is who he is. His dream of reaching the top of the mountain, any mountain, is so strong that he has no choice. He endures because he must.

As a famous French philosopher once wrote, "Those who can bear all can dare all."[4]

The Fifth Principle of Rhino Leadership:
Rhino Endurance

A leader's goal is not to survive but to thrive.

Margaret Okayo of Kenya was the first woman to cross the finish line in the 2003 New York City Marathon. She finished with a record time of two hours, twenty-two minutes and thirty-one seconds. Zoe Koplowitz finished in last place the following day with a time of just under twenty-nine hours and forty-five minutes. Like Okayo, Koplowitz is a spirited and fiercely competitive woman. At fifty years of age, she's completed sixteen marathons, finishing every one of them dead last. In fact, it has taken her more than twenty-four hours to complete every single marathon in which she has run. When you meet her, the reason is immediately obvious. Koplowitz has multiple sclerosis and walks the entire course with two canes, always in pain and never certain that she'll finish. Yet as she says to those around her who ask why she does what she does, "Either you have your dreams or you live your dreams. I'm not all that remarkable. I just keep putting one foot in front of the other until I get where I want to go."[5]

Whether a corporate leader takes his company public or Zoe Koplowitz bravely inches her way through the New York streets in the middle of the night, endurance isn't always about being first or being the fastest. It's about getting to where you want to go and accomplishing your objectives. It's about finishing the race you start.

And while speed is certainly important in today's competitive climate, as any marathoner will tell you, there's no reason to run faster if you can't finish the race at all. As leaders, we know where we need to go. Now we have to do what it takes to get there. We have the power and the people and the will. All we need is the endurance to finish the task. And we will do it as Koplowitz advises us, by "putting one foot in front of the other."

Talk about endurance, and people immediately think of strength, tenacity, power, willfulness, and stamina. While endurance does in fact take a "pedal to the metal" perseverance, it equally takes a wiser, more cautious approach and an "easing off the accelerator" reliance on pace, moderation, economy of motion, and, most important, balance.

This is the foundation for the Wisdom of the Odd-Toed Ungulate, the rhino's three-pronged approach to incorporating endurance into leadership practice. Just as the rhino has three toes that support its enormous weight, leaders need three foundational blocks that together will carry their weight, giving them the support that makes endurance possible on their journey. The rhino's three essential toes of endurance are strength, wisdom, and balance.

The First Toe of Endurance Is Strength

What would you do if you knew that in six months you had to run a marathon, swim the English Channel, or climb Mount Everest? You'd either crawl back under the covers in denial or you'd start to get in shape, beginning with an intense program of diet, cardiovascular training, and sport-specific drills. Whether you want to climb the stairs, climb Mount Everest, or climb your way to competitive greatness, you have to be strong enough to do it, and that starts with training. The simple question to ask is, What could stop you from achieving your goal? After all, you can't be expected to endure anything unless you know what you're up against.

To paraphrase Pogo, I have met the enemy and it is us. Sometimes, we can be our own worst enemies. Self-doubt, uncertainty, and fear can keep us from accomplishing our goals. Indeed, they can even freeze us in place and keep us not just from the finish line but from the starting line. How do we overcome those old tapes playing in our heads? We have to build strength in areas where, in the past, we have experienced resistance and fear.

Continuing the example of marathon runners, how does an ordinary person, a weekend runner who has done nothing more than a 5K race, learn to finish marathons? Jeff Galloway is one of America's most successful marathon coaches, training not just elite runners but also "the rest of us." He offers the "Galloway method," in which a runner runs for five to seven minutes and then takes a one- to two-minute walk break, repeating this process until the race is complete.

Why take walk breaks? Because if you charge hard throughout the first ten or fifteen miles of a marathon, you may have nothing left in the tank by the time you get to mile twenty—hence the dreaded "wall" that so many runners talk about with anxiety and fear. Galloway points out that by taking walk breaks, you get your heart rate down temporarily, and you take the strain off your running muscles, allowing you to go the distance. Galloway combines this unique approach to running with affirmations that he encourages runners to photocopy, carry with them during races or long training runs, and read to themselves during their walk breaks. The message of those affirmations is simple: "We're here to have a good time." "Let's enjoy the day." "Running is our natural heritage." "We're going to make it." As we move toward our goals, we need to pause every so often to give our "running muscles" a rest, and then we can make it to the finish line.

The Leader in the Mirror Any meaningful training program, whether for a marathon or another challenge or endeavor, must begin with an honest assessment of where you are at the present moment. You need to take a good, hard look at yourself and ask the same questions you'd ask about the people in your organization: Am I performing to the highest level of which I'm capable? Am I as efficient, energetic, and optimistic as I can be? Or have I slipped into that corporate quagmire of fatigue and burnout?

What's the first reaction when a CEO is discovered to be in ill health? The stock price plunges. Wall Street hates uncertainty, especially when it comes to the health of corporate leaders. Yet no matter what organization or enterprise you lead, whether you are the president of the United States or the head of your family, everyone around you is counting on you to maintain health, strength and balance in your life.

And yet we don't. We routinely try to cram twenty hours of work into sixteen-hour workdays, taking our work everywhere—to the airport, on vacation, to the dentist's waiting room. We surround ourselves with like-minded people so we don't feel quite so strange when we devote all of our time, effort, and energy to work and precious little to family, exercise, and play.

The lack of balance costs us in terms of health, energy, and flexibility. And yet society applauds this kind of behavior. Frequently, the term "workaholic" is applied reverently to some hard-charging business leader or politician in a front-page profile in the *Wall Street Journal*. The health-and-lifestyle columnist may preach balance, exercise, proper nutrition, and rest, but who gets the real laurels in the business sections of our newspapers? It's the people who work too hard, too long, too much, and without respite. Workaholism is nothing to be proud of. It's a compulsion no different from alcoholism, compulsive overeating, drug addiction, or any other self-destructive form of escapism that we choose when we seek to avoid facing the truth about our lives.

Simply put, we've got to take better care of ourselves. The challenge is to stay committed to our goals and remain driven to excellence while also staying strong, healthy, and balanced. It's not an impossibility. Plenty of highly successful individuals lead balanced lives, even if we don't get to read about them on the front page of the *Wall Street Journal*.

Life coaches are people who help their clients maximize their sense of fulfillment, achievement, and enjoyment. They typically create a "wheel of life" with these items around the center: family, physical health and fitness, friendships, finance, work, recreation and play, and spirituality. They ask their clients to reflect honestly on their lives and ask, on a one-to-ten scale where ten is total satisfaction and one is complete disarray, how they would rate themselves in each of these aspects of a balanced life. They then work with their clients to develop a plan to increase the low numbers to where they should be.

You can hire a life coach, or you can be your own life coach. Take a moment and score yourself in each of the above. Where do you find fulfillment? Where would you like to improve your life? Are you going to be a shooting star at work, one that creates a brilliant path across the sky only to flame out before the journey is complete? Or will you be the kind of star that offers light, warmth, and guidance—a star to steer by—for a long, long time? We can't control some things in life: the drunk driver crossing the line, the industrial accident, or the sudden act of nature. But we can control so much: specifically, our attitudes, our actions, and our words. Are we striving for balance? Or are we running from it?

Rhino's Seven-Step Program for Increasing Energy Finding our own strength takes a new type of energy, one that comes with purposeful and conscious "life conditioning." The result is not only good health but vitality, enthusiasm, and renewed purpose.

Step 1: Embrace a New Goal. For most leaders, professional and corporate growth is an easy concept to grasp: gather the necessary information, create a workable strategy, and begin. Personal growth is an entirely different matter. For many of us, it doesn't come easily, and it may even seem superfluous and counterintuitive to our "real" goal of growing a business and developing an exit strategy. And yet, as the rhino will teach us, personal growth should always be our first goal. Without it, nothing else can happen. It is the first cause for all success. Our primary goal is clear and simple: create the energy needed to complete the mission. Today's leaders need physical and mental health—not just for ourselves but also for the companies, organizations, and enterprises we serve.

Step 2: Embrace a New Mind-Set. As we begin our journey toward health in its broadest definition—emotional balance and physical well-being—we must shift our preconceived thinking and reframe how we work. In our constant efforts to drive profits higher and higher, we cram more and more into our days, tugging, pulling, and straining our bodies. Even our language speaks to our struggles, how we are forced to "bend over backward," "keep our nose to the grindstone," "work our fingers to the bone," "sweat blood," or "bust our buns." It's no wonder that our bodies are often as broken as our spirits.

As leaders, we must remember the point of diminishing returns, the moment at which the hours we spend no longer increase our productivity in a meaningful way. We need to worry less about how much effort we exert or how much time we spend and focus more on how much energy we have, and the quality of that energy. We must come to the realization that working sixteen hours a day avails us nothing if during the remaining eight hours we are impatient, edgy, irritable, confrontational, and, worst of all, unproductive in our private lives.

Step 3: Embrace a Strategy of Focused Energy. Twenty percent of our day is spent on tasks that do nothing to advance the company's mission. A strategy of focused energy means that we eliminate those nonessentials from our workday and concentrate only on what's important, only on those actions that drive our business. If we're honest with ourselves, we all know the individual areas where we dawdle or waste time.

How much time do we spend organizing our e-mail, despairing at the hundreds of unread e-mails in our in-box, or surfing the Web and checking out our spouse's or daughter's MySpace page? How much time do we spend chasing down information that we really ought to ask others to find for us? How many other tasks do we perform out of a compulsive need to overcontrol our environment? Where do we fail to trust others to take the lead and to take responsibility? We are being compensated not for our e-mail skills but for our ability to create, communicate, and implement a vision. And yet we so often willingly choose to bog ourselves down in the minutiae of business life so that we can avoid our higher calling.

We're like Jonah. In the book of Jonah, God gives Jonah a vital mission: go to the people of Nineveh and inform them that unless they change their ways, their city will be destroyed. What does Jonah do? He gets on a boat headed in the opposite direction! And then he goes down to the hold and falls asleep. It's not until a serious storm comes up that he is spurred into action by those around him. And what action do they take? They throw him overboard!

This story is a perfect parable for the modern CEO. We know that our responsibilities are in one direction, but we choose to go in the other direction. Worse, we lull ourselves into a state of unconsciousness, seemingly uninterested in the fact that we're going in the wrong direction. Finally, those around us—team members, coworkers, stockholders, regulators, the media—notice that we are going the wrong way. And what do they do with us? They toss us overboard!

What Nineveh needs to hear your message? And how are you avoiding that responsibility? Focused energy means relying less on multitasking and more on the concentrated effort that comes from working on one task at a time.

Regardless of how much our society values multitasking, we cannot judge our worth based on how well we juggle ten tasks. Instead, the question is, How skillfully can we focus on each task that we do? Success is a matter of quality over quantity. The era of the multitasking generalist is past. People want to find the best specialist in any field. Are you that man or woman?

One of the biggest mistakes made by students applying to colleges is their choice to participate in as many activities as possible during high school. "I want my application to look good!" they think, and so they dabble in sports, drama, extracurricular clubs, honor societies, and band. But admissions counselors at colleges nationwide have expressed an increasing interest in students who show a strong sense of focus, students who made a commitment to one or two areas during their high school experience and followed through on that commitment with passion and energy. The business world is the same way: hone your craft and be a specialist. Your skills will put you in high demand.

Of course, leaders must do many things well. A lack of the requisite multiple skill sets of leadership often leads to failure. And we don't always have the luxury of concentrating on only one task at a time. But this should be our aim. If we can focus on one task for part of the day, we increase not only our energy but our productivity. We can do in one hour what might take a distracted colleague two or three hours or longer to complete. We will not only see our productivity rise, but we will see our physical and mental health increase as well. More important, we will see the quality of our work improve. The true leader must always pay attention to not just the quality or quantity of work but the integrity that underlies it.

Step 4: Reward Yourself. Just because you saved all that time and energy doesn't mean you replace it with more items to put in your BlackBerry. The idea behind focused attention is to achieve extraordinary results with an economy of energy, not to kill yourself by piling more work on your desk. Instead, reward your hard work and focused energy with time off.

Whether we take off ten minutes or sixty minutes, one day or one week, leaders must commit to the simple idea that we become efficient and purposeful so that we can work less and enjoy more, following our forefathers' wisdom to seek life, liberty, and the pursuit of happiness. That's *happiness*, not more work, longer days, and even bigger headaches. When we take time to replenish our bodies and minds, we can then go back to work and do an even more powerful job, enhancing not only our lives but also the organizations we serve.

As recently as two generations ago, people did not work the insane hours that we do today. Somehow, Franklin Roosevelt and Winston Churchill led the Allies to victory in World War II without a laptop, without a BlackBerry, and without an iPhone. Churchill did his best work in the bath, where he would smoke a cigar and read papers on a small portable desk. He took naps and drank plenty of sherry. While this kind of behavior might be hard for a CEO to explain or justify to shareholders, it shows that a relaxed frame of mind creates an environment that allows for a much greater level of productivity. The memoirs of all the great leaders of the twentieth century—until the age of personal electronics—are replete with memories of time off, vacations, and relaxation. The rise of the Type A executive, aided by an increasingly sophisticated array of gadgetry, is our dubious contribution to history.

A conversation was recently overheard between two people in a New York airport. "Work or pleasure?" the man asked the woman, in regard to her purpose for travel.

"Pleasure, for once," the woman responded. "Everyone at my office jokes that I have separation anxiety from work."

"Ha," the man chuckled. "I'm institutionalized, too."

As leaders, we must "deinstitutionalize" ourselves. And there's no better time than now.

Step 5: Admit to the Stress. Nothing zaps our energy faster than negative stress. People experience stress when they feel that they're unable to cope with the pressures or demands put upon them. The problem with stress is not that leaders have it but that they won't admit to having it. Admission of stress is often seen as a weakness, tantamount to admitting you can't handle the workload. As the old saying goes, "If you can't handle it, they'll find someone who can." And so we leaders often live in denial, pretending the problem doesn't exist or concocting elaborate ways to cover it up. We fail to realize that we can never cover it up; we can only mask it, the equivalent of sticking our finger in a leaky dam. Of course, the dam will burst, causing much more damage than if we had taken care of it properly in the first place. Just ask the people of New Orleans.

While a certain amount of stress is normal, and while positive stress—the enjoyment of digging deep inside ourselves and finding what's there—can be good, too much negative stress will eventually manifest itself in a myriad of physical and psychological symptoms. Untreated negative stress leads to headaches, backaches, muscular pains, poor memory, limited concentration, loss of energy, lack of motivation, anxiety, feelings of helplessness, fear, apathy, sleep difficulties, exhaustion, depression, ulcers, cancer, and worse. It's just not worth it. While most of us won't experience all of these symptoms and illnesses, we will experience many of them unless we stop and examine our lives. The only question is whether we'll do something about it in time. As an insurance salesperson will tell you, it's better to handle a situation a year too soon than a day too late.

Step 6: Deal with the Stress. Treating stress is very much like treating a cold. There are all kinds of remedies, and usually a combination of treatments works best. While you search out the remedies that work best for you, you can immediately incorporate some universal stress-alleviation techniques into your work life. For example, exercise regularly.

One look at the high rates of obesity, diabetes, hypertension, heart disease, and osteoporosis in our country and we quickly realize that our sedentary lifestyle is killing us. If it's not killing us, it's certainly sucking our energy and making us feel weak and ineffective.

Our need to stay in good physical shape is as important for us as it is for any marathon runner or triathlete. Performance psychologists Jim Loehr and Tony Schwartz explain why in their important book *The Power of Full Engagement*: "Because the rest of us are evaluated more by what we do with our minds than with our bodies, we tend to discount the role that physical energy plays in performance. In reality, physical energy is the *fundamental* source of fuel, even if our work is almost completely sedentary. It not only lies at the heart of alertness and vitality but also affects our ability to manage our emotions, sustain concentration, think creatively, and even maintain our commitment to whatever mission we are on."[6]

Many leading companies across the country, such as Coors, DuPont, Johnson & Johnson, and PepsiCo, are integrating exercise programs into their corporate culture. In return, they are experiencing reduced absenteeism, fewer health-benefit claims, and a dramatic rise in productivity. Participants in their fitness programs are more alert, maintain better rapport with coworkers, and enjoy work more than those who do not participate. In other words, reducing stress is not just good living. It's good business.

So whatever you decide to do—join a gym, hire a trainer, take up a new sport, buy an exercise video, walk during lunch, take the stairs, do yoga, sign up for a Pilates class, jump rope in your office—just start. Then watch your energy and productivity soar.

Step 7: Don't Forget to Train the Mind. Ted Williams, the baseball legend, said, "Hitting is fifty percent above the shoulders."[7] He knew what all great leaders know: achievement begins in the mind with our thinking, not with what we see but with how we see. As Shakespeare told us, "There is nothing either good or bad, but thinking makes it so."[8]

Of course, if achievement begins in the mind, so does failure. For as big an obstacle as our physical bodies may be, even greater obstacles are the ones we create and allow to rent space in our brains: boredom, criticism, fatigue, inertia, doubt, worry, laziness, and ego. These are the great roadblocks of our lives, the barriers to our success and personal happiness. If we hope to overcome these insidious habits, we will need the inner strength to take back control of our minds.

Norman Vincent Peale once told the story of a tattoo shop he stumbled upon in Hong Kong. When he saw a sample in the window that read "Born to lose," he asked the tattoo artist if people actually asked to be permanently marked with that terrible phrase. When the artist replied yes, Peale said, "I just can't believe anyone in his right mind would do that." That's when the tattoo artist made a very revealing comment: tapping his forehead, he said in broken English, "Before tattoo on body, tattoo on mind."[9]

What's tattooed on a leader's mind affects the entire organization. When an organization has become bored, apathetic, and restless, the leader needs the strength to stay committed with constancy of optimism, purpose, and principle. When the journey becomes stalled with fear and indecisiveness, the leader needs the strength

TIPS FOR DEALING WITH STRESS

Eat Regularly and Well

If you took a poll asking leaders to rank what they felt were the most critical elements of doing their job, eating well would end up dead last. However, poor eating habits plus stress create a potentially harmful and even life-threatening situation. The more stressed we become, the more likely we'll make even more destructive nutritional choices, and these choices can actually *increase* our stress levels to create even more health problems. It's tough to get a balanced meal out of snack machines. Stress and poor eating habits create a vicious cycle that may be easy to get into but very hard to get out of. We may gain weight by eating to relieve stress or lose weight due to stress-related loss of appetite.

We often skip meals, compensating with caffeine, fast foods, and mindless munching, and then we try to remedy the situation with crash diets. Why are they called crash diets? It's because eventually our metabolisms crash and we find ourselves eating more food and gaining more weight than we had lost. Our eating becomes as inconsistent as our busy schedules. Our diets therefore suffer and so do our energy, health, and productivity.

To reclaim your health, you must find creative ways to incorporate good habits into your schedule. Plenty of information is readily available to help you take the first step, but make this your mantra: What we put into our bodies is just as important as what we put into our minds.

Take Vacations

We have to stop thinking of vacations as selfish and counterproductive interruptions. Instead, we must recognize them as effective methods for boosting creativity, efficiency, and energy. Vacations need to be a genuine part of our corporate strategy, our opportunity to gain perspective and renew ourselves mentally and physically.

Remove Toxic Vampires from Your Workplace

We have enough stress to deal with without having colleagues and coworkers sucking our energy. Nothing is more destructive than the negative forces that drain the lifeblood of our organization. As leaders, we have a responsibility to get rid of influences that detract from our mission, and that includes the very individuals lurking in our organizations who may lack the requisite mental health to contribute in a positive way. They've got to go.

Leave Your Power at the Office

Perhaps the best stress alleviator of all can be found in the principles we discussed in chapter 4. The advice is simple: leave the job at the office where it belongs. Take just this one piece of guidance and you will change your life forever.

to jump in and take control, to embrace change, risk, and forward thinking. When the organization's mission becomes increasingly difficult, the leader needs the strength to persevere, turning setbacks into learning experiences and challenges into opportunities. When outside factors (such as earthquakes, floods, wars, financial crises, election results, and other challenges of man and nature) threaten the organization and the mission, a leader needs the strength of mind to know that in spite of everything she cannot control, she can always control what matters most—her mind and their attitude.

We want to recall the heroic lesson of Zoe Koplowitz, who, after running sixteen marathons with multiple sclerosis, offers us all inspirational proof that endurance takes more than strength of body; it takes strength of mind and character.

The Second Toe of Endurance Is Wisdom

An aging father in Neil Simon's drama *Broadway Bound* tells his son, "I thought wisdom came with age. It doesn't. Wisdom comes with wisdom."

All the strength and power in the world mean nothing if we don't know how to use them. The story of the tortoise and the hare reminds us that it's not the fastest out of the gate that ends up winning. It's not the most powerful, either. Victory goes to those who know how to use their strength and energy to their best advantage, the ones who can keep themselves moving in spite of their circumstances. To put it another way, if strength is the energy to run the race, wisdom is knowing how to run the race. Endurance will always take equal parts of strength and wisdom. And one without the other will take us only so far. Cicero said, "The function of wisdom is to discriminate between good and evil."[10] For leaders, it's also the ability to discriminate between the essential and the nonessential, fact and fiction, fast and slow, left and right. Wisdom is a leader's ability to make sensible judgments and the choices necessary to finish the race.

> Nine-tenths of wisdom consists in
> being wise in time.
> *Theodore Roosevelt*

The Wisdom of Time and Pace Imagine running a marathon. You train for months and you are in the best physical shape of your life. But on the day of the race, you start out too fast, trying to catch an early lead or to keep pace with someone much faster than you. What happens? You burn out early and don't finish, or your finishing time is much slower than what you could have achieved.

As leaders, we have to realize that running a race is as much about *timing* and *pacing* as about strength. It's knowing when to slow down and when to speed up, when to look at the clock and when to ignore it, when to run with the competition and when to cut loose and run at our own pace. This takes instinct and reliance on our own inner awareness. In the Boston Marathon, the first twelve miles are all downhill. The race starts in Hopkinton, Massachusetts, an inland community, and makes its way in an easterly direction toward Boston and the sea. The first half of the race, therefore, is deceptively easy. Wise runners know to save their strength for the hills of Wellesley and Newton.

"Heartbreak Hill" is actually a series of hills that cruelly challenge fatigued marathoners less than ten miles from the finish line. The hills stretch for four or five miles, going up higher and higher and higher. The stretch received its name because of runners' propensity to move ahead of the pack too early in the race, thus dooming them to heartbreak as other runners, who paced themselves more wisely, shoot past them on the way to the finish line. It's great to have the energy to create a burst of speed that leaves competitors in the dust. We just never want to peak too soon.

We can't escape the reality that we are a culture that values speed. We want results, and we want them sooner rather than later. We also can't deny that we are influenced by what the "other guy" is doing, or at least what we think he's doing.

This is an inevitable part of business. We must stay connected with our competition, but we can't allow ourselves to consciously or unconsciously get hooked into the timetables and pacing of our competitors. It doesn't work in the Boston Marathon, and it doesn't work in the business world. If we hope to achieve our own long-term goals, we must see the big picture when no one else will, slow down when everyone else around us is running full speed ahead, and then charge like a rhino while others are calling for caution and reserve.

We must have the wisdom to see the big picture and then act in accordance with our own organization's strengths and weaknesses, coupled with our own inner guidance. Most important, we must allow the timing and pacing of our own mission to unfold according to the needs of the mission, not according to what others think it needs.

All the greatest athletes of our time—Tiger Woods, Michael Jordan, Joe Montana—have a common belief: worry less about what the competition is doing and more about what we ourselves can accomplish. Worry less about being better than someone else and more about being better than ourselves. It's called "running your own race," and it's the ultimate key to genuine and lasting endurance. It's said that no one sleeps worse than the golfer who has a two-shot lead on Tiger Woods going into the final day of a tournament. That golfer is so fixated on what Tiger is going to do that he can forget his own game plan. And we all know what the results will be: Tiger holding the trophy and the golfer who held that two-shot lead a day ago skulking off in second place.

> I never lost a game. I just ran out of time.
> *Vince Lombardi*

The Wisdom of the Future While having a goal is important, how we strive to reach that goal will ultimately determine our success or failure. Leaders must create the right environment for their organizations' goals to be realized. And the longer and more arduous the journey, the more care we need to put into that environment. As George F. Will wrote, "We make our buildings, and our buildings make us."[11] What is the physical reality of your workplace? Trader Joe's, the unique specialty foods store, usually buys or leases real estate in second-class shopping centers. But on the inside, Trader Joe's stores are beautifully designed and maintained to give customers the feeling of being on a tropical beach. The team members all wear Hawaiian shirts, the handwriting on all the signs is fanciful, and the atmosphere is festive. This predisposes customers to feel relaxed, and when they feel relaxed, they buy more. Again, what's the environment in your workplace?

Every major accomplishment in our country's history—from independence to the light bulb, from the automobile to space travel—began with the same daunting sense of fear and impossibility. Did Joe Coulombe, the founder of Trader Joe's, create his first store convinced that before long he would be running an international phenomenon? It's doubtful. But he never listened to dissenters, those in his own psyche or those surrounding him in the business world. Somewhere along the way, "It can't be done" was replaced with "Why can't it be done?" which is always the precursor to "We did it!"

Leaders who expect to reach the promised land of accomplishment will need to commit themselves to incorporating the following principles into their leadership practice.

Ignore Reality Fyodor Dostoyevsky said, "In order to act wisely, it's not enough to be wise."[12] It's also not enough to be well-educated, intellectual, and profound. A leader's true wisdom comes from perception originating from imagination and possibility not from logic or sense. We can never allow reality and all its limitations to stop us from dreaming and, more important, from taking those first few tentative steps. In spite of those who would try to stop or ridicule us, we must remember that our primary function is to make our own reality and to step forward with the courage to believe that anything is possible.

Everything you see in the business world—every store, every product, every service—began with a vision. What's your vision?

Cut Your Goals into Eighths Henry Ford said, "Nothing is particularly hard if you divide it into small jobs."[13] As if they were running a marathon, leaders need to break down their epic journeys into stages with quantifiable milestones, to turn long-term goals into short-term and more manageable ones. They need to see these stages clearly themselves and then communicate them to their organizations.

Marathon runners have the benefit of seeing signs every mile that inform them of their progress. At most marathons, those signs are accompanied by clocks showing much time has elapsed since the start of the race. This allows runners to take a moment to congratulate themselves on reaching another milestone (in this case, a literal milestone!) and also to recalibrate their success based on the time on the clock. What milestones can you offer yourself and your team?

Allow Many Successes along the Way When the United States put a man on the moon in 1969, it was seen as one of the great successes of the modern age. Yet that achievement wasn't just about going to the moon. It encompassed the *first* geometric equation that gave us the *first* theorem that allowed the *first* unmanned aircraft to take flight, which led to a hundred more *firsts*, eventually leading to Neil Armstrong taking that historic *first* step on the moon. That's how achievement happens—one first step after another. Wise leaders will recognize all the important steps their organizations take, realizing that successes build confidence, and confidence fuels the engine that allows us to continue our journey.

Enjoy the Journey As Robert Pirsig, the author of *Zen and the Art of Motorcycle Maintenance,* reminds us, "It's the sides of the mountain that sustain life, not the top." For leaders, it's the journey that makes us grow, blossom, and become what we are capable of becoming. We need to be filled with a sense of accomplishment and completion not only at the end of the journey but also at every step along the way.

The endurance to succeed doesn't develop over a lifetime; it happens one day at a time. How can you reward yourself and your team members today so that all of you can pause and reflect on your successes instead of allowing everyone to be swallowed up in the endless quest for more?

> If you have one eye on yesterday and one eye on
> tomorrow, you're going to be cockeyed today.
>
> *Anonymous*

The Wisdom of Now Philosophers, poets, and sages throughout the ages have espoused the virtues of present-moment awareness. The sum total of their advice comes down to this: creativity, joy, and happiness live now, in this very moment. And if that wasn't enough, now is also where a leader's creativity, efficiency, and power reside. Two things cannot occupy the same space at the same time (unless you happen to be attending Hogwarts School of Witchcraft and Wizardry). You can't dwell in the past or fear the future and do your job well at the same time. You need to be like the great ball-players mentioned earlier who are able to put an errant play behind them and move on mentally, freeing themselves to experience the challenges and joys that exist in the present moment.

In contrast to those ballplayers, Mark Langston was a successful California Angels pitcher whose perfectionism nearly destroyed his career. Langston would make letter-perfect pitches for the first four or five innings of a game. And then he would start to feel fatigued and make a physical or mental error. Unable to put the error behind him, he would struggle harder and harder on the pitcher's mound until he found himself putting too many men on base or allowing too many runs to score. He could go from throwing a nearly perfect game to getting tagged for an ugly loss in a matter of minutes.

We're all going to throw an errant pitch or leave a curve ball hanging for the batter to hit. Yet the degree to which leaders live in the past or future, mulling over previous mistakes or fearing potential crises is the degree to which they will lose energy for present-moment activity. That's a luxury that no leader can afford. Yes, we must certainly learn from the past and anticipate the future, but we can never forget that in order to harness our entire energy, we must live our lives with a strong sense of present-moment awareness.

The Third Toe of Endurance Is Balance

The final toe—the middle toe of the rhino—represents balance, something every leader must have in order to master endurance. Strength gives us the grit to power through obstacles, and wisdom gives us the foresight to properly strategize our paths, but balance offers an intangible quality that gives us a foundation from which to grow. Balance offers the firmness of conviction that fuels our inner strength. Without balance, the greatest strength and the wisest strategy are vulnerable to failure.

As an exercise, take off your shoes and socks. Now lift all your toes off the ground and try walking. Try moving to the left and then to the right. Now try running. You can do it, but it's not easy! Now try these activities again with your toes down on the ground where they belong. Notice the firmness, the stability, and the balance. Without your toes in place, you feel as though someone could give you a good push and knock you right to the ground. But with your toes firmly planted, you have the center of gravity to protect yourself and keep your balance. When your toes are firmly planted on the ground, it's much harder for someone to knock you off course.

Toes are a small part of our overall anatomy, but they're critical for balance. The same is true for rhinos, whose middle toes offer most of their stability. Without their middle toes, rhinos can be easily pushed off balance and sent tumbling to the ground.

In a similar way, a tree seedling is weak and vulnerable. Any good wind or rain can easily uproot a young tree because it hasn't established the root system that provides balance. It has within it the qualities necessary to grow big and tall. But until it's firmly rooted—until it's balanced—it is a system that can fail.

Now imagine the same tree one hundred years later: it has a giant trunk and deep, firm roots. Its balance is so strong that almost nothing can knock it over or impede its growth. With a strong foundation and firm roots, the tree can grow to almost-unimaginable heights. As leaders, we need to firmly plant our own roots. We need to find our own balance. In other words, we must engage in the search for equilibrium: the perspective to know when we have tipped the scales with too much of one thing and not enough of another. We need to find the right blend of work and play, thought and action, dreaming and reality.

People who visit the redwood forests of northern California marvel not just at the astonishing size of the trees but also at the fact that trees as large and tall as redwoods can grow so close to one another. How could there be enough room for their roots? The answer is fascinating: the root systems of redwood trees intertwine beneath the surface, thus providing stability to the entire grove of trees. So it is with leaders and great organizations: their roots intertwine beneath the surface, therefore providing the stability and balance that all need in order to grow and reach to the sky. On a more profound level, balance comes from knowing who we are and where we're going. Balance comes from having faith in our judgment. It derives from having a firmness of conviction, knowing that we are centered enough in our beliefs that we can withstand the greatest of storms. And finally, balance comes from knowing that we stand for something larger than our organizations: we stand on principle, integrity, and a vision that serves to create a better life for those we lead.

We can't see balance any more than we can detect those interlocking roots of the redwoods in their groves. Yet this intangible quality fosters the deep-rooted confidence and determination that fuel our endurance with strength and wisdom.

When others doubt, when others tire, when others lose their vision for the future, a true leader's balance will prevent the organization from being knocked off course. A true leader's balance gives the organization the endurance it needs to move forward toward success.

The Wisdom of Rhino Endurance

Business, like life, is challenging and difficult. At times, it can be downright dispiriting. For every great idea that makes its way to the marketplace and for every brilliant invention that finds its way into our households and our culture, ten thousand more go nowhere, dying great deaths in briefcases and computers. The difference between success and failure, between *what is* and *what could have been*, isn't always talent or brilliance but rather perseverance and old-fashioned stick-to-it-iveness. The edge that every leader needs is the simple ability to endure, to keep going when no one else wants to. This aspect of character will always be the great differentiator between what we want to achieve and what we will achieve.

We have often discussed runners in this book. Perhaps you are familiar with the story of Marlon Shirley. Abandoned by his mother at age three, Shirley lost his foot in an accident involving a lawn mower at age five. After surviving in the foster care system, he was adopted by a family in Utah who saw him on television. Shirley discovered that with a prosthetic foot in place, he had the capacity to become a highly successful athlete. Today, Marlon Shirley is one of the most successful Paralympic athletes of all time, the winner of several ESPY awards, and an internationally famous motivational speaker. Every day, he made a choice: either to give up and surrender to his disability or to become a stronger person than he ever thought possible. His goals must have defied reality, but he accomplished them all and continues today with tenacity, optimism, and an uninhibited faith in himself and where he wants to go. He endures as we must all endure—with strength, wisdom, and balance, symbolized by the three toes of the rhino.

A FINAL RHINO THOUGHT

While we dare to dream and believe, we must remember that we can go only as far as our feet will take us. And our feet are only as strong as we make them.

CHAPTER SIX

The Rhino's Skin

A Leader's Conviction

To avoid criticism, do nothing,
say nothing, be nothing.
Elbert Hubbard

The symbol for success in corporate America used to be the key to the executive washroom. If you were admitted to that hallowed sanctum, you had it made. Or so you thought, because the fellow slapping you on the back to congratulate you was most likely slapping a bull's-eye on you.

Leaders don't just stand in the front of the room. They're on a pedestal, wearing neon yellow like the front runner in the Tour de France, challenging the audience to work harder, achieve more, and do it in less time. This make leaders the great American target. They're public, powerful, influential, demanding, seemingly privileged, and surprisingly vulnerable, with no place to hide. The impressive-looking rhino is all too often the perfect sitting duck.

And because leaders must answer to everyone from shareholders, team members and the board of directors to the federal government, local neighbors, spouses, and children, there is no shortage of people either pinning bull's-eyes to the leaders' backs or taking shots at them. So what's a leader to do?

Duck, dodge, and, when necessary, take one for the team. Whereas the rhino's feet represent endurance and the ability to stay strong and keep moving, the rhino's skin is the ability to stay still and take the blows that come with the job and, more important, not let those blows destroy you or turn you into something you're not.

No matter how good you are at what you do, no matter how many successes you enjoy or accolades you receive, the blows will still come. It's impossible to go through life without experiencing the storms of adversity. Sometimes they'll come at full force, strong and obvious, and other times they'll sneak in, subtle and disguised. Customers disappear. Competition increases. Profit margins wither. Key personnel leave and start competing businesses. And those who stay will doubt you, accuse you, and quietly turn their backs on you. Add scandal, disaster, and betrayal, and you'll find that with each crisis, the burden of your responsibility becomes even greater. And with responsibility come criticism, blame, culpability, and, if you let them, guilt, shame, and doubt, which can turn rhinos into mice and leaders into followers.

We must do everything to prevent that, to rise above the fray and not let adversity destroy us. We must be like President Harry S. Truman, who took the heat for everything that ended up on his desk, always with the same "the buck stops here" conviction. We must take personal responsibility for the events and circumstances of our organizations, whether we're directly responsible or not. Unfortunately, many of the crises we face have nothing to do with our own personal actions. They are runaway trains, and we must somehow jump on top of them, like action heroes in the old silent movies, and halt them before they take our organizations—and us—over the cliff.

The challenge of taking responsibility and accepting criticism doesn't always come from having problems. In reality, the challenge arises when a leader is unable to do anything about those problems. We leaders like what we can control. When faced with a problem, we want to identify it, find a solution, and then implement that solution. That's our comfort zone.

Just as often, however, a crisis requires us to do nothing but take the hit, to be the lightning rod for the inevitable storms that rain down on our organizations. Whether these storms originate from our own actions, the actions of our own team members, or other causes, we need to prepare for them. We can wear a coat, use an umbrella, seek shelter, and take any number of proactive measures, but we must first understand how to handle the cold and stormy elements in the first place. To put it another way, we need to toughen our skin.

The first step you can take is to realize that the elements that affect your organization are as unpredictable as the weather. The only certainty in life is uncertainty. This guarantees that there will be highs and lows, ups and downs. One day your earnings triple and you are the executive of the year, and the next day you have *60 Minutes* at your doorstep with compromising footage of your staff. Running an organization is like being on a roller coaster: uncertainty creates anxiety because you never know when and where and from what direction the adversity will arrive.

We will all be faced with storms of adversity at some point in our lives and careers. Rare is the leader who will not go through some dark night of the soul, where his vision becomes clouded or his goals seem impossible to achieve. What sustains us through these hard times isn't always a matter of will power and force but instead the ability of our skin to deflect the blow.

To survive, we will need Rhino Armor.

Rhino Anatomy: The Skin

Rhinos are often called "living tanks." Their skin appears to be divided into plates. The bumps on their skin look like rivets, thus creating the illusion that they are armor-plated. While rhinos' thick skin may protect them from sharp twigs and thorns, it's surprisingly sensitive and scratches easily. This contradiction serves as the foundation for the rhino's lesson on how leaders will protect themselves from the elements that attack them and their organization. But first, we must realize how we protect ourselves now—or at least how we think we protect ourselves.

Hide and Seek: The Flight of the Leader

To paraphrase the Zen koan, "If someone whines, moans, and complains and no one is around to hear it, did that individual really make a sound?" Some leaders practice the hide-and-seek approach to conflict. In other words, when the going gets tough, the not-so-tough get going—literally—as far out of the office as they can possibly get. Psychologists call this avoidance and denial the "flight response," our body's automatic intention to flee from perceived attack, harm, or threat.

In the business world, we may find ourselves "conveniently indisposed" when crisis arrives. Suddenly we have meetings, busywork, or that trip to Alaska we've been meaning to take. Sometimes our decision to flee is conscious, and sometimes it isn't. In either event, we're still hiding, and those around us know exactly what we're doing. This often exacerbates the situation.

While it's obvious that dealing with conflict by avoidance is about as effective as a double scotch for breakfast, the flight strategy occasionally has its place. Often, all a challenging situation calls for is time, perspective, and the space for people to gather their thoughts and emotions. As is the case with bad weather that blows over quickly, time can sometimes clear the darkest skies. What does a president of the United States do when domestic crises sap his energy and threaten to take down his presidency? He boards Air Force One, takes off and visits foreign lands, where he gets to look and act presidential. By the time he returns to the United States, the storm has passed. In these cases, the leader is wisely stepping back and giving space to the situation. He's not thinking that if he runs away, the problems will go away. (At least we hope that's not what he's thinking!)

Ready, Set, Attack: The Fight of the Leader

A child on the playground calls another child "ugly." The second child retorts and calls the first child "stupid." Someone cuts you off on the freeway, so you purposely rear-end her car. A punches B in the nose, so B punches A in the eye. Psychologists call this the "fight response," the flip side to the flight response. Instead of running, we stay and fight. In business, we think of not backing down, standing up for ourselves, and, in those especially brave moments, sticking to our guns. The adrenaline rush that comes with the fight response usually makes us feel better for the moment, but in the long run, it's a hollow victory and about as effective at relieving tension as pouring gasoline on a raging fire.

Obviously, leaders can't back down at the first sign of challenge and division. The "fight response" strategy also has its place. We certainly need to stand up for ourselves. We have a right to protect ourselves and defend the principles we believe in. In 1982, a crazed individual tampered with bottles of Tylenol pain reliever, adding poison, killing seven people in the Chicago area. James Burke, the CEO of Johnson & Johnson, the company that manufactures Tylenol, made a $100 million decision to fight back without waiting for the government to tell him to do so. He pulled from the shelves of every store in America every container of Tylenol and had it destroyed. He then announced that Tylenol would go on a crash program to create a tamperproof bottle. In the process, he transformed the safety of drug delivery not just for his company but for the entire industry. He stood his ground, fought, and won. Burke was widely hailed for his courageous and timely leadership. By contrast, in 1990, when state health officials found traces of benzene in Perrier sparkling water, that company's CEO received widespread criticism for failing to address the problem head-on.

We cannot fight unconsciously at the first sign of trouble, allowing our unchecked emotions to get the best of us, dictating the nature of our response. To do so is to court defeat, not at the hands of others but through ourselves. But we must face facts, and the world must know we are facing the facts, no matter how difficult, unpleasant, or unprofitable they may be.

Standing Firm: The Conviction of the Leader

How we protect ourselves from our environment is less about what we do than how we do it. The intention behind our actions is what matters most. Do we protect ourselves from a position of weakness, vulnerability, and fear or from a position of strength, power, and necessity? Leaders shouldn't run or attack out of a perception of danger or misplaced emotion. Instead, they need to deal with their storms of adversity logically and without emotion. Each time they do so, they diffuse a potentially volatile situation, as well as make themselves and their organizations even stronger.

Whether we choose to listen or talk, apologize or fight, take responsibility or walk away, get tough or laugh, we need to act for one reason only: the situation calls for a specific action at that particular moment. By making the best choice, leaders never sacrifice who they are; they always stand firm and are true to the convictions and core values in which they believe.

The Sixth Principle of Rhino Leadership: Rhino Armor and the Rhino Shield of Protection

A leader's goal is not to defend but to embrace.

We'll always need thick skin to protect ourselves from the internal and external pressures that come with the role of leader. Rhino Armor is that protection and is based on the fundamental principle that our skin must be tough and soft, strong and vulnerable. Leaders need to grow thick skin not to keep the world out but to connect with it and to bring us closer to our mission and the individuals who bring that mission to life. Through the lesson of Rhino Armor, leaders will learn to stay firm and unwavering in principle, simultaneously embracing the world around them while protecting themselves from the world as well.

Rhino Armor ultimately teaches leaders that what protects them in difficult times is not external armor but internal core values. These core values make up the rhino shield of protection, which helps leaders deflect the blows that come with the storms of adversity and limit the amount and severity of the blows as well. The six values of the rhino shield of protection are humility, humanity, integrity, surrender, humor, and optimism.

The First Core Value: Humility

If I only had a little humility, I'd be perfect.

Ted Turner

"Humility" comes from the Latin word *humus*, meaning "ground," so humility means to be grounded. It means to know who we are. It also implies that we are free from pride and arrogance. Humble people are conscious of the defeats they have experienced in life. They don't think they are perfect. The word "humility" is linguistically very close to another word: "human."

Unfortunately, when it comes to the qualities that a leader needs, being human rarely makes it to the top of the list. We want our leaders to be superhuman instead. Leaders are expected to be above the ordinary, able to transform their organizations into greatness with a few inspirational words and the wave of a magic wand. When we say, "We're human," we're implying that we're flawed, which means that we make mistakes, slip on occasion, and use the erasers on the ends of our pencils. And if that's true, who needs leaders? Shouldn't leaders be better than everyone else? The rhino answer is a resounding no!

Leaders aren't supposed to be better than everyone else, contrary to popular expectation. They might be wiser and more experienced, but they're definitely not better people. It's arrogant to say we are better than others simply because of our position or title. That's about as far away from humility as we can get. Every leader from George Washington to Bill Gates has had flaws. Name the leader, read the biography, and you'll find the flaw or, in many cases, multiple flaws.

The need to be perfect actually separates you from the organization you serve. Perfectionism keeps out the world. Instead of empowering you, it makes you more vulnerable to getting hurt. After all, what is the first thing people want to do to perfectionists? Find their flaws, of course! Perfectionism encourages people to take even more shots at you. If you stand on a pedestal and tell everybody how perfect you are, the bullets will come flying before you know it. If people weren't shooting before at you, they will start. And their aim will improve to the exact degree of perfection you claim for yourself.

This is the same principle that makes all of those tabloid magazines so popular. While we may admire the talent and seemingly perfect lives of the rich and famous, we love to see them fall.

Perfection is an unreal and moving target. The dictionary definition of "perfection" is "to be beyond criticism." But being perfect doesn't mean that other people are going to stop criticizing you! You can never actually achieve perfection anyway. It becomes a tiresome slave driver, depleting your energy as you spend your time and resources trying to live up to its illusive promises. Perfectionism makes you defensive and combative, which in turn makes you run, hide, or attack and stops you from listening and understanding what you need to hear or doing what you need to do in the moment.

With humility comes an *acceptance of our limitations*. When we acknowledge that we can't do our job alone, we empower those around us so that they are more likely to come to our aid when times are tough. Our humility, by its very nature, invites others to join in our cause because they want to, not because they have to, because they see themselves in us. In our humility, we reveal what we all know but too frequently deny: we need each other to realize our individual dreams. As the Roman philosopher Seneca said, "God divided man into men that they might help each other."[1]

Regardless of our title or the size of our paycheck, from the boardroom to the mailroom, we're truly all in this together. The thread that unites us is our humility, our humanity. Humility is and always will be the great equalizer. We won't eliminate the blows we're bound to face as leaders, but we can soften them, deflect them, and make them easier to bear.

With humility comes *empathy*: an acknowledgment of the law of reciprocity. If we don't allow ourselves to be imperfectly human, then we will never allow others to be imperfect, either. This means that we'll never be satisfied. No matter what our teams bring to the table, it will never be good enough for us. On the other hand, the more we allow others to be imperfect, the more likely we'll create a culture of acceptance in our teams—a top-down commitment to less blaming, faultfinding, and attacking and more understanding, tolerance, and cooperation.

With humility comes *global understanding*. We embrace not only our own organization's imperfections but the world's imperfections as well. If we can allow an imperfect world in all its chaos to exist around us, then we will be neither surprised nor unnerved when chaos inevitably enters our personal world. This global understanding is essential to growing Rhino Armor and mentally preparing for whatever challenges we may embrace in the future.

With humility comes the *embracing of dissension*. The more we invite criticism as a constructive part of the growth process, the less likely the entire organization will be to see it as a negative. Once those who attack realize that we're not threatened by criticism, that we welcome it, the less likely they are to come at us with guns blazing.

Finally, remember that humility has nothing to do with lack of confidence. As a leader, you must have a healthy ego to demonstrate confidence and a strong belief in yourself, your abilities, and the value you bring to your organization. Conversely, you can't allow that self-assuredness to cross the line into arrogance and self-importance. George Foreman likes to say his mother taught him that it's better to have people say about you, "There he goes!" than "There he lays!"[2] In other words, leaders have to have tough skin to take some blows and know when it's best not to fight back and instead to live to play another day.

The Second Core Value: Humanity

Make a career of humanity . . . You will make
a greater person of yourself, a greater nation of
your country, and a finer world to live in.

Martin Luther King Jr.

While humility connects us with ourselves, humanity connects us to the entire human race. It says that we are human and that we are obligated to join and serve others. Our humanity brings kindness, compassion, and a deeper understanding of the world we live in, allowing us to step back and see the world as it really is, not as how we think it should be. Our humanity helps us realize what is important, essential, and meaningful in our lives, thereby showing us how to protect ourselves and also what we need to protect in the first place.

Humanity in action is illustrated by former president Jimmy Carter, who became involved with the organization Habitat for Humanity, which builds homes for the poor. Former U.S. presidents can make hundreds of thousands of dollars for a single speech or public appearance, but Carter did not join the organization as a board member or as a "brand name" to be trotted out in fund-raising appeals. Instead, he picked up a hammer and a saw and started to build houses with the rest of the members of the team. As the president of the United States, he rode in Air Force One and in motorcades protected by the Secret Service. As a member of Habitat for Humanity, he rode Trailways buses, slept in sleeping bags, and never used his position as former leader of the free world to demand special perks for himself.

Humanity Brings Perspective In business as in life, it's easy to get caught up in the drama of a crisis, to get sucked into the adrenaline rush that comes from the day-to-day struggle to survive. Conflict becomes a drug that we can't live without. Like junkies, we seek the "attack and defend" high that is becoming the new way of life in the business world. And if we don't seek it, we certainly don't hide from it, either. Each in our own way, we feed the beast that keeps drama alive.

The problem with drama is that it invariably leads to loss of perspective. Our crises become magnified, along with our pain. Two people fighting can spend so much time screaming at and insulting each other that they forget what they were angry about in the first place. It's the same with any dramatic event—getting in an accident, being fired, even falling in love. The greater the drama, the more our imaginations go wild. While this heightened sense of drama may feed our addiction, it does nothing to help resolve the crisis we face.

When we forget the issues and concentrate on the fight, we enter an artificial world where we believe that life is the crisis. In the process, we become less effective, spending our time and energy fighting not for a cause but for the preservation of our own egos and our not-so-subtle need to be right or to win. We may think we're tough, waging our wars to the bitter end, but in reality, we are only fighting ourselves, a phantom adversary that leaves our skin soft, pliable, and ultimately defenseless.

Of course, if we recognize our humanity by reaching out to others, we will then be able to see the larger picture, thereby broadening our point of view. We will no longer identify with the fight but with the individuals. We can ignore the crisis and deal with the situation. We can forget the drama and deal with the reality.

The perspective that humanity brings can be boiled down to three main concepts we need to remember if we wish to keep our skin thick:

- *Don't make a mountain out of a molehill.* We have enough real crises in our lives without creating new ones. As Richard Carlson suggests in his popular book *Don't Sweat the Small Stuff*, we can't allow ourselves to be bothered and diminished by inconsequential matters. Nor can we allow the "small stuff" to be turned into matters of consequence. Many of our problems exist only because we allow them to exist in our minds. We interpret, judge, arbitrate, and second-guess, allowing our thoughts to become like a broken tape in our heads. Instead of being big rhinos, we become Chicken Littles. Every time that broken tape plays, it becomes louder and stronger until it eventually takes on a truth of its own. Soon, we're not just talking ourselves into this new reality; we're believing it.

- *Don't let others make a mountain out of your molehill.* While leaders need many eyes and ears in their organizations, they can't let anyone else's assumptions and beliefs become their own. The number and severity of the crises you face are often a matter of interpretation. If someone yells, "Fire!" you don't necessarily have to call the fire department. A simple extinguisher might be all that's called for. Listen to the information you're presented without allowing someone else's agenda, insecurities, or biases to dictate how you should act or, for that matter, how you decide what is important.

- *This too shall pass.* The Bible says, "and it came to pass," not "and it came to stay." This concept should find its way into every leader's tool kit because it makes our skin tough. Whatever trials and tribulations our organizations may endure, they don't last forever.

    If every time you got hurt you thought the pain was never going to end, you'd live your life in fear. This just intensifies the pain. Knowing that time heals all wounds helps you to endure conflict and to avoid the trap of forcing a resolution because you want the conflict to end quickly.

A doctor doesn't "heal" a broken arm. She just sets it so that the natural healing process can take place. Athletes cause themselves the most damage not when they injure themselves but when they attempt to come back too quickly from an injury. The weekend player doesn't take the cast off his arm too early so he can start playing tennis again. He knows that if he lets his arm heal properly and then gradually starts using it again, he'll be able to enjoy playing tennis for the rest of his life. We need to handle each crisis we face in a similar way. We can allow the storm to hit, confident that "this too shall pass." This gives us the perspective not to overreact.

Humanity Brings Detachment Detachment has gotten a bad reputation. People often misinterpret it as a sign of aloofness or of being unaffected and without emotion. On the contrary, detachment is merely a process by which we do not identify with the drama, pain, and emotions of others. Empathize, yes. Identify, no. Having a detached point of view means that we allow events to take their course without becoming emotionally invested in the outcome. Just because others feel angry, outraged, hurt, and betrayed doesn't mean we have to feel the same way. Leaders need to stay calm and steady, not allowing others' emotions to become their own. Detachment allows us the wisdom to honor each other's experiences and to refrain from judging or interfering with them. This can be a tough lesson to learn. By our nature, we are a culture that wants to fix things, to put on a bandage and make everything better. Most of us find it hard to watch someone struggle or suffer. While this makes us empathic, compassionate, and human, it also makes us emotional and potentially weak, especially if we try to control factors that we can never change.

A caterpillar turns into a butterfly within a self-created chrysalis. Someone who reaches into the chrysalis to "help" in the process of transformation only ends up killing the butterfly. Sometimes, we can accomplish more by refraining from action than by charging ahead. Take, for example, the story of a woman whose younger brother was an alcoholic. Because she loved her brother dearly, the woman had always been the person to get him out of trouble: she paid his outstanding debts, let him live with her when he needed a place to stay, and even posted bail on several occasions when he was arrested for drunk driving. But after many years, the woman finally realized that she was doing her brother a disservice. Not only was he taking advantage of her, but her willingness to rush in and "save the day" only made her brother more dependent and helpless because he had no motivation to take care of himself and face his addiction. She finally had to make the difficult decision that she wouldn't rescue her brother anymore, a painful but worthwhile choice to detach.

A rhino never charges unless the situation requires it. If we charge in when we should refrain from action, we run the risk of denying others the right to experience life in all its manifestations, especially when life may be tough and challenging.

Face it: earthquakes happen. So do fires, floods, and hurricanes. Businesses close. Downsizing happens. We can get sick, hurt, laid off, or fired. And as much as we'd like to stop all the pain and wish it away, we can't stop it. Life is tough, and we can either bemoan that fact with self-defeating cynicism or we can embrace the reality with detachment, accepting our world for what it is, and invite challenges to become opportunities that help us grow and uplift our spirits. The good news is that the choice is ours. The Reverend Norman Vincent Peale liked to say that the only people with no problems are in cemeteries. And whenever he experienced a period in his life when he had no problems, he would look up at the heavens and say, "Lord, don't you trust me?"[3]

Setbacks can lead to redemption. While we never wish adversity and hardship on anyone, and while we certainly don't believe it takes suffering to evolve as a human being, through pain and loss come rejuvenation, strength, and greater understanding. Through the power of detachment we can lead with the good of the whole in our minds, recognizing that not everyone will have his needs met. Through the power of detachment we can allow ourselves to stay strong and compassionate, knowing that while all problems can't be fixed, the human spirit can transform obstacles into life-affirming experiences.

Detachment: The Human Side Detachment isn't just about what happens but also about how we react to it—or, to be more precise, how we respond to the way *others* react. Leaders do not have the responsibility or right to judge the emotions of others, arbitrarily deciding how another human being should or should not feel. This is more than allowing others the freedom to be who they are, to experience life on their terms. It's also a self-preserving mechanism that leaders can use to thicken their own skin. Why? Because the less we judge, the less we'll be hurt.

When someone is personally attacking us and we don't judge those attacks as being rude, angry, disloyal, or insensitive, then we can't be hurt by them. In reality, only our judgment of what someone does causes us pain. Zig Ziglar says that if you treat all others as if they were hurting, you're probably treating just about everybody you meet exactly the right way. In other words, when people say mean words or do mean things to one another, they are more often than not acting out of a sense of self-hatred or frustration with their own circumstances. This is not to suggest that we can allow our organizations to attack or be attacked but that we must control how we respond to attacks. Again, the choice is ours.

Detachment Brings Compassion and Kindness Beat a dog long enough and eventually you'll get that dog to obey you and follow your rules. But what you gain in obedience you lose in loyalty and trust. Using fear and oppression may seem like an easy solution to get what you want, but in the long run, not only are your actions counterproductive, but they immediately put you on the defensive, at odds with those in your organization. To protect yourself from the world around you, you actually need to reach out and show compassion and kindness to others, sending a clear message that you empathize with and understand them.

Bill Clinton was an unknown governor of a small state, politically untested at the national level, when he ran for president in 1992. But he said four simple words that demonstrated a sense of empathy with the average American—"I feel your pain"—and he was rewarded for his empathy with eight years in the White House.

Are you conscious of the pain of the people around you? Almost everybody's suffering in one way or another. A team member or a loved one may have a serious physical ailment. Perhaps money is tight. Perhaps a team member has unmourned losses, disappointments, frustrations. Good leaders are aware of the birthdays, favorite recipes, children's names, and other happy details of the lives of their team members. Great leaders know and understand the pain of those who serve them and whom they serve. What kind of leader are you?

The Third Core Value: Integrity

If you stand straight, do not fear a crooked shadow.
Chinese proverb

Eleanor Roosevelt was more than a great first lady. She was an ambassador for change and social development. She fought for equality, education, and the oppressed. She chaired the commission that drafted the Universal Declaration of Human Rights. In spite of her positive impact on society, she often elicited deep feelings of negativity and criticism. She was often told that since she wasn't elected, she had no right to tell others how to live and what to do, that she had no credentials to back up her ambitious agenda. The first lady responded patiently, realizing as other leaders have that as long as you live your life in the public eye, you're going to be damned if you do and damned if you don't.

Eleanor Roosevelt could have easily slipped into the woodwork and done nothing. Women in her day were not expected to take a role in public life. "No human being enjoys being disliked," she said. "So it would be normal to try to avoid actions which bring criticism."[4] But she chose not to hide, believing that you must never, for any reason, turn your back on life. Instead, she lived by the straightforward philosophy that you should do what you feel in your heart to be right, for in the end, it's inevitable that you will be criticized anyway.

She is an example of integrity, which means "wholeness"— wholeness of spirit, mind, and body and wholeness of vision, purpose, and passion. Integrity is not something that can be seen and touched but instead a code of behavior by which people choose to live because it symbolizes who they are. As Thomas Jefferson said, "The moral sense, or conscience, is as much a part of a man as his leg or arm."[5] As soon as we lose sight of this fact, allowing our commitment, character, principles, honesty, and sincerity to be compromised, we lose a part of ourselves and we cease to be whole. In the process, our vitality is diminished. And it doesn't happen all at once but in stages. As the great motivator Tony Robbins points out, our standards diminish gradually until the point at which we have no standards at all.

We become a little less honest but a little richer, a little less sincere but a little more famous. We let go of a principle here or a character trait there, all in the name of achievement, as we make our way up the ladder of success. Unfortunately, by the time we get to the top, we are merely shadows of our original selves. We have sold out.

Theodore Roosevelt once said, "I care not what others think of what I do, but I care very much about what I think of what I do."[6] That is integrity in a nutshell, a guideline to live and lead by. Every leader needs to live by the four simple principles of integrity:

- Be true to yourself.
- Be true to your principles.
- Be true to your people.
- Be true to your mission.

If you commit to staying strong in character and integrity, truthful, ethical, and principled, then you can pretty much be guaranteed that you won't bend at the first sign of trouble, dissension, or disapproval. People may still disagree with you and your policies, and in the spirit of growth you should hope they will. Yet these disagreements will be tempered out of respect for your moral convictions. And if they're not, that's okay, too, because your strong-minded convictions, your Rhino Armor, will always protect you from the harm those around you may try to inflict.

If you stand on principle and character, it's harder to be knocked down and easier to get up. More important, you should aspire to reach your dreams as the same person you were when you began: honest, sincere, truthful, and whole.

The Fourth Core Value: Surrender

The greatness of a man's power is the
measure of his surrender.
William Booth

Let go of control. For many of us, these just may be the four most difficult words we will ever have to hear. Leaders can delegate, share responsibilities, even empower the people in their organization with a sense of ownership and duty. But to truly let go and surrender is tough. And yet if we are going to weather the storms of adversity, we must do exactly that. President Carter was often ridiculed during his presidency for his tendency to micromanage every last detail, down to who got to play when on the White House tennis courts. Micromanaging insults and frustrates our team members because it gives them the (all-too-accurate) impression that we don't trust them to handle anything of importance. It also wastes our time because a leader's job is to lead, not to micromanage.

Leaders can begin by realizing that surrendering does not mean giving up, quitting, or abdicating responsibility but rather relinquishing control of their environment and, more important, the need to have everything go exactly as they think it should go. Leaders certainly need to chart the course for their organizations and to implement concrete plans to reach their goals, but they also need to allow the journey to have a life of its own, to take its own needed direction. If we try to control the journey from A to Z, we may find ourselves confining that journey to a limited outcome instead of allowing it to take us to unexplored horizons, perhaps even beyond our wildest imaginations.

This is why it's important for businesses to determine not just whether consumers are buying their products but also how consumers are using those products. Often, consumers use products in ways that are very different from the original expectations of the manufacturer. In Italy, for example, an American undergraduate student conducted a research project on how other Americans abroad used bidets, the low-mounted plumbing fixture that sits by the toilet in most Italian apartments. Her findings? Not one person she surveyed actually used the bidet as it was intended. Instead, people stacked extra toilet paper on it, stored magazines and cosmetics on top, and even soaked dirty shoes inside. This goes to show that unless the proper research is performed, organizations will never know how consumers *really* use their products. That vital information could lead to changes in marketing or packaging that lead to radical new increases in profitability.

Unfortunately, in their single-minded devotion to their jobs, many leaders get caught up in the trap that "my way is the only way." This control isn't limited to what to do but how to do it, when to do it, why to do it, and who's going to do it. Frank Stanton, the executive William Paley chose to run CBS, became so involved with minor details that he often failed to see the big picture at the network, allowing competitors to steal both audience and advertising dollars. Stanton even picked out the paper, the font, and the ink for CBS's business stationery and went so far as to dictate the margins of the stationery and how letters should be typed. Instead of focusing on his main task—creating a vision—he allowed his focus to be spread into areas that were not really his business.

Like conflict, control can be a drug. The more control we wield, the more control we demand until we find ourselves in the debilitating position of wanting to control everything in our world. No matter how much we try, we can't control everything. Perhaps the best example of this truth comes from Dr. Seuss's children's book *Yertle the Turtle*, which tells the story of an autocratic turtle who demanded that more and more turtles pile themselves up underneath him so that he could be the ruler of all he surveyed. The only problem was that the turtle at the bottom of the pile, Mack, got fed up with his distant and domineering "boss" and dumped the whole lot of turtles off his back, ending Yertle's rule.

The degree to which leaders try to control their environment is the degree to which they will become immobilized when matters aren't "just so." Conversely, the more you surrender, the less you will be negatively affected. With surrender comes the freedom to let the world exist as it is, even with its conflicts, imperfections, and dissension.

Surrender liberates us to let go of what we cannot change in order to have time to work on what we can change. Not surprisingly, this is the same wisdom found in the Serenity Prayer written by Reinhold Niebuhr: "God, grant me the serenity to accept the things I cannot change; the courage to change the things I can; and the wisdom to know the difference."[7]

Besides surrendering our control over people, we need to surrender our control over events. While individuals in our organization certainly have to maintain codes of conduct and performance, we can't always control the exact means by which they achieve their results, nor should we want to. Let somebody else figure out the company stationery! The way that others choose may not always be our way, but our way is not always the best way. And the sooner we realize this, the easier our jobs will become and the faster we will maximize our teams' potential. Ultimately, the more we try to control behavior, like Yertle the Turtle, the less productive and the angrier our people will be. Eventually, they will become like caged animals who, with their first smell of freedom, will either attack their oppressor or run away. Neither alternative helps the organization! Taking surrender to heart allows leaders to spend less time and energy fighting phantom ghosts and more time on what is most important: driving the business. Surrendering control of a thousand little tasks gives us the freedom to concentrate on the one major task for which leaders are compensated: defining and disseminating a vision and making that vision a reality.

The Fifth Core Value: Humor

Humor is just another defense against the universe.

Mel Brooks

JUDGE: Is there any reason you could not serve as a juror in this case?

JUROR: I don't want to be away from my job that long.

JUDGE: Can't they do without you at work?

JUROR: Yes, but I don't want them to know it.

This old joke comes right out of an actual courtroom, shedding light on the worst-kept secret in America: we take ourselves and our importance way too seriously. The fact is, we're all expendable. What does it mean when there's a snowstorm in Washington, DC, and all "nonessential" government employees are allowed to go home early? Why are they even working for the government in the first place?

A twist of fate here and there and we could all be replaced by newer and more inexpensive models. This is exactly what happened at Circuit City: thousands of the highest-paid workers in all of the company's stores were summarily fired and given the opportunity to compete for their old jobs but at lower pay. It's not exactly a corporate policy to admire or emulate.

If we left our jobs tomorrow, life would go on in most of our organizations. This isn't to suggest that what we do lacks importance but is merely intended as a collective wake-up call: we need to lighten up.

If we don't, we're going to work ourselves into an early grave or, at the very least, make our world so somber that no one wants to be around us. It's said that the degree to which we take our work seriously is the best predictor of a heart attack. Yes, the world is complex and dangerous. Yes, there is much to be serious about. But still, we need to prevent this grim mentality from taking over our lives and dictating how we do business. Being tough and stoic has its place as we survive challenges, but so does humor and levity. Bill Cosby put it this way: "If you can find humor in anything, even poverty, you can survive it."[8] And survival is what the rhino shield of protection is all about.

Running an organization is hard work, with enough responsibility, liability, and culpability to fuel a thousand gastrointestinal diseases. The only way to handle it all is to find healthy alternatives—with humor at the top of the list. For example, after Ronald Reagan narrowly survived an assassination attempt, he looked up at the doctors as he entered the operating room and said, "Please tell me you're Republicans."[9]

Laughter truly is the best medicine. Published studies have shown that laughing lowers blood pressure, reduces stress hormones, boosts immune function, and triggers the release of endorphins, the body's natural painkillers, producing a general sense of well-being and comfort. Laughter helps us cope, easing frustration and anxiety and helping us to tolerate the unpleasant, unexpected, and unbearable. No prescription needed.

Laughter is also a feature of our humanity: we are the only species capable of developing a sense of humor. People say that it takes thirty-seven muscles to frown but only one to smile. Why not take the path of least resistance?

Incorporating humor into the workplace isn't a matter of bringing comedians and clowns into the break rooms. It involves bringing in a sense of lightheartedness and joy, recognizing our human flaws and being able to poke fun at them. It's about seeing humor in everyday situations and knowing when a joke is more useful than an admonishment in relieving tension and getting your point across. If you fly with Southwest Airlines, you might be struck by the levity that accompanies the flight crew's information about safety systems onboard their jets. The reason the crew tells you this information with a lighthearted air is that passengers are more likely to pay attention. Fear or boredom makes people tune out the flight attendants when they demonstrate life jackets or show where the emergency exits are. A little bit of levity gets the point across where a more serious approach would not.

Humor lightens our load, allowing us to work longer, harder, and with greater joy. It knocks the chip off our shoulders and keeps resentment and self-importance at arm's length while simultaneously lifting the gravity out of the crises we face. And this lightness of spirit will make our skin tougher, protecting us in challenging times.

The Sixth Core Value: Optimism

When you have vision . . . your attitude is optimistic
rather than pessimistic.
Charles R. Swindoll

What's the difference between an optimist and a pessimist? An optimist created the airplane; a pessimist created the seat belts. Optimism is the most profound quality a leader can hope to embrace. It is an essential ingredient in the rhino shield of protection, offering a glimpse into one inescapable truth: leaders need to believe that great things can happen. As the Chinese proverb suggests, "The man who says it cannot be done should not interrupt the man who is doing it."[10]

In the darkest nights, when everything seems hopeless and irreparable, all the humility, humanity, integrity, surrender, and

humor in the world mean nothing if leaders don't believe somewhere down deep, that tomorrow is going to be a better day. Without
optimism, there is no hope, and without hope, there can be no fight.
When President Reagan took over the White House, he inherited
double-digit inflation and double-digit unemployment—a record-
high "misery index." But his core optimism led America out of the
period of self-doubt that had been fostered by Vietnam, Watergate,
Nixon's resignation, the sudden rise in oil prices, and the uncertainty of the Carter years. The 1980s were a time of renewed faith
and optimism in the nation because its leader embodied and com-
municated those characteristics. Optimism is a mysterious force
that says we will receive what we expect to receive. Everybody
knows about Murphy's Law, but how many people know about
Bijan's Law? Bijan Anjomi, a motivational speaker and the author
of many books, says, "Whatever can go right, will go right. Expect a
miracle."[11]

We are what we believe. Our inner world creates our outer
world. This is the secret of the book *The Secret*, but this idea has
been known for centuries, even millennia. In the book *As a Man
Thinketh*, James Allen tells us that as we think in our hearts, so we
make our outside world. And he was basing his book, not surprisingly, on the Bible.

The world of the optimist is generally a more pleasant place to
live than the world of the pessimist or the person who is simply
indifferent. While no one is suggesting that we should live in a
Pollyannaish world where we blindly and foolishly believe everything we're told, we leaders need to have a lot of faith in everyone
else, knowing that the only difference between a stumbling block
and a steppingstone is the way we approach it. If we take on the
world's despair and pessimism, agreeing that this is what life is all
about, then we turn that despair into our own reality.

Franz Kafka wrote, "There is plenty of hope . . . but not for us."[12] But if we recognize the despair, deal with it on a practical level, and then turn our focus instead on what we'd like to see happen—what we *believe* will happen—then we empower ourselves and our organizations with the gift of hope. The half-full glass is the smart leader's number one survival tool. Optimism doesn't soften us: it makes us tougher. With the optimist mind-set, we are saying that we refuse to be stopped and defeated. When we get knocked down, we're going to get right back up, convinced that with hard work and the right attitude, our troubles will pass. With the optimist mind-set, we are sending a loud and clear message to all those in our organization: nothing is impossible.

When you have a negative thought, tell yourself, out loud, "Thank you for sharing! But I don't believe that for a minute. Next thought, please!" This is the rhino shield of protection.

The Wisdom of Rhino Armor

To survive in the corporate jungle, leaders need a thick skin. We're on display, as if in the zoo, with everyone staring at us, gawking, judging, wondering what we're going to do next. How we handle this challenge—our public displays of leadership—will determine our longevity and our success in achieving our mission. Thomas Holdcroft said, "Life is a grindstone. But whether it grinds us down or polishes us up depends on us."[13] More accurately, it depends upon our Rhino Armor.

A FINAL RHINO THOUGHT

*That which would destroy us will make us
stronger only if we embrace our challenges with
the power of humility, humanity, integrity,
surrender, humor, and optimism.*

CHAPTER SEVEN

The Rhino's Back

A Leader's Support System

The smartest thing I ever said was, "Help me!"

Anonymous

I t's not a coincidence that the quotation that leads off this chapter is sourced to "anonymous." We never want to admit that we need help. Leaders are especially prone to this syndrome. They tend to believe that they can do it all. Like a Hollywood auteur who writes, directs, produces, and stars in his own movie, we want to do everything—from establishing the vision to masterminding the mailroom.

But take a look at the crawl of credits that follows any feature film and you'll see that hundreds of people are involved in the creation of a movie. If we are doing anything of great importance, we need others to work with us. A female comic once quipped about this, saying, "If I ever have kids, I want somebody to film the birth so that I can roll credits at the end. Producer? That would be me. Director? That's the doctor. Best boy grip? Probably my husband . . . depending on how hard I'm squeezing."[1]

The successful birth of a child does require a dedicated team of people, and so does almost everything else in life. It takes not just a village but a whole army of hardworking, motivated people to get anything of importance done. You can say it's your show all you want, but the fact remains that you can't go it alone. No one can.

This doesn't stop leaders from trying, though. Call it compulsiveness, impatience, arrogance, or goodwilled intention, but we are all guilty at one time or another of biting off more than we can chew. We are like Atlas from Greek mythology, taking the weight of the world on our shoulders. According to legend, Atlas stormed Olympus during the war of the Titans, unwisely threatening the gods. To punish him, Zeus condemned Atlas to hold up the heavens and bear their weight on his shoulders forever—a mythical explanation of why the sky never falls. (Take that, Chicken Little!) Since the sky didn't seem heavy enough, history eventually gave Atlas the job of holding up the whole world as well. Thus the god of weightlifting and carrying heavy burdens was born.

Of course, when leaders take on the weight of the world, it's usually self-inflicted punishment. Most leaders don't even realize they're doing it, lifting vigorously and unconsciously, until finally the weight adds up and the strain becomes unbearable. Suddenly something gives, and they buckle, unable to take another step.

While we have already learned to toughen our skin, one fact of leadership remains: the world is heavy. Leaders always need to carry much of the weight on their own shoulders. But as any weightlifter will tell you, you can only lift what you can lift! If you try to lift even one pound more than you're capable of, something is bound to snap.

In today's busy and complex world, the responsibility for the organization you serve is great—not just your responsibility to the people but to the mission itself. With so much to shoulder, you need to use conscious effort and the Rhino Nuchal Crest.

Rhino Anatomy: The Back

A large adult male white rhino can stand up to six feet tall at the shoulder and can weigh up to five thousand pounds. That amounts to carrying around thirty professional football players on your back. The rhino's head alone can weigh over two thousand pounds (a mere eight football players). Carrying that much weight is obviously challenging. It takes muscle and a strong back, both of which rhinos fortunately have. This explains their ability to move quickly and efficiently despite their heavy weight. In fact, a great deal of a rhino's enormous weight is solid muscle, including the exceptionally large and oddly shaped hump on its back: the nuchal crest, which supports its enormous head and body weight.

The message of the Rhino Nuchal Crest is clear: if today's leaders are to carry the weight and responsibility of their leadership roles, they must have not only a strong back but also a different type of back—their own nuchal crest support system. Without genuine, lasting support, leaders can't be expected to handle the heavy workload of their jobs. But before the rhino can teach us how to create this support system, we must understand how we currently support ourselves—or at least how we *think* we support ourselves.

Working Hard

Nothing beats hard work. Hard work builds character, makes us tough, and gets the job done. Something about working up a sweat is intensely satisfying, and the world will always need people willing to roll up their sleeves and make things happen. But while hard work gets you to the top of your profession, it's not always what keeps you there. Hard work is valuable only in proportion to the manner in which you work hard. To work tirelessly is noble. To work tirelessly on the wrong things or, even worse, on everything is foolish. Leaders can't allow themselves to waste time or energy in pursuit of an outdated work ethic. The "work till you drop" or "if you want a job done right, do it yourself" mentality will undoubtedly create a workforce of busy bees, but it will do nothing to lighten the load of its leaders or to move the organization forward.

Hard work does have its place, but to generate real support, leaders need to work more selectively, like Tom Hanks. When Hanks was a younger actor, he took on role after role, many of them in eminently forgettable movies: *Dragnet, The Money Pit*, and *Nothing in Common*. But as his career progressed, Hanks has taken on fewer and fewer roles, all of them meaningful and memorable—*Big, Forrest Gump, Apollo 13, Saving Private Ryan*, and *Sleepless in Seattle*. Working feverishly made Tom Hanks a household name. Working selectively made him a true Hollywood icon.

Working Smart

"Working smart" is the new buzzword for today's corporate culture; it's the collective call to refocus our attention on maximizing effort to increase results. Working smart comes in many shapes and sizes and often comes disguised in other corporate buzzwords: "streamlining efficiency," "time management," "the 80/20 principle," and the like. Put them all together and we realize that we must lighten our load by finessing our energies, consciously directing our actions as well as our motivations. Of course, while the value that comes from working smart is immeasurable in helping us handle our workload, if we are to build an enduring support system, we need to do more than work smart. We need to work together with others.

A parable illustrates this concept. An expert in time management was speaking to a group of business students. To drive home a point, she used a powerful illustration. As she stood in front of the group of high-powered overachievers, she said, "Okay, time for a quiz." She reached into her bag and pulled out a one-gallon wide-mouth jar and set it on the table in front of her. She also produced about a dozen fist-sized rocks and carefully placed them, one at a time, into the jar. When no more rocks would fit inside, she asked, "Is this jar full?" Everyone in the class nodded. The time-management expert replied, "Really?" She reached under the table and pulled out a bucket of small beans, poured some of the beans into the jar, and shook it, causing the little beans to work themselves down into the spaces between the big rocks. She asked the group once more, "Is this jar full?"

By this time the class was on to her. "Probably not," one of the students answered.

"Good!" she replied with a gleam in her eye. Next she reached under the table and brought out a bucket of sand. She started dumping the sand in the jar and it went into all of the spaces left between the rocks and the beans. Once more she asked the question, "Is this jar full?"

"No!" the class shouted in unison, now wise to the game.

"Good," she said again. This time she grabbed a pitcher of water and began to pour it into the jar until it overflowed and liquid splashed onto the floor.

The woman looked at the class and asked, "What is the point of this illustration?"

One eager beaver raised his hand and said, "The point is, no matter how full your schedule is, if you try really hard you can always fit more in it."

"Wrong," the speaker replied, "that's not the point. The illustration reveals that if you don't put the big rocks in first, you'll never get them in at all. What are the 'big rocks' in your life? Time with loved ones, your faith, your education, dreams, goals, a worthy cause, teaching, or mentoring others? The others things in your life are inconsequential—they're the beans, sand, and water. But it's awfully easy to fill our lives with them until we can't possibly take any more. That's a recipe for disaster," she said, looking at the puddle of water on the floor.

"Be vigilant about your time. It's your greatest gift. And if you don't see to the matters that are truly important, your life will become filled with all the little things that don't add up to a hill of beans in the end."

Being efficient with our time means knowing how to zone in on our "rocks" while cutting down on the time we spend doing all the other things. Sometimes the beans, sand, and water have to be taken care of, too, but not necessarily by us.

As it turns out, efficiency is a double-edged sword. Efficiency usually brings in its wake more responsibility, not less. No matter how hard you work, no matter how efficient you become, there will always be more to do. Turn around one organization as a CEO and five others will be clamoring for your services. This unspoken law of human nature is the reason we're always giving the most work to the person whose plate is the fullest. We know he'll find a way to get the job done. And yet we are not Atlas, nor are we gods. The only way leaders can handle the weight of their jobs is by realizing that they cannot do them alone, that we are all on a shared journey and the only way we can lift what we need to lift is by doing it together.

The Seventh Principle of Rhino Leadership: Rhino Nuchal Crest

A leader's goal is not to lift but to help others lift.

To carry any significant amount of weight, you need a finely tuned support system. For the rhino, as we have seen, this includes a back that is both muscular and uniquely designed. Your support system also begins with a strong and muscular back, which ironically comes from adding weight, not from losing it. Of course, leaders need to take their cue from the rhino and make sure they're adding the right kind of weight: muscle mass, not fat or what is unflatteringly called "deadweight."

The weight leaders add must serve a purpose, increasing their power and ability to handle responsibilities even more effectively. The weight leaders add is people.

The Rhino Nuchal Crest is a leader's ability to put talented and committed individuals on her back, knowing that with each valuable person she supports, she carries the potential to effectively lift ten times as much as she could on her own. In addition to muscle mass, the Rhino Nuchal Crest requires the leader's back to be as unique as the rhino's. While we would agree that having a hump on our back would be useful only if we were going to portray Quasimodo in *The Hunchback of Notre Dame*, for the rhino, it is an ideally constructed support system. Just as their oddly shaped middle toe provides the perfect balance for endurance, rhinos' oddly shaped nuchal crest provides the perfect support for the heavy loads they need to bear.

The lesson of the Rhino Nuchal Crest is that you need to find the right support system uniquely suited to your individual needs. As no two leaders or organizations are the same, no two support systems will ever be the same. The Rhino Nuchal Crest entails a five-step plan to create your unique and individualized support system.

Step 1: Create an Inner Circle of Excellence

What would you do if you were going to be stranded on a deserted island and you could bring only three people with you? What if your survival depended on the choices you made?

Whether we're on a deserted island or in the executive suite of a Fortune 500 company, we leaders must question what we need to survive and thrive. What will make us stronger, healthier, leaner, and more effective? This is fundamentally the most important question a leader can ask. In answering this question, we must begin with the people with whom we work and, more specifically, our inner circle.

Think of a leader as a pebble thrown into the middle of a lake (the organization), creating a ripple (the leader's vision), which will then slowly extend outward to the rest of the organization. But in accordance with the laws of nature, the ripple will go only so far. Leaders must therefore surround themselves with individuals who will continually empower the rest of the organization, extending the ripple outward to their own inner circles and then onto the rest of the organization like a brand-new ripple. Leaders cannot allow the ripple to fade until it has clearly reached every individual in the organization. The line of communication must travel through the entire chain of command, from the CEO to the newest intern. A broken link weakens the whole organization. Like a slipped vertebra, it will influence the overall effectiveness and strength of the organization's spine. More important, with every break in the chain, leaders must pick up the slack, adding to their already heavy burden.

Creating effective communication between you and your organization requires a support system that begins with an "alone on an island" mentality. This is your personal commitment to invite into your inner circle only those individuals you would want around if your life depended on your choices. And while your inner circle will undoubtedly be made up mostly of coworkers, it will also include trusted friends, family members, and mentors—anyone on whose contributions you can rely to make you a better leader and your organization more effective as well.

These people should not be yes-men and flatterers, sycophants who will quickly rubber-stamp your ideas in deference to your position. Instead, you need individuals who will tell you the truth, offering their advice, their counsel, and, when appropriate, their dissent. These individuals might argue with your strategies but will just as quickly turn around and implement them with the same passion they'd have if they were their own.

Leaders must be on a constant lookout for the best, brightest, and strongest backs they can find, and they shouldn't stop until they're satisfied they've found them. As John F. Kennedy said, "Once you say you're going to settle for second, that's what happens to you."[2] And once we allow subpar performers to grab a foothold in our inner circle, we've conspired to allow mediocrity to seep into our organization. This is unacceptable. If we seek to create an environment where accomplishment and excellence are the norm, then we must demand the same excellence from those within our ranks.

It sounds so simple, but why don't more leaders follow this advice? Certainly no one goes out of her way to create an inner circle that is average. No one consciously tries to surround himself with yes-men and deadweight. But in spite of our best intentions, we often do it anyway. We allow time, energy, political correctness, tenure, guilt, external pressure, and, even worse, our own insecurities and fears to dictate with whom we choose to surround ourselves.

Other people's talent, hard work, and charisma often lose out to our egos, as if our own importance and value would somehow be diminished by the ability and accomplishments of others. But if we are going to truly ease our burdens and allow our organizations to thrive, we must not be threatened by how talented others are, fearing these individuals will move on, get promoted, or take our jobs. Rather, we need to surround ourselves with the best people we can find.

The smartest executives are those who find people even smarter than themselves. It takes a combination of self-confidence and humility to turn the reins over to such people, but the results are always extraordinary. After all, if you really were on that deserted island, you wouldn't get rid of the castaway who knows how to catch fish, build a hut, and sing by the campfire. You'd keep him around because he was keeping you alive and entertaining you. Before long, he might be charging a cover and a two-drink minimum to come to the campfire, but it's always worth paying great people what they deserve.

Back in the real world of our offices, however, people are watching their leaders for a shift from humility and the sharing of a vision to an increasingly relentless ego. We may not all be guilty of this sort of shift, but most of us have the *potential* to fall into this trap if we aren't careful. At all costs, we must stay vigilant, reminding ourselves that water rises to its own level. The support we seek will be only as strong and powerful as the people with whom we surround ourselves. Dictators choose yes-men and they inevitably fall, collapsing under pressures from within or without. Statesmen and stateswomen choose wise individuals—people who are confident and capable of challenging their leaders when appropriate.

Step 2: Match the Right Person with the Right Job

On the surface, the challenge of a coach or manager seems simple: field the most talented players, and then let the best team win. In reality, a coach's job is much more complex. Besides recognizing talent, a coach must put the best talent in the right positions. This may seem obvious. After all, in baseball, a pitcher pitches and a catcher catches. Likewise, in corporate America, most workers know exactly what they will be doing when they're hired, whether accountants, managers, sales directors, executive assistants, or technology officers.

But the truth is that once we enter the workplace, we often find ourselves becoming jacks-of-all-trades, suddenly asked to wear many hats. An athlete who joins a team as a starting pitcher is asked to relieve. A shortstop is moved over to play third base. While some individuals may grumble, "This wasn't what I was hired to do," if they are flexible and open-minded, they will soon realize that the change is the quickest way to become noticed and move up through the ranks. For a leader, team building offers the ideal opportunity to recognize the flexibility of team members and to discover whatever hidden skills they may have to offer.

Reviewing a résumé and conducting a job interview are only the first steps toward reaching common ground, the mutual understanding that a potential worker has the skills and mind-set to fit into the workplace. Unfortunately, résumés and job interviews often tell us nothing about how good people's analytical or communication skills are; how competitive people are; what kind of discipline, focus, and self-reliance they possess; or whether they are fair, honest, and dependable. It's hard to tell from a commercially crafted résumé whether a potential hire will interact well with others, whether she is a good team player, or if she is independent and self-reliant. These are the qualities we need to be on the lookout for, but regrettably, many of them are impossible to ascertain from even the most probing of job interviews.

So we hire on credentials, recommendation, or instinct, and then we hope we have made the right choice. Sometimes we do, and sometimes we don't. But only after an individual is hired will a leader see exactly how important that person can become to the organization. Only under the trial of the job and the interaction with the rest of the team will the truth of the person's character be revealed.

Like any good coach, a leader will see how best to use a player only after he has stepped out onto the field. Only then will the leader know what to do with him: move him to the top of the lineup, change positions, trade him, or send him down to the minors for seasoning.

This is where true team building begins: finding the right job for the right person, a skill that is predicated on our ability to recognize the natural talents and individuality of those in our organizations. We can start by reminding ourselves of the obvious: we are not all created equal. Our talents and skills are as varied as our personalities. Some of us are better at working with numbers; others, with people. Some of us are strategists, while others are motivators, salespeople, enforcers, mediators, designers, teachers, or writers.

What's more, we have no time frame for learning what we're good at or what we're meant to do in life. Sometimes our strengths are obvious, but more often they're not. A wise and observant leader will see what others can't see, recognize talent where others don't. Tom Brady, considered one of the greatest quarterbacks in the NFL today, wasn't selected until the sixth round of the draft. Give credit to the New England Patriots for choosing him.

A great leader will care less about why someone was hired and in which department she works and focus more on putting the individual in the position where she will be of the greatest value, the place where she can use her natural talents to generate the most productive results. Just because someone is an incredible salesperson doesn't mean that she will make the ideal corporate sales trainer. A personal assistant may be great at his job, but that doesn't qualify him to be the perfect human resources director. The ability to match the job to the person takes open eyes and an open mind. Most of all, we must dismiss the preconceived notion that all talented individuals must travel down a certain same path.

In seeing what others don't see, leaders find their most powerful team-building weapon: unrealized potential. Some great individuals simply need to be discovered. They're out there, often right under our noses. But we will find them only if we understand that a support system is a living, breathing, and changing entity. We need to stay flexible. Running an organization is like working on a crossword puzzle: trying out people at different tasks, putting them in different situations with different people, searching for an "exact fit" in a place where they can stand out and flourish.

As leaders, our job is to do more than run an organization. We must help people find purpose, meaning, and value in their jobs. Just as we can't fit a square peg into a round hole, we can't fit the right person into the wrong job—unless we're willing to settle for mediocrity. Remember the Peter Principle, first enunciated by Laurence J. Peter more than three decades ago: "In an hierarchy, every employee tends to rise to his level of incompetence."[3] In other words, we generally tend to keep promoting people until they're in a position they can't handle. There they languish for the rest of their careers, creating chaos in the organization because they are not capable of doing the new tasks with which they have been charged. On the other hand, the more leaders care enough to put the right people in the right slots—and not promote them any higher than that—the more they will make those people feel valued and empowered, setting them on a course that may change not only the lives of the individuals but the life of the organization.

Step 3: Empower Others through Shared Responsibility

To share the burden, you must give away the burden. It's not enough to have the right people doing the right jobs. Leaders also need to have individuals involved in activities that significantly lighten their own loads. But like parents who won't leave their children with "just any" caregiver, most leaders won't leave their responsibilities with "just any" team member. Leaders rely on the people they trust, naturally sharing their burdens with only those individuals in whom they have complete confidence. The problem is that confidence, like trust, doesn't happen by accident. It needs to be cultivated and, more important, earned. Leaders can facilitate the process by creating an environment where mutual trust is fostered—one where the leader wants to share her burdens with those around her and, in return, where those around the leader will feel as if their contributions are encouraged, valued, and needed.

Of course, this process takes time, patience, and the leader's commitment to *empower others through shared responsibility*. This means more than sharing the work. It also means sharing the power, the influence, and the opportunity to make a difference. Some basketball players, such as Michael Jordan, make the players around them better. In contrast, some have criticized Kobe Bryant for his willingness to take the whole game on his shoulders, not trusting his teammates with the ball and reducing them to spectators at the "Kobe Show."

If we are going to say to our people, "We want you to make a difference," then we must hold them accountable for the outcomes, and we must hold ourselves accountable to dish out power the way a point guard passes a basketball. In order for mutual trust to exist, real, measurable stakes must always be on the line for both parties. Having something on the line means more than valuing our teams' contributions. It is the very groundwork for peak performance. Ask competitors in any sport what makes a winning team, and most will undoubtedly give you one common answer: it's the competition. Muhammad Ali's greatness was tested because he came of age at a time when so many great boxers were competing, including Sonny Liston, Joe Frazier, and George Foreman. We're all familiar with teams that win games against tough competition and can't really motivate themselves to beat a weak team. That's because great competitors rise to the occasion, to the level they're asked to face. Pro golfers will tell you that winning isn't about beating the course or the record or their own insecurities. *It's about beating the other guy.* This sense of competition is the driving force behind the desire to win and become the best possible.

John Wooden, the great UCLA basketball coach, once wrote, "You are in the presence of a true competitor when you observe that he or she is indeed getting the most joy out of the most difficult circumstances. The real competitors love a tough situation. That's when they focus better and function better."[4] As leaders, we must provide to those around us the opportunities to excel. We must offer up those great and noble challenges that will enable our people to become great and noble themselves.

And if you believe sharing responsibility seems like a troublesome and needless path to follow, think of the alternative. Give away little or no responsibility and there is only one inevitable outcome: everyone in your organization will believe no one is watching, and if no one is watching, then no one cares. This can only lead to neglect, procrastination, and indifference. If you do not empower through shared responsibility, you will suffer the unpleasant consequences.

As we have discussed, Ted Williams was one of the greatest baseball hitters of all time. In 1941, he was one game shy of joining the elite few in baseball who hit .400 for an entire season. On the last day of the season, because he was already hitting .400, his manager suggested that he sit out the last game so he would not jeopardize his batting average and thus would guarantee his place in immortality. Williams laughed at the idea and said he wasn't going to slip into the .400 club through the back door.

That's the mark of a true competitor: the courage to put one's record on the line. Whether in baseball or business, if we don't care about the results, our people will know we don't care. The impression we make on those around us is indelible. If they sense that we don't care about the job we gave them to do, if we diminish the responsibility we offer them, we will suffer the consequences.

If we hold our people accountable, clearly letting them know our expectations, they will realize we trust them and genuinely believe in their abilities. By making accountability an absolute requirement, we create individuals with a vested interest in their results and also a culture of leadership, whose basic premise is that we are all leaders. Although we might not be in positions of leadership, managing people and dictating policies, we can all influence others as we implement positive action and effect change. We can all make a difference. In doing so, we can all become leaders.

Of course, if people are given responsibility and accountability, they must also be given autonomy to see the job through. Leaders must resist the urge to save the day when the going gets tough, vigorously avoiding the temptation to micromanage. Kobe Bryant's style may be flashy, but without a trustworthy team around him, championships are likely to elude him. Dotting the *i*'s and crossing the *t*'s of everyone else may give a leader temporary satisfaction, but it only leads to organization-wide resentment and the stifling of creativity. We need our people to run with the responsibility we give them. In the words of Theodore Roosevelt, "The best executive is one who has sense enough to pick good men to do what he wants done, and self-restraint enough to keep from meddling with them while they do it."[5]

Finally, leaders must realize that trust doesn't develop overnight and that it won't happen without hiccups or mistakes. Trust is earned through trial and error, success and defeat. Think of two battle-weary soldiers sharing a foxhole: only through adversity and challenge do they learn unquestionably to trust the other.

The wait is worth it, though. Empowering the people in your organization with responsibility, accountability, and autonomy will offer the leader lasting support as well as strengthen the entire workforce. Like a chain reaction unfolding, responsibility leads to initiative, initiative to an increase in confidence, and increased confidence to self-respect, pride, and ultimately, ownership. And what more can you want than to have the individuals in your organization feel as if they own the place where they work? These are the people with whom you want to share your burdens. This is the kind of support you can count on, support you can trust.

Step 4: Recognize That Support Is a Two-Way Street: You Scratch My Back and I'll Scratch Yours

You can't expect the people in your organization to stand on their own two feet unless you give them the foundation and support that allow them to stand in the first place. Having all the responsibility in the world means nothing if the person can't handle it. Your team members are all different, and they all have different needs. Perhaps one person needs more computer training to feel confident at work. Another person wants to be able to telecommute part of the week. Yet another wants to be able to fit the demands of the workplace around family concerns and not the other way around. The only way you'll know what your people need is if you ask them. You may not be able to meet every one of their desires, and it may not be in the best interests of your business to do so. But unless you ask, you'll never know. The flip side of responsibility will always be the inescapable truth that the people in your organization need your help—not to squash incentive but to strengthen it.

According to a Buddhist saying, "If you light a lamp for somebody, it will also brighten your own path." In the corporate world, this translates to, "If you want others to help you achieve your own goals, help them achieve theirs." Helping others isn't just good karma. It's good business, and a prerequisite for leadership success. But what kind of help are we supposed to offer? How can we lend a meaningful hand to the individuals in our organizations? Before we send them to workshops, seminars, and off-sites for training, we must step back and see the big picture. We must realize that our ultimate responsibility is the same as it always has been: we must help our people prosper and live good lives of growth, value, and purpose. We must value our people as much as we value our profits, dedicating ourselves to enriching their lives because we're expecting them to do the same for us.

In Silicon Valley, the second most powerful form of currency, after cash, is stock options. New companies pay their employees with stock options, which cost the company little and offer the employees an ownership stake in the future of the enterprise. If the company succeeds and goes public, the employees will be rich. During the dot-com heyday of the late 1990s, and even again today, companies not only paid employees with stock options but used options to pay their attorneys and other professionals and even their office-rental fees. Giving people an ownership stake ties them to their organization's success in an exciting and meaningful way.

We must find ways to help our people succeed. And the best way is to embrace the three main commitments that follow.

Help Your People Overcome Their Fears Most of the things that hold us back in life are fear based. We don't raise our hands in school, volunteer at work, reach out to others, or take risks because we're afraid. While we could psychoanalyze all the reasons for the fear, we can safely assume that for most of us, fear comes down to a lack of confidence.

While we know that shared responsibility leads to confidence, it will do so only if people feel they can handle the responsibility. What about those people who want nothing to do with responsibility—the ones who recede into the woodwork when they are called to action or asked to perform at a higher level? Are they lazy or uninterested? Or do they just need the confidence to step up their game? And who will give them that confidence?

Athletes have people standing by to give them confidence. Golf is a solitary sport, but the professionals walk the course with their caddies, who offer the players everything from advice on club and shot selection to whispered words of encouragement. In professional tennis, coaches and other supporters are visible to the players on the court because these spectators are sitting in the boxes closest to the action. In baseball, coaches stand near the foul lines along first and third base, ready to pass on encouragement and guidance to hitters and runners. If athletes can have coaches right in the middle of the action, why can't we?

A baby's first step will almost always take place within a few feet of a beloved parent; Mom or Dad stands, arms open wide and face beaming, a pillar of strength and comfort. Part of leadership involves being that coach or parent, always ready to cheer from the sidelines and support the team. Why can't we provide the same kind of confidence building to those people who are "on the court" in our businesses? Despite what popular opinion tells us, confidence is not a matter of personality but a matter of competencies. So leaders must continuously ask the same question of everyone within their organizations: what can we do to make you more self-confident?

Most organizations train their people to perform only the jobs they were hired to do instead of training them to become what they are capable of becoming. Of course, leaders must deal with skill sets, techniques, and procedures in order to maintain the integrity and efficiency of their enterprises. Knowing the job is always the first step to competency. But if we want people to step up to the barbells and really start lifting, we need to give them not only the tools we think they need but also the tools they think they need.

However, we don't always ask people what they need. The Strategic Coach, a consulting company run by Dan Sullivan, preaches that the most important tool in the entrepreneur's arsenal is confidence, and everything the entrepreneur does, from the selection of team members to the selection of technology and other tools, must reinforce and increase his sense of confidence. What can you provide your workers, individually and collectively, to protect their confidence?

Once we help someone achieve the confidence she needs to succeed, we must complete the cycle by letting her know that she has done a good job, a job that has earned our trust. This small effort on our part will always increase the confidence she has already gained.

Show Your People the Way: The Lost Art of Mentorship The term "mentor" originated in Greek mythology with a character named Mentor, who was a faithful friend of Odysseus. When Odysseus went off to fight in the Trojan War, he put his son Telemachus into Mentor's care. Mentor was a tutor, guide, and protector to the boy.

While mentorship continues to have value, it is largely underutilized. For the most part, we offer skills but not individual attention. We train, but we don't mentor.

By definition, becoming a mentor means accepting responsibility to guide someone in his personal and professional growth, a process in which the mentor shares life experiences, knowledge, and skills. A good mentor will model appropriate skills and behavior for an organization. Mentorship also fosters accountability, instant feedback, and external validation.

But more than that, mentorship is a personal pledge by which one individual—and by extension, the whole organization—promises to guide and protect another. This is the leader sending a clear and important message to his people: "I will walk with you, side by side, doing whatever it takes until you succeed."

A popular story offers a perfect illustration of what it means to be a mentor. One night, a woman dreamed that she was walking along the beach with God. Across the sky flashed scenes from her life, and for each scene she noticed two sets of footprints in the sand: one belonging to her and the other to God.

When the last scenes of her life had flashed before her, she looked back at the footprints in the sand. To her surprise, she noticed that many times along the path of her life, there was only one set of footprints. Upon closer observation, she realized that this happened at the very lowest and saddest times in her life.

She was perplexed and frustrated, so she questioned God.

"Lord," she said, "you said that you'd walk with me all the way. But I've noticed that during the most trying times of my life, there is only one set of footprints. I don't understand why you would leave me when I needed you the most."

God replied, "My daughter, my child. I would never leave you. During your times of trial and suffering, when you see only one set of footprints, it was then that I carried you."

Mentorship means supporting the other individuals on our teams and, when necessary, carrying them to help them meet their full potential.

Most of us can fondly recall the mentors in our own lives. They might have been former employers who took the time to cultivate relationships with us, or they may have been people we met in a nonbusiness realm. Mentors are the people who have shaped and inspired us, helping us become who we are today. It is now our time to mentor others. It is our responsibility to convey an unwavering message of support and encouragement to our team members.

The symbolic and practical value of this message is immeasurable, especially when we consider that those we mentor will often turn back to us with the same message of solidarity and go on to mentor others in our organizations.

Go the Extra Mile for Your People The exchange is ageless: we give a paycheck, and in return we get a job well done. Throw in some health insurance and two weeks off a year, and everybody is happy, or at least coming back day after day. On average, each of us will spend more than a third of our adult lives at work. That's a lot to give. As leaders, we generally give back to our people something that falls between what the law requires and what the market will bear. The question is, What more should we offer? Should we go the extra mile for our people, and if so, how?

The choice is ours. So, too, are the consequences. If we choose to do the minimum, then we can expect like results: the organization will give back only what is required. On the other hand, if we choose to extend ourselves, believing that leaders have a moral responsibility to do more than what is necessary, then we can expect, by the same kind of logic, that the organization will repay us in kind. When it comes to lending a hand to those around us, we must realize that by virtue of our position, we can create our own support systems, whereas the rest of the organization often cannot. All the other members of the organization must take personal responsibility for themselves, but in many matters they are at the mercy of the day-to-day policies and guidelines set down by those in charge. They have families to support and careers to think about, but they must sit back and take what is given.

In this vacuum of insecurity, there exists an opportunity for leaders to step in and make a profound difference in the lives of their people. Leaders have the chance to go the extra mile, to do what is unexpected and unasked for. Wise leaders take these steps not for themselves but for those who devote their lives to their organizations.

What this "extra mile" means to you as a leader is as individual and personal as your own organization. You could offer day care, gym facilities, flexible hours, job sharing, bonuses, four-day work-weeks, free lunches on Thursdays, or casual dress Fridays. Some-times going the extra mile simply requires a phone call or e-mail. One worker reported being overwhelmed by her boss's thought-fulness when, after a meeting had been scheduled for 11:30 a.m., she received a personal call from her boss, who wanted to make sure that the meeting wouldn't interfere with any lunch plans she might have with her children. But whatever you do, it's your obli-gation to help your people enjoy the third of their lives that they spend with you. Help them find joy and purpose every day, not just on the weekends. Help them believe in a new mantra for your organization: TGIM, thank God it's Monday.

Step 5: Don't Look a Gift Horse in the Mouth

It doesn't matter where an idea comes from. We've demonstrated that we need to look inside our organizations for guidance and sup-port. But we must look outside as well, to the wealth of people upon whom we can and must rely: spouses, children, relatives, and friends; consultants, specialists, and coaches. Even our adversaries and competition can offer support. And of course, there is the indi-vidual who had your job before you—and that person's predeces-sor as well. All we have to do is open our minds and egos to the idea that we can learn from anyone, anywhere, anytime.

Unfortunately, we often ignore the support that is right in front of our noses, either because we have preconceived ideas regarding where help should come from and what it should look like or because we feel an undeniable urge to put our stamp on everything we do. Some leaders erroneously believe that any outside help, especially from their predecessors, would somehow diminish their legacies. In truth, we shouldn't care where the help comes from, only that we are being helped and that our organizations are growing in the right direction.

If your mother can still ease your burden somehow, let her do it. If your spouse comes up with a solution to a problem that's been keeping you up at night, accept it. If the individual you replaced had great ideas, use them. If your competitor is using an innovative process that might work for you, adopt it. Leaders should have the objectivity, wisdom, and strength to recognize what is being offered on merit alone, regardless of where it comes from.

We often place unnecessary weight on our shoulders by needing to reinvent the wheel, by having to do everything by ourselves. The world—past, present, and future—is littered with good ideas, and we should use them all, if only because every time we implement a good idea, we increase the odds of our success. If we stick to our own limited ideas, we put a stranglehold on our possibilities, shortchanging our sphere of influence and potential power. We're like a farmer planting one tiny apple seed, hoping for an orchard to grow. It's certainly not impossible, with plenty of time and a healthy degree of optimism, but it would probably be a lot easier to sow hundreds of seeds, with many workers tending the land.

Every apple seed contains the same elements, but certain seeds take root and others do not. Fortunately, we don't need *every* seed to take root. Farmers don't care which seeds grow, as long as enough do. They want the orchard to bloom as fully and richly as it possibly can. This is a lesson for all leaders.

Isaac Newton said, "If I have seen further, it is only because I have stood on the shoulders of giants."[6] Today's leader needs to stand on the shoulders of those who have gone before him and those who are with him now. After all, who is more valuable: the person with the great idea or the one who recognizes the idea and effectively implements it. A patient in the hospital bed doesn't care who developed the medicine that gets him well. All he cares about is the doctor who has chosen that medicine and then kindly administers it to him. If you truly aim to create a support system that will ease your burdens, you need to be strong enough to accept help from wherever it comes.

Some businesses have used an effective trust-building activity to illustrate the importance of a support system, though the exercise is customarily reserved for children's classrooms and athletic-team warmups. In the exercise, all the members of a group stand in a circle and join hands. Then, slowly and carefully, everyone leans outward while still holding hands. Everyone must move at roughly the same pace. If one person is too fast or too slow, for example, she will fall and pull the rest of the group down with her. But if the entire group moves as one unit, each applying the same amount of force and adjusting for the force applied by others, people will be able to lean very far back without losing their balance. In this way, the team can achieve something that the individual members could never do on their own. Only through the strength and power of the group as a whole can people achieve what they never before thought possible.

The Wisdom of the Rhino Nuchal Crest

More than 50 percent of Americans will suffer from some sort of back problem during their lives. Some problems may be congenital. Others may be the result of an accident or a sports injury. But most back problems are due to tension and muscular tightness, which comes from poor posture, extra weight, inactivity, and lack of abdominal strength. In other words, back problems are preventable. With proper methods of stretching, strengthening, standing, sitting, and, of course, lifting, they could be entirely eliminated.

It's no different for today's leaders. The back pain that comes from taking on the burdens of the job is just as preventable, provided that leaders allow those around them to share the burden. No man is an island, able to make it through life without the assistance of others. If we try to go it alone, bearing more than we're capable of carrying, something will inevitably break, leaving us ineffective and unable to continue our journey. Relying on others is not a matter of pride but a matter of necessity.

In the words of John Andrew Holmes, "The entire population of the universe, with one trifling exception, is composed of others."[7] And we need those others. We need their talents, their energy, their enthusiasm, and their heart. We need their support to make our dreams come true.

A FINAL RHINO THOUGHT

The weight on your shoulders becomes more like a feather with each person who lends you a hand. Reach out and share your journey. Teach. Validate. Empower. Trust in the greatness of others and their capacity to lighten your burden.

The Rhino's Heart

A Leader's Life of Passion and Service

The best and most beautiful things in the
world cannot be seen or even touched.
They must be felt with the heart.

Helen Keller

O ne of the most heartwarming sports stories ever turned
into film is *Rudy*, the account of Daniel "Rudy" Ruettiger,
a young kid who grew up in the blue-collar community
of Joliet, Illinois. After graduating from high school, Ruettiger went
to work in the steel mill alongside his father and brothers, seemingly destined to live the same life as everyone else in his town.
Only Ruettiger had other plans—his own impossible dream. He
wanted to play football for the Fighting Irish of Notre Dame.

Of course, as everyone was quick to point out to him, Ruettiger
lacked the brains, the brawn, and the financial means to ever achieve
his goal. But he didn't listen, and in spite of everyone's doubts, he
set out for South Bend, Indiana, where he enrolled in a junior college across the street from the university. He applied to Notre Dame
three times before he was finally accepted. Then he boldly walked
onto the football field and told Coach Ara Parseghian that he
intended to play on the team.

Ruettiger stood five feet six inches tall and weighed only 165 pounds. The idea of such a fragile individual playing football for Notre Dame was laughable. Ruettiger refused to take no for an answer, though, and eventually his tenacity and perseverance earned him a spot on the team's scout squad. He displayed such a strength of heart and fierceness of will that he touched and inspired all those around him. He stayed on the practice squad, being pummeled day after day by men twice his size, until he was finally given his greatest honor: the chance to play in an actual game.

As eighty thousand fans chanted his name, Ruettiger entered Notre Dame folklore, sacking the opposing quarterback in the last twenty-seven seconds of the sole play in which he participated, in the only game of his college football career. To this day, Rudy Ruettiger is the only player in Notre Dame's history to be carried off the field on his teammates' shoulders.

Ruettiger's story is timeless and universal, showing us all what we can achieve—not necessarily with talent or size or brains but with heart. A plot like this has always been a Hollywood favorite— the ordinary guy doing what no one else thinks he can do. It's the plot of *Hoosiers, Braveheart,* and, of course, *Rocky,* who we all know should never have been in that ring. He was too old, too small, and outmatched, but he hung in there and fought to the end because he had heart.

The lesson for leaders is obvious. It takes more than strength and a vision to lead, more than personality, energy, and drive. It takes heart—not just the muscular organ that pumps blood throughout the body but that imperceptible something that gives us our spirit, our pluck, our passion, our joy, and our love.

Yes, love, the word that changes everything. Now we are headed into uncharted waters. Business, like science, doesn't like what it can't see, touch, and quantify. Matters of the heart—especially love—top the list of suspects in this regard. We prefer our reality in black and white, as something that is safe and easy to understand, like an Excel spreadsheet or a PowerPoint presentation.

Yet as much as we might be comforted by what we can see and touch, that's not what makes or defines us. In short, every visible part of the rhino we've discussed so far—the eyes, the ears, the mouth, the horns, the feet, the skin, the back—would all be completely useless were it not for the unseen heart, pumping blood, life, and spirit into each of them. For leaders, the heart gives our eyes vision, our mouths the ability to communicate, our feet the endurance to carry on. Heart gives our flesh and bones the capacity to achieve what others consider impossible. Still, we ignore and mistrust the heart, which is understandable considering that we have always been told that the heart has no place in the business world. And yet Mother Teresa, who made an entire life and legacy out of loving others, said, "We can do no great things; only small things with great love."[1]

We've convinced ourselves that the heart is wishy-washy, unreliable, and too emotional to serve any practical purpose. Because of this tenuous logic, many of us have found ourselves obligated to turn our hearts off as we enter our workplaces. We have forced ourselves to live in two worlds: our home world of family, friends, joy, love, and passion and our work world of colleagues, clients, tenacity, perseverance, and will power.

At home we slip off our shoes, put a child on our lap, and talk about the goodness of life and the need to be kind, considerate, and gentle. We allow ourselves to smile and laugh, to be silly, passionate, honest, and grateful. In short, we allow ourselves to be human, unguarded and free to express our emotions as we see fit. It's no wonder that when the end of the week rolls around, most workers become like giddy children shouting, "Thank God it's Friday!"

But come Monday morning, we enter into the other world: our work life. Now we get serious. We are tough and strong, taking no prisoners while quietly separating the two worlds, sacrificing our home-life ethics with the self-delusion that we act the way we act because we have no choice. It's just business, we tell ourselves.

Admittedly, this is an exaggeration, and the two worlds of home and work are almost always separated. Unless you're Hugh Hefner, you can't run around in your pajamas at work any more than you can run your home with the efficiency of a boardroom. If we didn't separate the two worlds, we'd never get any work done and our home lives would be miserable.

The problem is not really that our *worlds* are different but that we are so different within those worlds.

From a practical point of view, we certainly should conduct ourselves differently at work than we do at home. But down deep, at the core of our beings, we should not be any different. Every time we act one way in one situation and another way in a different situation, we are selling out, giving all our humanness and authenticity in exchange for some false ideal of what we think we should be or what those in our organizations think we should be. Until recently, the disparity between these personalities had never been seen as a problem. It didn't matter if we acted different at work than at home. It was understood and accepted, even admired. But that was before Enron, WorldCom, Adelphia, and HealthSouth came crumbling down, before CEOs were indicted and jailed for their malfeasance. Greed and scandal infested these organizations, robbing thousands of people of their livelihoods and pensions. Suddenly, the rules changed. What worked before was no longer acceptable, let alone tolerable.

Organizations now look for new qualities in their leaders, for the kind of honesty and integrity that transcend place and position.

They want leaders who can be tenacious, serious, straightforward, and relentless but also kind, considerate, and fair. It is "what you see is what you get" leadership, a simple idea that leaders should bring their authentic and human selves to work instead of checking their integrity at the door.

Rhino Anatomy: The Heart

The rhino once again proves that you can't judge a book by its cover. On the surface, rhinos seem temperamental and menacing. Photographs of them fiercely charging cars full of tourists on safari seem to prove this. However, nothing could be further from the truth. Rhinos are actually easygoing creatures. Not only do they keep their young with them for years, but they also teach them everything they need to know to survive on their own. The quiet tenderness that rhinos share with their young clearly illustrates that to be strong and powerful doesn't rule out being compassionate and gentle.

The rhino teaches us that what will make the greatest difference in our lives is not our power but our love, as well as our ability to give without expecting anything in return. This takes a big heart, a rhino-sized heart.

The rhino can show us the way, but first we must understand how we use the heart in the first place—or at least how we *think* we use the heart.

The Beating Heart

The average heart beats seventy-two times per minute, over a hundred thousand times per day, and almost 38 million times per year.

By the time you are seventy, your heart will have beaten approximately 2.6 billion times. That's a lot of work for any one organ, especially when you consider that the heart is nothing more than a pump and, like all pumps, can easily clog, break down, and need repair.

Most of us already know that heart disease is the leading cause of death in the United States. Almost two thousand Americans die of heart disease daily, which works out to about one death every forty-four seconds. We also know we can significantly reduce our risk of heart disease if we exercise, eat right, watch our cholesterol, and avoid smoking and excessive drinking. Fortunately, many of us will act on this information, but just as many of us won't, choosing instead to react only when an obvious pain in the chest forces us to pay attention.

The Feeling Heart

Certainly we must pay attention to the heart that beats. But more than that, we must take care of the heart that feels.

The heart is more than an organ. It is also a metaphor for the center of our emotions. To say we "have a heart" is to say that we experience life-affirming emotions: joy, sadness, sorrow, and love. We can't see them, touch them, or quantify their existence with an EKG, but we know they exist because we feel them—the lump in our throat, the shiver down our spine, the clamminess of our hands, the warmth in our cheeks. We may dismiss or ignore our feelings, but we can't deny their existence, nor should we undervalue their importance in our becoming well-rounded leaders. Whether we choose to pay attention to the heart that feels is another choice that we have to make. This choice will determine the degree of emotional health we will enjoy, as well as our ability to connect with those around us.

The Giving Heart

Besides taking care of the heart that feels, we must also take care of the heart that gives. It's not enough to register and feel emotion. We need to do something with that emotion. It is certainly important to *experience* love, passion, and joy, but it is much more noble and useful to *share* our love with others, to give it away. In the gift of sharing, the true power of the heart is realized. Our emotional heart becomes stronger the more it is connected and shared with others. It is not enough to love. We need to give away our love unconditionally, through service, gratitude, and compassion.

The Eighth Principle of Rhino Leadership: Rhino Heart

The greatness of a man's power is the
measure of his surrender.

William Booth

You can have all the vision, power, endurance, and leadership skills in the world, but if your heart isn't in it, as the expression goes, you will be doomed to mediocrity. You may get where you want to go, but you run the risk of having no one care that you arrived. The heart is not only what pumps life into your organization but what makes the journey memorable and enduring. The heart is what brings your organization together, uniting everyone in a common purpose.

The rhino teaches us to incorporate Rhino Heart into our leadership practice by leading with the three heartstrings of leadership. Before we can receive these lessons we must open our minds, but more important, we must open our hearts.

The First Heartstring Is Love

From a great heart secret magnetisms flow
incessantly to draw great events.
Ralph Waldo Emerson

Without exception, love is what gives your journey its meaning, truth, and longevity. More important, it is what will draw others in your organization to follow you.

Before we go on, let's define "love" as it applies to the life of a leader. Of course, leaders do not throw their arms around their co-workers and promise their undying love. We save this kind of personal love for our family and close friends. Rather, the love leaders need to bring to their professional lives is of a different, more universal nature, incorporating two common principles that will uplift and enrich the leaders and, in the process, the lives of everyone in their organizations. These principles are *passion* and *compassion.*

Passion and the Power of Transformation Passion is the burning fire that compels us to do more than we ever thought possible. To be passionate is to be enthusiastic, inspired, and motivated for the simple reason that we love what we do.

What happens when we love what we do? The same thing that happens when we fall in love: the world changes. When we love what we do, we do it more often and better, living with more intensity, drive, and purpose. This adds meaning and joy to our lives, as well as productivity to our workplace. Without a doubt, passion is the great transformer in our organizations. Its power belongs to us all—not just to rock stars, astronauts, firefighters, or workaholic CEOs featured on the front page of the *Wall Street Journal* but to anyone who chooses to live a life of purpose.

Let's face it: we're not all in glamorous professions. Some of us make pencil erasers, shoelace tips, soda cans, paper clips, eyeliner, and magnets. We can lead highly productive yet conventional lives. It doesn't matter. The shoelace executive has the exact same potential to be passionate or passionless in life as does an astronaut or a top fashion model.

Passion is not job dependent but people dependent. It's not about what you do for a living but how you do it. In fact, when it comes to living a rich and passionate life, your chosen profession is the least important factor in determining your success.

Erin, for example, was twenty-two years old and worked in the copy room of a large business, managing the never-ending flow of documents that needed to be copied, collated, and bound. It was a demanding job, noted more for its tediousness than anything else.

Erin easily could have coasted through her day. The job didn't require more than two hands and an occasional bit of mental focus. Besides, she was paid little and wasn't looking for career advancement in the organization; she held the job in order to support herself through graduate school. But that wasn't Erin's style. Instead of slacking off, she made it a point to know everything about her job— not just paper, toner, software, and the 800-number for the repair service but all the different ways to increase her speed and efficiency. She could even fix problems that would normally require a technician's visit, saving both time and money.

Erin mastered the small world of her copy center, understanding the subtleties of her machines and deftly handling the needs of demanding coworkers. She took pride in delivering work ahead of schedule and always with an extra touch thrown in: a fancy binder around a document, a cover sheet no one asked for, or a card that wished someone a happy birthday. She even made deliveries on her lunch hour. Because Erin never saw herself as less important than anyone else in the organization, she had a quiet strength to which people naturally gravitated. People wanted to be Erin's friend, and they looked forward to seeing her every day. Perhaps it was the way she smiled, laughed at their jokes, or genuinely cared about what they had to say. But when she walked into a room, the energy changed immediately, becoming lighter, stronger, and more balanced.

Like all genuinely passionate workers, Erin didn't flaunt her efforts or her charisma. She had no hidden motives; she had nothing to prove. She just loved doing what she did and took pride in being good at it, in mastering her world. Erin did her job in service to others and always with flair, style, and efficiency. She proved that even the most menial of tasks, if done with passion, can be rewarding and make a difference in the lives of others.

When the time came for Erin to leave the organization to focus on her graduate school studies, everyone was sad to lose her. Her coworkers chipped in and threw her a big good-bye party. All the people at the party recounted what they would miss about Erin. They cited her work ethic, her positive attitude, her joyful spirit, and even the excellent quality of copies the organization had enjoyed ever since she began working there. Above all, they loved Erin for her heart.

After the party, the CEO took Erin aside and told her he'd be happy to promote her if she stayed. Erin thanked him for his gracious offer but said it was time for her to move on. And although she moved on, she left a positive and lasting impression on everyone who worked there.

A few years later, when she'd earned her MBA, Erin returned to that organization, and people remembered her. After only a few years, she worked her way up the ranks to a top executive position. Her passion for her work continued, except now Erin wasn't dealing with copiers; she was in charge of millions of dollars of assets and an impressive client base that stretched across the nation.

Conventional wisdom says we become passionate about the things we love: cars, computers, clothes, sports, or gardening. Or we become passionate about the causes in which we believe: ending world hunger, fostering world peace, helping the homeless, confronting the AIDS crisis, or stopping global warming. Or we might even become passionate about particular fields in which we are involved: medicine, law, music, art, or teaching.

Yet while we may indeed care about something and value its importance, this wisdom suggests that our passions are outside ourselves and therefore out of our control. This couldn't be further from the truth. The passion we're discussing springs from the very core of our being. It comes not from things or causes or careers but from how we approach these outside issues, the intensity, sense of purpose, commitment, and love we bring to bear on what we do. Our passion comes from our attitude, from our desire to master ourselves in pursuit of our interests, whatever they may be. Erin was not passionate because of her interest in copiers. She was passionate because of her approach to the copiers and the way she chose to live her day.

Leaders must ignite the same passion in their own lives, expressing themselves through the work they love and strive to master. Remember the lesson Erin taught: passion is contagious and it takes only one individual to help everybody catch it. That individual is you.

Compassion and the Power of Transformation Compassion is many things. It's kindness, forgiveness, charity, and acceptance. It's also a leader's quiet, invisible power, which is all the more remarkable since most leaders don't even want to acknowledge it. A certain amount of compassion is necessary, but most people in business fear that they will be ostracized and ridiculed if they become known for being compassionate people.

The loss of compassion in the workplace always begins with a small white lie. Our *work self* tricks our *home self* into believing that compassion doesn't fit in an office cubicle. We tell ourselves that we don't have time to coddle and babysit all the individuals in our organization, that these are grown adults who have jobs to do. If they can't work without a group hug, then we'll find someone who can.

While this line of thinking has an element of truth, in reality, the compassion and kindness that come with an open heart take no time or energy at all but only an unwavering commitment to treat others with fairness and honesty. Besides, no one is suggesting that leaders don't have tough decisions to make. Reprimanding, disciplining, and even firing others is a necessary part of leadership. We can forgive and forget, but we should also hold people accountable.

For example, companies vie with each other to sell their products to Wal-Mart, the world's largest retailer, because when Wal-Mart is your customer, you can count on huge orders. The flip side is that you can also count on Wal-Mart to expect you to cut your price 5 percent a year. At some point, you will find that it is simply impossible to make a profit by maintaining the high standards that attracted Wal-Mart to you in the first place. You must either lower the quality of the product you make or send the manufacturing jobs offshore to a region of the world where employment costs are much lower. The owner of Huffy, a bicycle manufacturer, was faced with this painful choice: accept an order from Wal-Mart and with it the need to possibly compromise his manufacturing standards, fire his workers and move the jobs offshore, or reject the order. He led with his heart and made the tough decision to say no to Wal-Mart. Today, Huffy bicycles are still made in America. You can't buy them at Wal-Mart, and they aren't coming down in price every year. But the company survives and thrives even without Wal-Mart as a customer.

Rhino Heart teaches us that power and strength must come with equal doses of love and compassion. The owner of Huffy made his decision based on the love and compassion he felt for his employees, for his customers, and for the products themselves. You can be strong and duty bound while recognizing that all individuals should be treated with respect and compassion. There's never a good reason to be curt and insensitive, intentionally embarrassing or belittling those in your organization, treating them as if they were faceless numbers on a payroll sheet instead of the human beings they really are.

If you treat them this way—as if they were your own personal property—you will become like the spoiled athlete who believes he can behave any way he wants because of his unique position or the spoiled heiress who thinks she can act however she pleases because of her wealth and social status. Behavior like this diminishes leaders in the eyes of the staff and separates them from their teams. The larger the chasm between the leader and the team, the harder it is for both sides to reconnect when they really need each other. And in today's changing world, they always will need each other.

We could advocate the golden rule—"Do unto others as you would have them do unto you"—but many leaders have such tough skin already that they don't care how they're treated. They don't need to be liked, admired, or respected, or at least that's what they'd like you to believe. Just the same, perhaps we'd be better served if we updated the golden rule so that it reads, "Do unto others as you would have them do unto your son, daughter, wife, husband, brother, or best friend."

The rule takes on a whole new meaning when you think of how someone might treat those you love. How do you want your son or daughter to be treated by the bosses? Most likely, you would say fairly, honestly, and kindly, recognizing his or her individual worth, dignity, and humanity—nothing more, nothing less. Each person you employ is someone's son or daughter. Doesn't each deserve that same kind of treatment?

This kind of thinking is illustrated by a fascinating social exercise developed by a friend after she moved to New York. She'd been living in the city for only a few months, but she was already feeling frustrated and worn down by her New York experience: the noise, the hustle and bustle, the pollution, and, perhaps worst of all, New Yorkers' attitude. One evening as she sat squeezed between two fellow commuters on the subway home, she realized she didn't like the way she was regarding (and subsequently judging) the other people on the train. So she decided to try looking at her fellow passengers through a different pair of glasses. Instead of staring past people or being aggravated at the fact that there were so many people in such a small space, she focused on each person in the subway car and tried to imagine what someone who loved them saw. By putting herself in the place of a wife, mother, daughter, sister, or best friend, she was no longer looking at the people as passengers; they became humans with rich backstories and histories, people who loved and were loved in return.

The result was a total transformation of the way my friend perceived people. Suddenly, the older gentleman in a bowler hat had three grandchildren who adored the candy he brought with him on visits; the unwashed woman became a mother to a baby who lovingly tugged on her long braid; the large mole on a commuter's nose was now a lovable characteristic that his wife found endearing. My friend learned a powerful lesson that day: when we pause long enough to treat people as real human beings, our perceptions of them begin to change. We more fully understand and appreciate who they are and how they might feel. Such an exercise awakens the compassion in the deepest parts of our souls.

As leaders, we must all strive to reach this level of compassion. We can do it only if we commit to opening our hearts and bridging the gap between our home world and our work world, between who we are in our finest moments and who we often pretend to be at work.

The Second Heartstring Is Gratitude

Gratitude is not only the greatest of virtues,
but the parent of all the others.
Cicero

"Gratitude" is a word very much like "love" in that it makes many of us roll our eyes and wonder skeptically what it has to do with running an organization. Yet gratitude has everything to do with success as a leader, and this doesn't refer to an incentive or a reward program. Instead, gratitude implies genuine appreciation for what we have in our lives—with no expectations that our grateful state will yield any results.

Of course, no one can artificially inject this feeling into an organization, let alone into our hearts. Only we ourselves can create an atmosphere of gratitude. Gratitude must be practiced and consciously incorporated into our *personal lives* before it can be authentically integrated into our *work lives*. We cannot "turn on" the heart for work and ignore it in the rest of our daily activities.

What's more, it would be self-serving and disingenuous if, in the spirit of "What have you done for me lately?" we were grateful only during the good times. After all, it's easy to be grateful when you triple your earnings or win the lottery, but what about all the days when nothing eventful and fantastic seems to be happening in your world? This is where real gratitude must be found. Albert Einstein said, "There are only two ways to live your life: One is as though nothing is a miracle. The other is as though everything is a miracle."[2] And if everything is indeed a miracle, our days will take on new and hidden meanings, and we will undoubtedly find that we have much to be grateful for.

As Dostoyevsky remarked about the human spirit, "There is such a longing for what is beautiful!"[3] But that longing need not go unfulfilled; we can find beauty in our daily interactions, whether it's the smile on a child's face or the way a leaf falls from a tree. John Ruskin, a nineteenth-century artist and critic, devoted his life to teaching others how to appreciate the beauty around them. Ruskin claimed that he was motivated by a desire to "direct [people's] attention accurately to the beauty of God's work in the material universe."[4] He was a strong believer in drawing; he thought that people could best appreciate beauty when they understood it, and drawing enabled the viewer to possess the beautiful thing—at least on paper. Ruskin believed that we could best express our gratitude for all the beauty in the world by opening our eyes to it. Indeed, in a world of increasingly busy schedules and agendas, we are all guilty of often being blind to the glory that surrounds us.

How often do you take the time to savor a beautiful sunset or watch the way an oak tree bends in the wind? You can't be grateful for what you don't see.

Be Grateful for the People You Lead One of the biggest complaints workers have is that their leaders see only the negative in what they do—or, at the very least, it's what leaders focus on the most. We leaders walk a fine line between making our people accountable and making them feel guilty and anxious about their shortcomings. Every time we focus only on people's faults and deficiencies, we diminish their contributions and worth, decreasing their efficiency and undermining their morale.

While we certainly need to correct the shortcomings of our team members in appropriate ways, we cannot do it while ignoring what they do right. We tend to forget all about the collective contributions they already offer: all the times they showed up early and stayed late, when they selflessly took on a job nobody else wanted or supported us when nobody else would. What about all the times they worked when they were sick? Or when they skipped lunch and didn't complain, helped others when they didn't have to, or made us laugh when we felt like screaming?

These small, unsung moments create the positive energy that makes our workplaces enjoyable and productive. Yet because they're small, they tend to be forgotten or ignored, losing their significance in our big-picture vision. Deep down, we know better. We know that these small acts create our larger picture and shape our lives.

And every time we acknowledge this with gratitude, seeing the small miracles that occur within our organizations, we empower people to keep doing what they are doing. This cycle of evolution and development not only makes people feel better; it makes them act better, which in the long run makes the organization better as an enterprise.

What is the power of gratitude? In Alcoholics Anonymous, newcomers are encouraged to list daily five to ten items for which they are grateful. We tend to focus only on the problems and negative experiences of life. Focusing on what we are grateful for changes our mind-set and ever so slowly turns us from negative to positive. The "attitude of gratitude" is a hallmark of sobriety in Alcoholics Anonymous, where it is said that "a grateful heart doesn't drink."

Just as gratitude is essential for an alcoholic, so it is essential for a leader. If we don't acknowledge our people with gratitude, we run the risk of leaving them feeling emotionally shortchanged and resentful. Work then becomes an uneven transaction, which can put a proverbial chip on anyone's shoulder. Failing to acknowledge with gratitude the efforts of our team members pushes them to balance the scales on their own. In other words, they will withdraw their positive attitude and, with it, their peak performance. This situation leads to individuals who leave their jobs—but not before they foul up computer systems, files, or other vital sources of information within a company. A profound truth in life and business is that we can't expect to keep a miracle alive unless we acknowledge and honor it. Besides, the appreciation we show for all those incalculable moments does more to change unwelcome behavior than all the tongue lashings, reprimands, and "notes to the file" that we could give. Mom was right: we do get more flies with honey than with vinegar.

Be Grateful for the Experience When we actively look for something for which to be grateful, we discover an unexpected benefit. In time, gratitude will inevitably extend to areas of our lives where we thought we had nothing to be grateful for. We begin to see our experiences, even the challenging and seemingly negative ones, as positive lessons.

For example, a man developed a debilitating case of tinnitus—a profound ringing in his ears—that forced him to give up a promising musical career. While the event was tragic for him at the time, altering his entire way of life, he eventually came to see it as a blessing that allowed him to stop traveling and spend more time with his young son. To this day, he is grateful for the gift he received. His son feels the same way.

Being grateful for our experiences is often not easy. Embracing the painful lessons we need for our growth may take concerted effort, but the value gained is immeasurable. To be grateful for our experiences not only strengthens our hearts but keeps us from playing the victim, allowing us to see that there are no mistakes or coincidences in the world. All events can be hidden blessings if we open our hearts to see them.

Take the story of John, a boisterous and joyful man who always had something positive to say. If someone asked him how he was doing, he would reply, "If I were any better, I'd be twins!" He was grateful for everything in his life. He was a natural motivator and a fabulous leader to his team. If someone was having a bad day, John was right there telling the individual how to look on the positive side of the situation. John explained his attitude this way:

"Each morning I wake up and say to myself, 'You have two choices today. You can choose to be in a good mood and be grateful for the day you've been given, or you can choose to be in a bad mood.' I choose to be in a good mood.

"Each time something bad happens, I can choose to be a victim, or I can choose to learn from it. I choose to learn from it.

"Every time someone comes to me complaining, I can choose to accept their complaining, or I can point out the positive side of life. I choose the positive side of life."

When his coworkers said it wasn't that easy, John would respond, "Yes, it is. Life is all about choices. When you cut away all the junk, every situation is a choice. You choose how you react to situations. You choose how people affect your mood. You choose to be in a good mood or bad mood. The bottom line is, it's your choice how you live your life."

One day, John was involved in a serious accident, falling some sixty feet from a communications tower. After eighteen hours of surgery and weeks of intensive care, he was released from the hospital with rods placed in his back.

When one of his coworkers paid him a visit and asked how he was, John replied, "If I were any better, I'd be twins. Wanna see my scars?"

The coworker declined and instead asked him what had gone through his mind when the accident took place.

"The first thing that went through my mind was the well-being of my soon-to-be-born daughter," he replied. "Then, as I lay on the ground, I remembered that I had two choices: I could choose to live, or I could choose to die. I chose to live."

"Weren't you scared? Did you lose consciousness?" the co-worker asked.

"The paramedics were great," he continued. "They kept telling me I was going to be fine. But when they wheeled me into the ER and I saw the expressions on the faces of the doctors and nurses, I got really scared. In their eyes, I read 'He's a dead man.' I knew I needed to take action."

"What did you do?" his coworker asked.

"Well, there was a big burly nurse shouting questions at me," said John. "She asked if I was allergic to anything. 'Yes,' I replied. The doctors and nurses stopped working as they waited for my reply. I took a deep breath and yelled, 'Gravity.'

"Over their laughter, I said, 'I am choosing to live. Operate on me as if I am alive, not dead.'"

John lived, thanks not only to the skill of his doctors but also to his amazing attitude. John was ultimately grateful for his life, even the not-so-good parts. And it was his attitude of gratitude that got him through the difficult times when others would have cursed the heavens and given up.

Be Grateful for Where You Are A man who turned forty received the usual two ties from his mother, this time a paisley and a solid. When he picked her up for dinner that night wearing the solid tie, she took one look at his attire and snapped, "And what's wrong with the paisley?"

It's an old story: the demanding mother and her seemingly un-grateful son. Yet we can learn a lesson from this story. We leaders are sometimes like that mother, never satisfied, always wanting more—more money, more profits, more results, more favorable articles about ourselves and the organization (preferably about ourselves). While not being satisfied is not always bad, it can lead to a loss of appreciation and gratitude for what we already have. We certainly don't want to settle for anything less than our organizations are capable of achieving, but we also don't want to allow our people to be blindsided by artificial and unrealistic goals. Besides, the individuals in our organizations are wiser than that. They know that as soon as we set one goal with a, say, six-month deadline attached, we'll want them to do even more. If we don't stop and allow them to celebrate moments of success, they will become resentful and bitter. If we don't watch ourselves, we can become like that unsatisfied mother who slowly drives her children to rebel or, worse, run away.

As leaders, we must remember that contentment is not complacency. We have to appreciate where we are and find positive, creative ways to help our organizations grow and evolve. We must overcome whatever resistance we have and do whatever it takes to stop and enjoy the moment.

Gratitude is a twenty-four-hour-a-day job. We cannot appreciate what we do not notice. Perhaps we should heed John Ruskin's advice and take a notepad with us wherever we go, pausing to make sketches or "word paintings" of the world around us. Whatever we do, we must take every opportunity to be grateful. This takes vigilance, attention, and most of all, an open heart.

The Third Heartstring Is Service

> No person was ever honored for what he received.
> Honor has been the reward for what he gave.
> *Calvin Coolidge*

No matter what we do in life, we're all in the service business. We serve our families, our teams, our customers, our society, our country, and our faiths. We serve through our labor and our products, through the training and guidance we offer, the skills we share, and the money we give. Every individual or organization in the world serves something or someone in one fashion or another. That said, it's not the fact that we serve that matters; it's the manner in which we serve. The nobility of Rhino Heart is not to serve because we feel obligation or guilt but because we want to, because it's instinctive within us to do without any thought of "What's in it for me?" Our focus should always be, "What's in it for somebody else?" It's easy for us to fall into the trap of thinking that we are the center of the universe, the top rhino, with everyone and everything else revolving around us.

The problem with being at the center of the universe is that our world becomes incredibly small and finite. We can't see or do much in that tiny world. We create a lonely place for ourselves without much room for sharing or companionship, let alone acts of service. As the expression goes, when we are all tied up with ourselves, we make a pretty small package.

On the other hand, as soon as we realize that there is life beyond ourselves, as well as people who need us as much as we need them, our world changes. We must choose to reach out and connect with this larger world because when we do so, we open ourselves up to infinite possibilities. In the process, we strengthen ourselves and those around us, becoming much like a heart distributing blood to and from the rest of the body, delivering oxygen and nutrients necessary for life. This doesn't mean just goodwill and generosity but also the contagious and selfless mind-set that puts people before profits and the needs of others before our own. This is the service that connects us to one another and to life itself.

While no one expects us to be the next Mother Teresa, we can find plenty of ways to commit ourselves to the service of others. Sometimes we may find service opportunities in places we never expected. Princess Diana, who was known as the people's princess and widely lauded for her philanthropic work, said, "No one sat me down with a piece of paper and said, 'This is what is expected of you.' But there again I'm lucky enough in the fact that I have found my role ... I love being with people."[5] Perhaps we, too, will be surprised to find a niche in serving other people. And when we do, we ought to seize every available opportunity to improve the lives of others.

In 1985, Wilma Mankiller was the first female to be elected chief of the Cherokee Nation of Oklahoma, and during her ten years of service, she lost no time in creating better healthcare services and prospects for education, training, and employment for her people. We may not have a Cherokee Nation under our leadership, but we, too, can enact real and lasting change in our organizations.

The obstacles to overcome require a giant leap of motivation. Most of us are entrenched in the business of self-preservation. We have to take care of ourselves, our stakeholders, and our shareholders, which in business means cutting costs, maximizing profits, and finding new and different ways to make a dollar. In truth, if we didn't ask what was in it for us, we wouldn't survive and neither would the organizations we serve. The message of Rhino Heart is not to ignore our own needs but instead not to allow ourselves to be consumed by them or to start believing that the world revolves around us. Life is not about what we can take and accumulate from others.

To create balance in our lives and in our organizations, we need inflow and outflow, give and take, yin and yang. Consider any ecosystem and it becomes clear that if we take without putting back, our world will eventually crumble and become extinct. The law of nature says that we can take only to the degree that we replenish afterward. In our leadership practice, this means we must give back and serve. The best lumber companies don't plant just one tree for every tree they cut down to turn into paper and pulp. They plant ten.

How we choose to be of service is up to each of us to decide. While giving our money and resources is always good, nothing is more rewarding and energizing than giving of ourselves and of our time. It means the most and sets the greatest example to those in our organizations. There is no shortage of ways to serve. We can set up community outreach programs, corporate sponsorships, recycling incentives, scholarships, and 10K runs. We can become mentors, Big Brothers and Big Sisters, and volunteers for our favorite charities. We can match our workers' charitable donations and even help people in our organizations set up their own service programs. It doesn't matter what we do—only that we start, that we reach out beyond our own individual situations. For some of us, this will be our first foray into service, while for others the move will increase our presence in that world. In either case, we must all make a full and lasting commitment to integrate service and charity into our organizations' missions.

Charity Begins at Home Before we go out and do good in the world, we should make certain we are doing good in our own backyard first. Yes, charity begins at home. This means starting with the job we were hired to do. In truth, anything can be an act of service if we perform the work selflessly and honestly. If pleasure and gratitude motivate us instead of guilt, then service is the result. In fact, there is no greater service than doing our everyday jobs willingly, with love, with passion, and from an open heart. We learned this from Erin, our friend from the copy room, who served humanity as much as anybody. Her life was clearly one of contagious service, which was no doubt a bug caught and spread by everyone with whom she came in contact. This is the true power of service—to give of ourselves in everything we do.

Living Our Own Lives What happens if we fail to live by the values we espouse? What happens if we sacrifice integrity for expediency, letting go of what we think is important in order to be successful and prosperous? The answer is simple: we stop living our own lives, turning our futures over to false ideals or others' ideas of what we should become.

It doesn't happen all at once. As we have seen, the lowering of standards happens gradually, in stages, creeping up on us so slowly that sometimes we don't even notice until it's too late and the flow of life between the heart and the rest of the body is cut off, and we cease to be who we were.

We can ignore it, deny it, or even laugh it off, but we can no longer hide the truth: we cannot believe one way and behave in another without suffering consequences in our health, vitality, and peace of mind. The heart needs to pump as it was meant to pump: with love, gratitude, service, and a belief that anything is possible.

Consider the story of Wilma Rudolph, who weighed just four and a half pounds when she was born. At age three, she came down with double pneumonia and scarlet fever. Two years later, she was paralyzed with polio. At six, after losing the use of her left leg, she was fitted with metal leg braces. Doctors said she would never walk normally again. Her mother didn't listen and told her daughter that she could do anything she wanted if only she believed.

Rudolph didn't hesitate. She wanted to be the fastest woman on earth. At age nine, against her doctors' advice, Rudolph removed her braces and took her first unaided step. Eleven years later, at the 1960 Olympics in Rome, she won three gold medals. That's when she was recognized as the fastest woman on earth.

We must take our lesson from both mother and child. As leaders, we must empower and we must believe. We must help our people to do what they thought they couldn't do, inspiring them to tap into that unseen part of themselves that makes miracles happen. We must inspire them to live, as the saying goes, true to their hearts. And we must live true to own our hearts as well. It is the single most important thing we can do for our organization and for ourselves.

The Wisdom of Rhino Heart

We've been told for generations not to wear our hearts on our sleeves, that our emotions and feelings have no place in our corporate or political worlds. We have been told that using our hearts defies logic, convention, and popular wisdom. Yet this is absurd, considering that most of the world's problems, from poverty and addiction to violence, intolerance, and war, stem from a lack of the Rhino Heart qualities we have discussed here: love, gratitude, and service.

We have spent our lives trying to keep emotion out of the workplace, and it's not working. The Tin Man from *The Wizard of Oz* was right all along: it's the heart that makes us human. It's also what will solve every seemingly insurmountable problem we leaders will ever face.

A FINAL RHINO THOUGHT

We must all consciously and willingly open our hearts and feel the power of love as it pours over the world and transforms the lives of everyone it touches.

CHAPTER NINE

And Now,
the Journey Begins

Man does not simply exist but always decides
what his existence will be, what he will
become in the next moment.
Viktor Frankl

E verything you need to be successful on your journey is in
your possession: vision, influence, aptitude, talent, instinct,
power, and passion. As the Irish playwright George Bernard
Shaw wisely said, "Life isn't about finding yourself. Life's about creating yourself."[1] This leads us to the same question we asked when
we started this journey: Are great leaders born or made? The rhino
answer is simple: Leaders are born and made, or as Shakespeare
said, "Some are born great, some achieve greatness, and some have
greatness thrust upon them."[2] It doesn't matter where we fall on
that scale. All that matters is what we do once we are presented with
the opportunity to lead.

We each come into this world with different skills and predis-
positions. One person is good with wood and becomes a carpenter.
Another has a beautiful voice and becomes a singer. A third can
turn numbers into poetry and becomes a mathematician or an
accountant. But regardless of our natural proclivities and what we

choose to become in our lives—doctors, lawyers, teachers, land-scapers, actors, poets, or jugglers—we all share a common need for direction and guidance. We need someone who will lift us up and help us discover what we are capable of becoming. We all need leaders who will move their organizations forward. These leaders aren't superhuman. They're not heroes. They're everyday people, doing nothing more than responding to the call of duty.

At one time or another, most of us will be called upon to lead. We may be asked to lead a scout troop or the local PTA, coach a soccer or baseball team, head a small committee, organize a task force, run a division, or maybe even take over the helm of a multi-national corporation. We may lead one individual or ten or tens of thousands, but in the end, leadership is leadership—a matter of charting a course and then empowering those in the organization to make it happen. And when the time presents itself, when the call of duty comes knocking, we will either embrace the challenge or run from it. We will either believe in ourselves and our abilities or give into doubts and insecurities. But make no mistake: the choice will be ours.

To make that decision, you need to examine the three final laws of the rhino. If you can embrace these concepts, you will have taken your first step on the journey, the first step toward the life you have always imagined for yourself and for those in your care.

Rhino Law 1: We Are All Born with the Power to Become Leaders

Each of us has access to every leadership quality or characteristic mentioned in this book if we desire it. There is no patent on what it takes to be a leader, no monopoly on truth, no Holy Grail that will put us into the secret society of distinguished leaders—only hard work and determination. Some of us may be more qualified at certain parts of leadership than others. Some may have natural gifts as communicators, strategists, educators, or motivators that others must strive to obtain. But in truth, no one person is in a better position to lead than someone else.

We all come into this world with the same potential to learn and grow, and we all possess the same capacity to turn any quality and adversity into opportunity and accomplishment. Some tenacious individuals, without the privilege of money, influence, and connection, pull themselves up by their bootstraps and, in the true spirit of the American rags-to-riches story, find a way to make their dreams come true. In the film *Schindler's List*, three people whom Schindler had kept alive during the war later returned a similar favor. Abraham Zuckerman was one of Schindler's Jews, a teenager who had been deported from his native Cracow, Poland, first into a work detail and then into the concentration camps. Through a series of fortunate events, he was transferred to Schindler's factory, where he was able to survive the war.

After four years in a displaced-persons' camp in Bindermichl, Austria, Zuckerman came to the United States with little more than the shirt on his back. Today, he is one of the most successful builders in the United States, and he has put a Schindler Street, Schindler Boulevard, or Schindler Place into dozens of the communities he has built in New Jersey and throughout the Northeast. After the war, Schindler himself, a one-time industrial magnate and an extremely wealthy man, was destitute. Zuckerman and two friends supported Schindler in the last years of his life and saw to it that Schindler was honored with a plaque at Yad Vashem, the Israeli Holocaust memorial in Jerusalem, and at the United States Holocaust Memorial Museum in Washington, DC.

Abraham Zuckerman, like all of the examples in this book, found a way to make his dreams come true, and leadership is all about finding a way. Becoming a leader will always have less to do with education and privilege than with personal growth and an inner drive to realize one's potential.

You could argue that in the thousands of years since humans have been walking the planet and organizing themselves into groups for security and economic advancement, nothing essentially new has appeared in the field of leadership training. After all, how can you discover something that has already existed? In fact, you can only rediscover it, perhaps reinvent it. Certainly, no one has cornered the market on what it takes to be successful and resourceful. We are most likely using the same tools for organizing, motivating, and sharing a vision that early humans used. Portraits of deer, antelope, and, yes, rhinos, found on the walls of caves throughout southern Europe attest to the fact that humans have always dreamed big dreams, created a vision of what they wanted, and then gone after it.

I'm glad you've chosen the rhino way as an avenue to help you achieve your goals. The rhino way means that it doesn't matter how you do what you do, only that you do it with heart. This raises a question: If we have everything we need to succeed, just as the rhino does, and we all have equal access to these skills and talents, what separates us on the spectrum of leadership? What separates the manager from the visionary, the boss from the leader?

The answer is found in our passion and work ethic, along with our unrelenting spirit of persistence. What separates us is how deep each of us is willing to dig and, even more important, how long we will continue to dig. Perseverance and endurance are vital traits both for the rhino and for us.

As Confucius said, "If I am building a mountain, and stop before the last basketful of earth is placed on the summit, I have failed of my work."[3] This timeless reminder teaches us that if we care enough to help our organizations achieve greatness, then we must care enough to continue our journeys until they are unmistakably completed, until every last basket of earth is placed just where it needs to be placed.

In today's hypercompetitive world, we have no choice. The difference between the winner and the also-ran is slight. In the Olympics, a matter of centimeters or milliseconds could be the difference between success and failure.

The same is true for the leader, only it's the difference between running an organization and leading an organization, between managing your team for profits and inspiring them to greatness. The difference is not just a matter of tools, resources, and personnel. It is also in your commitment to keep pushing forward when everyone else around you wants to quit.

We may not all be athletes, but we're all in a race just the same—not merely to outwit our competitors but also to get where we want to go and to achieve what we believe we are here to achieve. The measure is not just financial. The measure is in terms of our character. We all begin the race in the same manner, with enthusiasm and a sense of purpose and duty. But as the race continues, we soon find out who becomes overwhelmed and who, despite their best intentions to succeed, will quit the race altogether. As most athletes will tell you, it doesn't matter how you start; it's how you finish. Most races aren't lost because someone lacks talent but typically because someone gives up too soon. The strongest individual going into a competition is not necessarily the last one standing. That would be the one who refuses to quit, who refuses to stop believing—the one with the most heart.

In 1952, Florence Chadwick attempted to become the first woman to swim the twenty-six miles from the coast of California to Catalina Island. After months of intense training—swimming day and night, always against the strongest currents she could find—she began her odds-defying swim. She started well and stayed true to her course, but after fifteen hours, she was numb, cold, and defeated. She couldn't go any further, and she asked to be taken out of the water.

When she recovered a little, she discovered that she had been pulled out of the water only half a mile from the Catalina coast. She realized she could have made it had the fog not affected her vision. If she had just seen the land, she would have had the heart to keep going.

How many of us have quit before we saw land? How many times have we changed course because we stopped believing or because our vision became foggy? How many times have our dreams become derailed because we failed to swim just a little bit longer?

Florence Chadwick promised herself that she would never let that happen again. She went back to her rigorous training and two months later swam the same channel. The cold and fatigue set in once again, and the fog obscured her view. This time, however, she kept going, kept swimming, even though she couldn't see her destination. She knew that somewhere behind the fog had to be land. This time she succeeded. She not only became the first woman to swim the Catalina Channel, but at thirteen hours and forty-seven minutes, she also broke the men's record by a good two hours.

So many of us are like Florence Chadwick. We have worked throughout our entire careers in pursuit of excellence. We're disciplined, hardworking, and committed. We're moving in the right direction. We just need to keep going, to keep swimming. It doesn't matter if we can't see land. The fog will lift, and when it does, everything we imagined will be waiting for us.

Rhino Law 2: Leaders Are Made by Their Own Hands

This law is short, simple, and to the point: we alone are responsible for our destiny. In the same way that an athlete knows what it takes to reach the Olympic gold medal platform, we already know what it takes to become leaders of substance and value.

Leaders need discipline, strength, boldness, courage, optimism, innovation, perseverance, integrity, creativity, sincerity, commitment, communication, honesty, humility, determination, vision, and heart. This isn't a secret. Anyone who has ever sought to lead has known or intuited that these qualities must be developed in order to succeed at the highest level. The question is, What are we going to do with this knowledge? How deep will we dig inside our own souls? Will we have the persistence of body, mind, and spirit to keep going? We must keep going until we can look in the mirror each day and say with complete confidence, "I am who I want to be." Or perhaps the real goal is to be able to say, "Today, I am a better version of who I was yesterday."

Personal achievement takes hard work. It's a proactive, ongoing, and never-ending process. We are not simply seeking to transform our organizations; true leaders are constantly seeking to transform themselves. This process requires a 100 percent commitment and calls for initiative and personal responsibility. When it comes to personal growth, it's do or don't, stand up and achieve or sit down and take your place among the complacent. There is no in-between, not when your organization's future—and the future of your own character—is on the line.

All of us need to do our own work. We need to remember that achievement is not something we are born with but something we develop over time, something we piece together, a tapestry of strength we stitch with our own two hands.

This is the inner challenge that will determine whether and how we become leaders that others will want to follow. And to those who wonder if they are up to the challenge of lifelong growth, we might consider the words of William Penn, who said, "No man is fit to command another, that cannot command himself."[4]

Rhino Law 3: Between Knowledge and Action Will Always Be Choice

Gandhi once said, "To believe in something, and not live it, is dishonest."[5] Our mothers imparted the same message in different words when they said, "You should have known better!"

With knowledge comes the moral responsibility to act, to listen to our gut and that nagging voice in our head that knows what we should do. This isn't easy. It's hard to act when we don't have to, when nothing appears to be on the line and we have no one to answer to. Lose weight? Get in shape? It's easier to stay in bed and pull the covers over our heads than to go for a run on a cold winter morning. Be creative? Take risks? Stand up for what's right? Why bother when no one's asking us to do so?

People don't solve small problems; they solve only big problems. It's much easier to act in a crisis, when we're forced to do something. Sometimes people need to suffer a heart attack before they change the way they eat and the way they live. Sometimes we need a bad review from a boss before we start shaping up our work habits. In such cases, threat and fear are immediate, making action not just a luxury but a necessity. Of course, once the threat is removed, so is our impetus to continue doing what we needed to do to get through the crisis.

Typically, when a sports team is doing badly, who gets the blame? Not the owner. He's not going anywhere. Not the players. They're signed to contracts. And the general manager is hardly likely to fire himself. It's the coach or manager who gets the ax. Then the "new broom" comes in and seeks to motivate the players by generally doing the opposite of whatever the last person did. And the players respond, at least for a while, before they tend to regress back to business as usual.

The world demands that we be only competent and moderately skilled, able to do just enough to slide by. The world does nothing to encourage us to do more. We tolerate the average in our workforce and above average in our leaders. But with the speed, danger, and complexities of the times in which we live, that is no longer enough. We deserve more than average. The people in our organizations deserve more. Our families deserve more. Society deserves more. Most important, the future we are creating for our children deserves more attention from us.

The Challenge of the Rhino

We need genuine and lasting change, a revolution led by individuals who will no longer settle for just getting by but who will demand of themselves and others that we rise up and challenge ourselves to become everything we can be. We need leaders who will embrace the challenge of the rhino.

The challenge of the rhino is to become leaders who will not just manage the nuts and bolts of their organizations but create a world in which people want to belong, a world where everyone is valued, respected, and empowered.

The challenge of the rhino is to become leaders who will embrace a culture of change, growth, evolution, and personal responsibility, creating an environment where all things are possible when we realize our full potential.

The challenge of the rhino is to become leaders who value substance more than style, who value the integrity and the heart of the organization as much as they do its public accomplishments and its balance sheet.

The challenge of the rhino is to become leaders who selflessly and unambiguously serve the organization's mission and not their own personal agenda. These are leaders who live exemplary lives in which character aligns with action, quietly inspiring others to follow not because they have to but because they want to.

The challenge of the rhino is to live a life that exceeds the boundaries of mediocrity, that goes beyond what others are doing—beyond what is safe, ordinary, and commonplace—to journey into uncharted realms.

The Wisdom of You

Embracing these challenges takes action, and action always begins with choice. The decision is not just whether to act or to not act. We must ask the all-important question that will define and shape our future: What do I want my life to stand for? As you complete this book, and as you begin and end each day, you must ask yourself that same question. What do you want your life to stand for?

We all have the capacity to become great leaders if we would only tap into the greatness within us that the rhino symbolizes. Only one person will make us great: ourselves.

As Albert Einstein said, "Try not to become a man of success, but rather try to become a man of value."[6] Greatness resides in our character, in those quiet moments when no one is watching but us. In these moments is where our future will be determined and our place in history will be revealed.

Follow the rhino, and let the journey begin.

NOTES

Introduction

1. Napoleon Hill, *Think and Grow Rich! The Original Version, Restored and Revised* (San Diego: Aventine Press, 2004), 52.

Chapter 1

1. Zig Ziglar, *See You at the Top!* 2nd rev. ed. (Gretna, LA: Pelican, 2000).
2. T. E. Lawrence, *Seven Pillars of Wisdom* (Ware, UK: Wordsworth Editions, 1999), 7.
3. Martin Luther King Jr., speech delivered on the steps at the Lincoln Memorial, Washington, DC, August 28, 1963.
4. Earl Nightingale, *The Essence of Success: The Earl Nightingale Library* (Niles, IL: Nightingale-Conant, 1997), audio CD.
5. Ralph Waldo Emerson, *Representative Men* (New York: Modern Library, 2004).
6. Ward Lambert, quoted in John Wooden, *Wooden on Leadership* (New York: McGraw-Hill, 2005), 36.
7. Katherine Mansfield, "Je Ne Parle Pas Francais," in *Bliss, and Other Stories* (New York: Alfred A. Knopf, 1920), 71–115.
8. Edwin Louis Cole, "Coleisms," The Ed Cole Library, http://www.edcolelibrary.org/coleism/.
9. Winston Churchill, quoted in David Cannadine, ed., *Blood, Toil, Tears, and Sweat: The Speeches of Winston Churchill* (New York: Houghton Mifflin, 1989), 79.
10. From Mark Twain, *Following the Equator*, vol. 1, quoted in *Respectfully Quoted: A Dictionary of Quotations Requested from the Congressional Research Service* (Washington, DC: Library of Congress, 1989).

11. Walt Disney, Pat Williams and Jim Denney, quoted in *How to Be Like Walt: Capturing the Disney Magic Every Day of Your Life* (Deerfield Beach, FL: HCI, 2005), 69.

12. Jalal Uddin Rumi, quoted in Arvind Krishna Mehrotra , ed., *A History of Indian Literature in English* (New York: Columbia University Press, 2003), 223.

Chapter 2

1. Buddha, quoted in Richard Alan Krieger, *Civilization's Quotations: Life's Ideal* (New York: Algora, 2002), 250.

2. Sherry Belle, Five Funny Females (live stand-up comedy show, McKinney Performing Arts Center, McKinney, TX, October 19, 2007).

3. Lev. 19:16 (New King James Version).

Chapter 3

1. William Aldis Wright, "The Life and Death of King John," in *The Works of William Shakespeare* (New York: MacMillan, 1891), 67.

2. Ann Landers, quoted by Brainy Quote, http:www.brainyquote .com/quotes/quotes/a/annlanders107915.html.

3. From Blaise Pascal, *Lettres Provinciales*, quoted in *The Columbia World of Quotations* (New York: Columbia University Press, 1996), also available online at http://www.bartleby.com/66/.

4. Gladys Bronwyn Stern, quoted in John Cook, comp., *The Book of Positive Quotations*, 2nd ed. (Minneapolis: Fairview Press, 2007), 79.

5. Robert Louis Stevenson, *The Novels and Tales of Robert Louis Stevenson* (New York: Charles Scribner's Sons, 1895), 143.

6. William Shakespeare, *The Tragedy of Hamlet, Prince of Denmark*, in *The Riverside Shakespeare* (Boston: Houghton Mifflin, 1974), 1147.

7. Sophocles, *Sophocles: The Plays and Fragments with Critical Notes, Commentary, and Translation in English Prose* (New York: Macmillan, 1913), 373.

Chapter 4

1. Abraham Lincoln, quoted in Richard Alan Krieger, *Civilization's Quotations: Life's Ideals* (New York: Algora, 2002), 228.
2. Casey Stengel, "Quotes," The Official Site, http://www.casey stengel.com/quotes_by.htm.
3. Mahatma Gandhi, quoted in Ralph Keyes, *The Quote Verifier: Who Said What, Where and When* (New York: St. Martin's Griffin, 2006), 75.
4. Earl Nightingale, *The Strangest Secret: Millennium 2000 Gold Record Recording*, read by the author (Keyes, 1999), audio book.
5. Napoleon Bonaparte, quoted by About.com, "Quotes by Napoleon Bonaparte," http://quotations.about.com/od/stillmorefamous people/a/NapoleonBonapa2.htm.
6. Quoted in John Cook, comp., *The Book of Positive Quotations*, 2nd ed. (Minneapolis: Fairview Press, 2007), 336.
7. Albert Einstein, quoted in Ralph Keyes, *The Quote Verifier: Who Said What, Where and When* (New York: St. Martin's Griffin, 2006), 98–99.
8. Michael Jordan, quoted in David L. Andrews, ed., *Michael Jordan, Inc.: Corporate Sport, Media Culture, and Late Modern America* (Albany, NY: SUNY Press, 2001), 157.
9. Wayne Gretzky, quoted in "Wit and Wisdom," *U.S. Society & Values: Electronic Journal of the U.S. Department of State* 8, no. 2 (December 2003).
10. Rosa Parks with Gregory J. Reed, *Quiet Strength: The Faith, The Hope, and the Heart of a Woman Who Changed the Nation* (Grand Rapids: Zondervan, 1994), 23, 25.

11. Helen Keller, *The Story of My Life* (New York: Grosset & Dunlap, 1905), 393.
12. Mark Twain, quoted in *The Columbia World of Quotations* (New York: Columbia University Press, 1996).
13. Gerald Ford, quoted in *Respectfully Quoted: A Dictionary of Quotations Requested from the Congressional Research Service* (Washington, DC: Library of Congress, 1989).
14. Ralph Waldo Emerson, *The Conduct of Life* (New York: Houghton Mifflin, 1904), 272.
15. Albert Einstein, quoted in Alice Calaprice, ed., *The Expanded Quotable Einstein* (Princeton: Princeton University Press, 2000).
16. Ronald Reagan, quoted in *The Columbia World of Quotations* (New York: Columbia University Press, 1996).
17. Barack Obama, interview by Oprah Winfrey, *The Oprah Winfrey Show*, ABC, October 18, 2006.
18. Martin Luther, quoted in Martin H. Manser, ed., T*he Westminster Collection of Christian Quotations* (Louisville, KY: Westminster John Knox Press, 2001), 211.
19. William James, quoted in Martin H. Manser, ed., *The Westminster Collection of Christian Quotations* (Louisville, KY: Westminster John Knox Press, 2001), 229.
20. From Margaret Mead, *Sex and Temperament,* quoted in David Sills and Robert Merton, eds., *Social Science Quotations: Who Said What, When, and Where* (Piscataway, NJ: Transaction Publishers, 2000), 158.
21. Al Capone, quoted in Fred R. Shapiro, ed., *The Yale Book of Quotations* (New Haven: Yale University Press, 2006), 130.

Chapter 5

1. From Winston Churchill, Speech at Harrow School, Harrow, England, October 29, 1941, quoted in *Respectfully Quoted: A*

Dictionary of Quotations Requested from the Congressional Research Service (Washington DC: Library of Congress, 1989).

2. Lance Armstrong, quoted in *Lance Armstrong: Historic Six-Time Tour de France Champion* (Champaign, IL: Sports Publishing, 2004), 33.

3. Friedrich Nietzsche, "Popular Quotations," The Nietzsche Channel, http://thenietzschechannel.fws1.com/popular.htm.

4. Marquis De Vauvenargues, quoted in *Webster's Online Dictionary*, http://www.websters-online-dictionary.com/definition/bear.

5. Zoe Koplowitz, quoted in Lorraine A. DarConte, ed., *Pride Matters: Quotes to Inspire Your Personal Best* (Riverside, NJ: Andrews McMeel Publishing, 2001), 15.

6. James E. Loehr and Tony Schwartz, *The Power of Full Engagement: Managing Energy, Not Time, Is the Key to High Performance and Personal Renewal* (New York: Free Press, 2003), 48.

7. Ted Williams, quoted in Andrew J. Maikovich and Michele D. Brown, *Sports Quotations: Maxims, Quips, and Pronouncements for Writers and Fans* (Jefferson, NC: McFarland, 2000), 190.

8. William Shakespeare, *Hamlet*, in *The Riverside Shakespeare* (Boston: Houghton Mifflin, 1974), 1155.

9. Norman Vincent Peale, *Power of the Plus Factor* (New York: Ballantine Books, 1996).

10. Marcus Tullius Cicero, *De Officiis: With an English Translation by Walter Miller* (New York: Macmillan, 1921), 341.

11. George F. Will, "The Stones of Treblinka Cry Out," *Washington Post*, September 10, 1989.

12. Fyodor Dostoyevsky, quoted in Anton Pavlovich Chekhov, *Notebook of Anton Chekhov*, trans. Samuel Solomonovitch Koteliansky and Leonard Woolf (New York: B. W. Huebsch, 1921), 41.

13. Henry Ford quoted in Larry Chang, ed., *Wisdom for the Soul: Five Millennia of Prescriptions for Spiritual Healing* (Washington, DC: Gnosophia Publishers, 2006), 472.

Chapter 6

1. Lucius Annaeus Seneca, quoted in Ralph Waldo Emerson, *The Complete Works of Ralph Waldo Emerson* (New York: Houghton Mifflin, 1904), 312.

2. George Foreman, *George Foreman's Guide to Life* (New York: Simon and Schuster, 2002), 105.

3. Norman Vincent Peale, *Have a Great Day* (New York: Random House, 1990), 76.

4. Eleanor Roosevelt, "How to Take Criticism," *Ladies Home Journal* 61 (November 1944): 155, 171.

5. Thomas Jefferson, quoted in John P. Foley, ed., *The Jeffersonian Cyclopedia: A Comprehensive Collection of the Views of Thomas Jefferson* (New York and London: Funk and Wagnalls, 1900), 591.

6. Theodore Roosevelt, quoted in John Cook, comp., *The Book of Positive Quotations*, 2nd ed. (Minneapolis: Fairview Press, 2007), 225.

7. Reinhold Niebuhr, quoted in Ralph Keyes, *The Quote Verifier: Who Said What, Where and When* (New York: St. Martin's Griffin, 2006), 190.

8. "Bill Cosby," *The Saturday Evening Post* (January/February 2007).

9. Ronald Reagan, quoted in James B. Simpson, comp., *Simpson's Contemporary Quotations* (Boston: Houghton Mifflin, 1988).

10. Ichak Kalderon Adizes, *Management/Mismanagement Styles: How to Identify a Style and What to Do About It* (Carpinteria, CA: Adizes Institute, 2004), 87.

11. Bijan Anjomi, "Bijan's Law," http://bijanslaw.com/.

12. From Walter Benjamin, *Franz Kafka: On the Tenth Anniversary of His Death*, quoted in James Whitlark, *Behind the Great Wall: A Post-Jungian Approach to Kafkaesque Literature* (Cranbury, NJ: Farleigh Dickinson University Press, 1992), 199.

13. L. Thomas Holdcroft, quoted in Vernon McLellan, *The Complete Book of Practical Proverbs and Wacky Wit* (Wheaton, IL: Tyndale House Publishing, 1996).

Chapter 7

1. Sherry Belle, Five Funny Females (live stand-up comedy show, McKinney Performing Arts Center, McKinney, TX, October 19, 2007).
2. John F. Kennedy, quoted in John Cook, comp., *The Book of Positive Quotations*, 2nd ed. (Minneapolis: Fairview Press, 2007), 469.
3. From Laurence Peter, *The Peter Principle* (1969), quoted in *The Columbia World of Quotations* (New York: Columbia University Press, 1996).
4. John Wooden, *Wooden: A Lifetime of Observations On and Off the Court* (New York: McGraw Hill, 1997), 86–87.
5. Theodore Roosevelt, quoted in Robert Hirschfield, ed., *The Power of the Presidency: Concepts and Controversy*, 3rd ed. (Edison, NJ: Aldine Transaction, 1982), 165–166.
6. From Sir Isaac Newton, letter to Robert Hooke (1675), quoted in *The Columbia World of Quotations* (New York: Columbia University Press, 1996).
7. John Andrew Holmes, quoted in John Cook, comp., *The Book of Positive Quotations*, 2nd ed. (Minneapolis: Fairview Press, 2007), 100.

Chapter 8

1. Mother Teresa, *Love: A Fruit Always in Season: Daily Meditations from the Words of Mother Teresa of Calcutta*, ed. Dorothy S. Hunt (San Francisco: Ignatius Press, 1987), 121.
2. Albert Einstein, quoted in David L. Cooperrider and Michel Avital, eds., *Constructive Discourse and Human Organization: Advances in Appreciative Inquiry* (Boston: Elsevier/JAI, 2004), 112.
3. Fyodor Dostoyevsky, "The Gentle Spirit," in *The Short Stories of Dostoyevsky*, trans. Constance Black Garnett (New York: Dial Press, 1946), 558.

4. Edward Tyas Cook, *The Life of John Ruskin*, vol. 1 (London: G. Allen, 1911), 391.

5. Diana Spencer, Princess of Wales, interview by Martin Bashir, *Panorama*, BBC, November 1995.

Chapter 9

1. George Bernard Shaw, quoted in Richard Alan Krieger, *Civilization's Quotations: Life's Ideal* (New York: Algora, 2002), 3.

2. William Shakespeare, *Twelfth Night*, in *The Riverside Shakespeare* (Boston: Houghton Mifflin, 1974), 422.

3. Confucius, quoted in James Freeman Clarke, *Ten Great Religions: An Essay in Comparative Theology* (New York: Houghton Mifflin, 1913), 51.

4. William Penn, *No Cross, No Crown*, 26th ed. (London: Society of Friends, 1896), 274.

5. Mahatma Gandhi, quoted in Stephen M. R. Covey and Rebecca R. Merrill, *The Speed of Trust: The One Thing That Changes Everything* (New York: Simon and Schuster, 2006), 69.

6. Albert Einstein, quoted in Richard Alan Krieger, *Civilization's Quotations: Life's Ideal* (New York: Algora, 2002), 250.

RECOMMENDED READING

Adair, John. *How to Grow Leaders: The Seven Key Principles of Effective Development.* New ed. London: Kogan Page, 2006.

Allen, James. *As a Man Thinketh.* New York: Barnes & Noble, 1992.

Bryant, John, and Michael Levin. *Banking on Our Future: A Program for Teaching You and Your Kids about Money.* Boston: Beacon Press, 2002.

Carlson, Richard. *Don't Sweat the Small Stuff . . . And It's All Small Stuff.* New York: Hyperion, 1997.

De Botton, Alain. *The Art of Travel.* New York: Vintage, 2004.

Fahey, Liam, and Robert Randall. *Learning from the Future: Competitive Foresight Scenarios.* Indianapolis: Wiley, 1997.

Ferriss, Timothy. *The Four-Hour Workweek: Escape 9–5, Live Anywhere, and Join the New Rich.* New York: Crown, 2007.

Finzel, Hanz. *The Top Ten Mistakes Leaders Make.* Paris, ON: David C. Cook Distribution, 2007.

Goodman, Gerald. *The Talk Book: The Intimate Science of Communicating in Close Relationships.* New York: Ballantine, 1990.

Hill, Napoleon. *Think and Grow Rich! The Original Version, Restored and Revised.* San Diego: Aventine Press, 2004.

Kouzes, James M., and Barry Z. Posner. *A Leader's Legacy.* San Francisco: Jossey-Bass, 2006.

———. *The Leadership Challenge.* 4th ed. San Francisco: Jossey-Bass, 2007.

Loehr, James E., and Tony Schwartz. *The Power of Full Engagement: Managing Energy, Not Time, Is the Key to High Performance and Personal Renewal.* New York: Free Press, 2003.

Maxwell, John C. *The 17 Indisputable Laws of Teamwork: Embrace Them and Empower Your Team.* Workbook ed. Nashville: Thomas Nelson, 2003.

———. *Failing Forward: Turning Mistakes into Stepping Stones for Success.* Nashville: Thomas Nelson, 2007.

Maxwell, John C., and Jim Dornan. *Becoming a Person of Influence: How to Positively Impact the Lives of Others.* Nashville: Thomas Nelson, 2006.

Murray, Alan. *Revolt in the Boardroom: The New Rules of Power in Corporate America.* New York: Collins, 2007.

Nightingale, Earl. *The Strangest Secret: Millennium 2000 Gold Record Recording.* Read by the author. Keyes Company, 1999. Audio book.

———. *Lead the Field.* Abridged ed. Niles, IL: Nightingale-Conant, 2002. Audio book.

Parks, Sharon Daloz. *Leadership Can Be Taught: A Bold Approach for a Complex World.* Boston: Harvard Business School Press, 2005.

Pirsig, Robert. *Zen and the Art of Motorcycle Maintenance: An Inquiry into Values.* New York: HarperTorch, 2006.

Secretan, Lance. *Inspire! What Great Leaders Do.* Indianapolis: Wiley, 2004.

Williams, Dean. *Real Leadership: Helping People and Organizations Face Their Toughest Challenges.* San Francisco: Berrett-Koehler Publishers, 2005.

Ziglar, Zig. *See You at the Top!* 2nd rev. ed. Gretna, LA: Pelican Publishing Company, 2000.

INDEX

ABOUT THE AUTHOR

Born in California and raised in the Pacific Northwest, Warren grew up in a classical music environment and spent most of his teenage and early adult life pursing an operatic career. While attending the New England Conservatory of Music, Warren realized that the financial demands of his music career were too great, so he began focusing on learning and mastering entrepreneurial and leadership skills that he could apply in the business marketplace.

In the early '90s, Warren started his first company, the Rhino Group, focusing on presentations to organizations and individuals on leadership, business concepts, personal development, teams and team building, creativity, and other topics. Warren's expertise in the areas of leadership, influence, sales, marketing, technology, and business acceleration has made him one of today's most dynamic and highly sought-after leadership and technology strategists. His executive leadership programs, workshops, and retreats have been instrumental in helping individuals from all walks of life increase their level of influence and leadership mastery.

Christian Warren currently lives in Orlando, Florida, with his wife, Jami, and four sons, Cameron, Chandler, Connor, and Chase.